International and Development Education

The *International and Development Education Series* Focuses on the complementary areas of comparative, international, and development education. Books emphasize a number of topics ranging from key international education issues, trends, and reforms to examinations of national education systems, social theories, and development education initiatives. Local, national, regional, and global volumes (single authored and edited collections) constitute the breadth of the series and offer potential contributors a great deal of latitude based on interests and cutting edge research. The series is supported by a strong network of international scholars and development professionals who serve on the International and Development Education Advisory Board and participate in the selection and review process for manuscript development.

Titles:

Post-Secondary Education and Technology

A Global Perspective on Opportunities and Obstacles to Development

Edited by
Rebecca Clothey, Stacy Austin-Li, and
John C. Weidman

POST-SECONDARY EDUCATION AND TECHNOLOGY

First published in 2012 by
PALGRAVE MACMILLAN®
in the United States—a division of St. Martin's Press LLC,
175 Fifth Avenue, New York, NY 10010.

Where this book is distributed in the UK, Europe and the rest of the world,
this is by Palgrave Macmillan, a division of Macmillan Publishers Limited,
registered in England, company number 785998, of Houndmills,
Basingstoke, Hampshire RG21 6XS.

Palgrave Macmillan is the global academic imprint of the above companies
and has companies and representatives throughout the world.

Palgrave® and Macmillan® are registered trademarks in the United States,
the United Kingdom, Europe and other countries.

ISBN: 978–0–230–33831–9

Library of Congress Cataloging-in-Publication Data

Post-secondary education and technology : a global
perspective on opportunities and obstacles to development/
edited by Rebecca Clothey, Stacy Austin-Li and John C. Weidman.
pages cm.—(International & development education)
Includes bibliographical references.
ISBN 978–0–230–33831–9
1. Education, Higher—Effect of technological innovations on.
2. Educational technology. I. Clothey, Rebecca A., editor of compilation.
II. Austin-Li, Stacy, editor of compilation. III. Weidman, John C.,
1945– editor of compilation.

LB2395.7.P67 2012
378.1'7344678—dc23   2012017746

A catalogue record of the book is available from the British Library.

Design by Newgen Imaging Systems (P) Ltd., Chennai, India.

First edition: November 2012

10 9 8 7 6 5 4 3 2 1

Contents

Illustrations

Figures

Tables

Abbreviations and Acronyms

AACC	American Association of Community Colleges
AARNet	Australian Academic and Research Network
ADB	Asian Development Bank
AICTE	All India Council for Technical Education
APDIP	Asia-Pacific Development Information Programme
APEC	Asia Pacific Economic Cooperation
BECTA	British Educational Communications and Technology Agency
CEC	Council for Exceptional Children
CHEA	Creating the Council of Higher Education Accreditation
CNE	Comité National d'Évaluation
CSLP	Centre for the Study of Learning and Performance
CTTC	Cyber Teacher Training Centre, South Korea
DBD	Digital Book Disk
DepEd	Department of Education of the Philippines
DE	Distance Education
DFAT	Department of Foreign Affairs and Trade, Commonwealth of Australia
DPA	Degree Program Advisor
eTQM	e-Total Quality Management College, UAE
EDUSAT	Educational Satellite
EU	European Union
EUROCALL	European Association for Computer-Assisted Language Learning
FDI	Foreign Direct Investments
FIPSE	Fund for the Improvement of Postsecondary Education
FYE	First Year Experience
GAA	General Appropriations Act
GAC	German Accreditation Council
GDP	Gross Domestic Product
GER	Gross Enrollment Ratio
HBMeU	Hamdan Bin Mohammed e-University, UAE

HEA	Higher Education Academy
HEI	Higher Education Institutions
ICJS	Institute of Criminal Justice Studies
ICONS	International Communications and Negotiations Simulations
ICT	Information and Communication Technology
ICT4E	Information and Communication Technology for Education
IDP	Internally Displaced People
IGNOU	Indira Gandhi National Open University, India
IHE	Institutions of Higher Education
IIT	Indian Institute of Technology
INMP	International Negotiation Modules Project
ISRO	Indian Space Research Organization
ITD	Information Technology Departments
IWS	Internet World Stats
JANET	Joint Network Team Association
JISC	Joint Information Services Council
LLAS	Languages, Linguistics and Area Studies
LMS	Learning Management System
M2M	Moving to Mathematics
MDNet	Mobile Doctors Network
MNE	Multinational Enterprise
MTS	Multimodus Teaching Strategy
NAFTA	North American Free Trade Agreement
NCERT	National Council for Educational Research and Training, India
NCES	National Center for Education Statistics
NCLB	No Child Left Behind
NEDA	National Economic Development Authority
NGO	Nongovernmental Organization
NICTE	National Institute for Technology for Education
NSDP	No Significant Difference Phenomenon
NWU	North-West University
OAC	Online Asynchronous Collaboration
OCDs	Online Course Developers
OECD	Organisation for Economic Co-Operation and Development
PG	Postgraduate
QIP	Quality Improvement Program, India
RSS	Really Simple Syndication
SABER	System Assessment and Benchmarking for Education Results

SAPA	South African Press Association
SEAMEO	Southeast Asian Ministers of Education Organization
SiMERR	National Centre of Science, Information and Communication Technology and Mathematics Education for Rural and Regional Australia
SMS	Short Message Service
TAFESA	Technical And Further Education South Australia
TRIPS	Trade-Related Aspects of Intellectual Property Rights
UAE	United Arab Emirates
UG	Undergraduate
UGC	University Grant Commission
UNCTAD	United Nations Conference on Trade and Development
UNDP	United Nations Development Programme
UNESCO	United Nations Education, Scientific and Cultural Organization
UNFPA	United Nations Population Fund
UNHCR	United Nations High Commissioner for Refugees
UNIFEM	United Nations Development Fund for Women
UoP	University of Portsmouth
USAID	United States Agency for International Development
VLE	Virtual Learning Environment
WEDIS	Women's Economic Development Personal and Social Impact Survey
WGC	Women's Global Connection
WTO	World Trade Organization

Series Editor's Introduction

Technology is driving changes worldwide at an unprecedented rate in all sectors. Businesses of all sizes rely on technology for communication, management, and innovation. The Internet is the general industry and the social network platform for many businesses in the present and will be increasingly so in the future. Yet there are great disparities in access to the Internet in different geographic regions of the world and among different socioeconomic groups. Although cell phone access has made great inroads in developing country contexts, the majority of people in Indonesia, Peru, South Sudan, and Zambia still do not have access to the Internet. Of the more than 1.037 billion people who reside in Africa, approximately 140 million (13.5 percent of the population) had access to the Internet as of December 2011. This is a tremendous increase in Internet access in Africa over the past decade, yet the region still lags far behind North America and Europe, where 78.6 percent and 61.3 percent of the respective populations were able to access the Internet as of December 2011 (Internet World Stats 2012). In many ways, educational changes, including those that involve technology are rooted in higher education institutions and organizations closely aligned with universities.

Post-secondary education is a subsector that is not accustomed to succeeding in an environment of ongoing and rapid changes. Higher education institutions, especially most traditional universities, are notorious for strong bureaucratic organizational structures that are often antagonistic to technological changes. The very nature of academic freedom—which is so cherished and grounded in the sciences and is fundamental to research—serves as both a deterrent as well as a facilitator to technological changes and innovation. The dominant educational paradigm often restricts or prevents changes including those in technology (Hawkins 2007). Those higher education institutions that are able to adapt and incorporate technology into curriculum delivery, management processes, and marketing programs are often the most successful in meeting changing student needs. If post-secondary education institutions are primarily responsible for training those who enter the formal employment sector in most societies, then instructors at these institutions need to be able to provide graduates with the necessary technological skills to contribute to society. Too often, however, students have more advanced knowledge of latest technologies than do their instructors. Such is the nature of technology access as it relates to higher education in the twenty-first century.

Open universities and distance education institutions have redefined the meaning of higher education curriculum delivery. Entire universities exist online, which include the registration and enrollment processes, coursework, examination, and granting of degrees. Those who are working fulltime but want to upgrade their skills or earn an advanced degree in their field of work often prefer to pursue a higher education degree by correspondence or entirely online.

It is within this complex technological context that we welcome *Postsecondary Education and Technology* as a volume in our International and Development Education Book Series. It is cosponsored by the Higher Education Special Interest Group of the Comparative and International Education Society and focuses on international perspectives that address challenges, obstacles as well as opportunities for the future of post-secondary education. Editors Rebecca Clothey, Stacy Austin-Li, and John C. Weidman have assembled a respected group of 25 international scholars and practitioners who have contributed 11 chapters to this volume. Even considering all the technological advancements that have been realized in recent decades, as well as the global expansion of higher education, inequalities in education persist in the post-secondary subsector. These inequalities are highlighted in this volume and include issues of gender, socioeconomic disparities, international refugees, and educational policy shortcomings. Several case studies of successes in these areas are also offered to readers. These include how to empower individuals through technology and access to higher education, and in meeting the dynamic changes of individuals and societies.

JOHN N. HAWKINS
University of California, Los Angeles

W. JAMES JACOB
University of Pittsburgh

REFERENCES

Hawkins, John N. 2007. "The Intractable Dominant Educational Paradigm." In *Changing Education*, ed. Peter D. Hershock, Mark Mason, and John N. Hawkins. Dordrecht, The Netherlands: Springer.

Internet World Stats. 2012. *Usage and Population Statistics*. Bogota, Colombia: Miniwatts Marketing Group.

Introduction

Education, ICT, and International Development

*Rebecca Clothey, Stacy Austin-Li,
and John C. Weidman*

Higher education has been identified in nations worldwide as an avenue for developing the local human resources and delivering the skilled expertise needed to promote economic development. This recognition has driven individuals, corporations, educational institutions, as well as governmental and nongovernmental organizations to make education a top priority.

As the global commitment to educational access has become integral in all levels of society, new technologies have also been developed that hold tremendous promise for expanding higher education's reach. The simultaneous demand for advanced education and the potential of technology to expand education access beyond national borders has resulted in previously unavailable and far-reaching, innovative ways to deliver educational programming.

The Internet and mobile communications have revolutionized the way people access and distribute information on a global scale. Distance learning, open source courseware, e-books, wikis, and many other innovative technologies have advanced education by providing the capability to connect any topic in any discipline to learners in almost any place, greatly expanding opportunities for access to post-secondary education. This new reality has generated vastly expanded possibilities for international collaboration, knowledge building, sharing of best practices, and new ways to teach—both inside the classroom and out—thereby providing the inspiration and impetus for this volume. However, even as modes of providing education proliferate, the digital divide continues to grow, raising new issues regarding effective ways in which to apply technology solutions to expand educational access and promote economic development.

This book looks at innovations in and challenges to the ways in which technology can be used to expand access to post-secondary education and contribute to a nation's economic development, through a set of case studies and analyses written by people involved in relevant projects around the world. The book builds upon the content of two virtual symposia jointly hosted in 2008 and 2010 by Drexel University, Wainhouse Research, and the World Bank's Global Development Learning Network in Beijing. The original concept for the symposia emerged from a desire to create a worldwide community of scholars and practitioners who were committed to cross-cultural collaboration and improved educational programming, without requiring the expense of travel across continents. The symposia offered content created by educators for educators, utilizing video technology and open source courseware to provide synchronous panel discussions and live keynote lectures from international experts based in the United States, Austria, the Philippines, China, and Japan (Clothey 2010). People were able to participate live from anywhere by simply clicking a link. In addition, the Web 2.0 tools enabled interactivity, so participants could also ask questions of the experts and communicate with other participants via chat modalities. Additional recorded presentations from five continents were available for viewing comments online, and all live sessions were also recorded for on-demand playback later (Clothey 2010).

The diversity of the symposium participants indicates the potential that information and communication technologies provide for global collaboration. For example, the 2008 inaugural symposium attracted registrants from 13 countries and 5 continents. Additionally, although the symposium was held in English, participants included native speakers of English, Chinese, Spanish, Korean, and Urdu (Clothey and Austin-Li 2009). This exchange was the inspiration for presenting a set of analytical case studies that highlight technology's diverse applications in education worldwide, offering real-life examples of uses of various technologies from authors around the world. At the same time, the conclusions and recommendations in the book are research based and therefore offer practical applications for education practitioners and policy makers. Beyond focusing simply on technology use, the book is framed within the context of expanding access to disadvantaged populations to whom post-secondary education has been denied for reasons including poverty, location, and gender. Although all the cases explored in this book promote the use of technology for expanding access, the book also takes a critical look at the realities of implementing these new tools and approaches, especially in, but not limited to, the developing world.

Higher Education in the Information Age

Philip Altbach, Liz Reisberg, and Laura Rumbley (2009, i) assert that "an academic revolution has taken place in higher education in the past half century marked by transformations unprecedented in scope and diversity." An increase in widespread participation in tertiary education, or the massification of higher education over the last several decades, has driven many of the key transformations (Altbach et al. 2009). The United States was the first country to achieve mass higher education, with 40 percent of the traditional 18–22-year old age cohort attending post-secondary education in 1960, but most countries have increased participation rates since then. The proportion of this age cohort enrolled in higher education has grown globally from 19 percent in 2000 to 26 percent in 2007, with a total of 150.6 million tertiary students of all ages enrolled worldwide (Altbach et al. 2009).

As a result of massification, new challenges have emerged for postsecondary institutions. Much of higher education's expansion is due to new avenues of access to higher education, which were previously closed to all but the elite. Never has the tertiary student body been so diverse in terms of age, race, ethnicity, and gender. For example, in 2009, 42 percent of US college–aged students were at least 25 years of age and 57 percent were female. In addition, the proportion of White college students in the United States has declined between 1990 and 2009 from 78 to 62 percent, while racial and ethnic minorities have increased—Blacks from 9 to 14 percent; Hispanics from 6 to 12 percent; and Asian/Pacific Islanders from 4 to 6 percent (Snyder 2011, 13). Such diversity requires new teaching strategies and learning supports, including new approaches for reaching student populations with various mother tongues.

In addition to the demands of serving more diverse student populations, the sheer increase in numbers also strains available resources in tertiary institutions. Institutions must ask faculty to teach larger classes, or hire more faculty. In fact, in many countries the average qualification for academics has declined because the supply cannot meet the demand. Altbach et al. (2009) estimate that as many as half of all university teachers in the world have earned only a Bachelor's degree. In China, which is now the world's biggest provider of higher education, only 9 percent of the university faculty have doctorates (Altbach et al. 2009).

The need for infrastructure to accommodate a growing student population is also a challenge for post-secondary institutions, particularly in a climate of decreased finances. Sub-Saharan Africa is a world leader in tertiary enrollment growth, having seen a 20-fold increase in the past 40 years. However, tertiary education systems there are not equipped to absorb the growing demand (UIS 2010). In India, half of the 1.2 billion population is younger than age 25, and the Indian government says the country must build 1,000 universities and 50,000 colleges within the next decade to accommodate them (Arnoldy 2012). At the same time, the worldwide shift to a knowledge economy also has led to the need for new skills in the labor market, requiring professional development, new credentials, and retraining. Not surprisingly, post-secondary institutions are increasingly being asked to address these societal needs as well.

Nevertheless, despite broader post-secondary participation globally, not all sectors of society have benefitted equally. Students from rural and impoverished backgrounds continue to be underrepresented at the tertiary level in most nations, and while strides have been made, there continue to be disparities across ethnic and gender lines in many places as well.

ICT as a Mechanism for Meeting the Challenges Tertiary Institutions Face

The potential connection between ICT (Information and Communication Technology), education, and national economic development goals has been enthusiastically promoted by international agencies and national governments alike. Crafting enabling legislation for more technology-based education is now one of the predominant global challenges across industrialized nations (Selwyn et al. 2001). International agencies such as the United Nations Development Programme (UNDP) promote ICT as an enabler to address socioeconomic variations in educational access, and the United Nations Educational, Scientific and Cultural Organization (UNESCO) advocates ICT for facilitating the modernization of education, improving the quality of learning, and enhancing the quality of life in general.

Among the more remarkable stories for promoting ICT for economic development is that of Rwanda, a nation with a per capita income of about US$560 per year (US Department of State 2011). The Rwandan government's 2000 report, *Rwanda Vision 2020,* proposed to make Rwanda into a technology and communications hub and to use the Internet to transform the country from an agricultural to a knowledge-based society by the year 2020. Since then, Rwanda has constructed approximately 2,300 km of optical fiber cable network across the country. The cost of the fiber optic cable network for this low-income nation was approximately US$95 million (Fiber Optic Mania 2011), an investment that demonstrates a firm belief in the ability of the Internet to promote national development.

Internet technology, in particular, has been advocated for its potential to broaden the reach of education beyond the brick-and-mortar confines of schools. In fact, the governments of many countries have supported distance education as a means of promoting greater educational access (Clothey 2008), and distance learning is becoming more commonplace across many educational sectors. The growth in online distance learning as a viable means of educational delivery has coincided with the expansion of technology use across the world. The Internet World Stats (IWS 2011) reports that there was a 440.4 percent growth in Internet usage throughout the world during the decade of 2000–2011, with a 78 percent Internet penetration rate across North America in 2010. Currently Asia accounts for 44 percent of the total world Internet usage (IWS 2011), and Asia also has the largest number of adult online learners in the world (Latchem and Jung 2010). Furthermore, more than 100 universities worldwide have placed *free* content online, and five thousand free online classes are now available through institutions in the United States, Japan, Vietnam, and India, among others (Bonk 2009). These trends, as well as pedagogical and technological innovations, have increased the potential for interaction and collaborative work in distance learning at the tertiary level.

Nevertheless, the best technology is useless if infrastructure and the proper training to use it remains inadequate. Both ICT and Internet availability are inconsistent from one region to another. The 2010–2011 Global Information Technology Report, which assesses "the conduciveness of national environments for ICT development and diffusion," did not rank a single Latin American country in the top 20, and most countries of sub-Saharan Africa ranked at the bottom of the scale (Dutta and Mia 2011, x).

Furthermore, while a UNESCO (2011) report shows that the penetration of computers in high-income countries is quite high (an average of 67 computers per 100 people), the penetration is still low in many parts of the world. In Eastern European, Central Asian, and Latin American countries there are 11 computers per 100 people; in East Asian, Pacific, Middle Eastern, and North African countries there are 6 per 100. In South Asian and sub-Saharan African countries, penetration is particularly low, with only 3 and 2 per 100, respectively (UIS 2011). Differences are even greater for Internet access.

Almost 80 percent of the world's Internet users are located in Europe, Asia, or North America (IWS 2011). Furthermore, although developing countries have 80 percent of the world's population, they have just 5 percent of the world's Internet hosts. In contrast, North America has only 5 percent of the population, and 65 percent of the world's Internet hosts (Bjarnason 2007).

In many places, this divide is also prevalent within countries where rural areas commonly have poorer ICT infrastructure than urban areas. China, for example, has a 30 percent Internet penetration, with over 500 million users (Kan 2012). However, rural users account for a mere 1.2 percent of that total (McQuaide 2009). Similarly, although information technology has been recognized as a means for sustaining development in

India, the International Energy Agency reported in 2010 that more people in India lack access to *electricity* than any other nation. There is also a digital divide between states in India. In 1994, electricity was available to 83 percent of households in the Punjab, but only 15 percent of households in West Bengal, and 404 million people nationwide remained without electricity in 2010 (Remme et al. 2011). In addition, while India claims only 0.37 percent of the overall population as Internet users, more than two-thirds of these users reside in either the capital city of New Delhi, or in one of India's state capitals. One-third of all Internet users are from one of only two cities, either New Delhi or Mumbai (Chandrasekhar et al. 2004).

ICT, Language, and Cultural Barriers

As Jayson Richardson (2009) reminds us, the digital divide is not solely about whether individuals have access to the Internet. It also involves the ability of the end users to access and apply information to create new knowledge (Richardson 2009). There are therefore many issues of access that even better technology infrastructure and training resources cannot address. Some of the most challenging are those related to language and culture. For example, the top two most used languages on the Internet are English and Chinese, together comprising more than half of the total number of websites, and 82 percent of all websites are in one of only ten of the world's languages (IWS 2011). However, there are 6,000 languages across the world, and most of these do not appear on the Internet at all.

A 2005 UNESCO study found that 80 percent of all web pages hosted on African domains were written in English. African languages accounted for only about 1.3 percent of the more than one million web pages examined in the study. The study also found that some of Africa's major languages were absent from the Internet altogether (Fantognon et al. 2005). In Southeast Asia, the diverse population utilizes some 15–20 different written scripts; in China there are an estimated 80–100 languages, many of which use different scripts or do not have written scripts at all (Clothey 2005). In any case, many of the major software packages are currently incapable of producing letters or characters for some local languages, meaning that providing a culturally relevant curriculum online for a linguistic minority student population may present an extremely difficult challenge to overcome.

Sedef Uzuner (2009) describes numerous studies that show students' cultural beliefs and practices affect the way they interact, even in online settings. He finds that cultural differences in fact hinder students' success in asynchronous online learning environments and cause them to experience "feelings of isolation, alienation, and dissonance out of conflict with the dominant educational culture" (5). Despite the existence of these studies, culture remains an underexplored facet of instructional design and technology use (Young 2008).

A key challenge faced by both established and new technology-enhanced educational programming worthy of consideration is related to the difficulty associated with assessment and evaluation. Altbach et al. (2009, xv) claim that there is a "pervasive disconnect between employing new ICTs and enhancing quality." Furthermore, UNESCO (2011, 15) reports that there is an "inconsistent relationship between the availability or use of ICT and student learning." Roger Harris (2004, 4) also states that "[m]uch of the evidence in support of the use of ICTs for alleviating poverty remains anecdotal, and initiatives are proceeding with little reference to each other." Even so, UNESCO strongly advocates the implementation of policies that support the development of ICT infrastructure and use worldwide (UNESCO 2011). This suggests that continuing assessment of the various educational programs that employ ICT is necessary, and that these results must be widely shared among scholars and practitioners—a motivating force for this book. As Harris (2004, 4) notes of ICT use, "As experience accumulates, we can begin to make general sense of it by detecting recurring themes and patterns of relationships that can be usefully carried forward."

Overview of the Book

This book tackles many of the issues outlined in the foregoing and covers not only a wide spectrum of educational programming and technology application but also cases from a variety of regions and countries. Since our original goal was to share experiences and best practices from both developed and developing nations, it was heartening to receive chapters from Africa, Asia, Europe, the Middle East, and the United States. The one region not represented is Latin America, perhaps due to our focus on circulating the call for papers via digital avenues. Chapters were selected both as representative of the experience of specific regions and for their relevance to the global community.

The first several chapters of the book focus on existing policy issues at the micro and at the macro level. The first chapter, by Mercedes del Rosario, analyzes specific policies that have been implemented in various countries of Asia to promote the use of ICT in education. She uses the frameworks of modernization and human capital theory to argue that such policies, though heavily pushed by international agencies and developing countries to promote economic development and modernization, often do not align with the actual contexts and needs of the countries in which they are implemented. As she points out, the existence of Internet connections or computers has little to do with their successful use; national technology policies, therefore, need to be reconsidered to meet practical goals if they are to contribute to a nation's economic development.

Robyn Smyth, Trish Andrews, Richard Caladine, and Jason Bordujenko (Chapter 2) discuss a survey of Australian universities where rich media technology is widely used. Their findings reveal that such technologies have great potential for reducing costs and environmental footprints across the higher education sector and also for improving the efficiency of administration and innovations in research and pedagogy. However, their research also indicates that a lack of coherent policy and planning for such technologies within the higher education sector is limiting their potential for maximum use. These authors argue that rich media technologies have not maintained their status as "lighthouse technologies," because their capability in a digital world is not well understood by managers and others beyond a small number of videoconferencing enthusiasts. Hence, to maximize the benefits of any ICT use, there must first be streamlined and transparent policies for its utilization.

In Chapter 3, Minghua Li addresses how to increase access to post-secondary education for nontraditional, working, and remote students by creating a virtual community of educators and educational programs built upon a common infrastructure of local learning centers networked into an educational grid. This open community college approach enables a broader array of services to reach these populations while limiting capital investment. Li addresses some of the challenges that this model faces, including the need for physical learning centers, monopoly providers, investment incentives, and assessment and accreditation of such educational programming.

The next chapters are case studies that look at ICT use for capacity building. Charl Wolhuter, Hennie J. Steyn, Elsa Mentz, and Ferdinand J. Potgieter (Chapter 4) discuss the increasing enrollments at South African universities, and the resulting strain of teaching larger class sizes on faculty. In this case, the authors have attempted to develop a strategy to deal with the large classes without sacrificing retention or student achievement. To do so, they launched a blended learning approach to teaching in which larger classes were supplemented with digital course materials in one of several South African languages. Students could select the language with which they were the most comfortable. In addition to relieving some of the burden on faculty who taught large classes, the student evaluations of the blended classes were more positive than those for the traditional face-to-face classes in the same subject! Furthermore, they found that providing the course materials in multiple languages also addressed the challenge of linguistic diversity that cannot typically be resolved in a traditional face-to-face setting.

Tricia Coverdale-Jones describes in Chapter 5 the implementation of distance learning within a single faculty at a university in the UK. She identifies sources of resistance among academic staff and describes the support system that was established to assist them with learning how to use ICT resources effectively. She argues for the importance of providing sufficient human resource support to augment technological infrastructure and facilitate use of eLearning techniques by sometimes resistant academic staff.

In India, where the need to expand university infrastructure for the masses is critical, the quality of the university level teaching faculty is low in large part, because many lecturers hold only Bachelor's degrees. In Chapter 6, Kalpana Kannan and Krishnan Narayanan focus on this concern, describing a nationwide online, live, synchronous teacher training workshop for teachers of engineering at the tertiary level. The distance modality of the workshop, which was designed to increase the professional credentials of university-level faculty, enabled facilitators to reach a large number of people across the country and at a lower cost than comparable face-to-face training. In addition, they were able to reach individuals located in rural and remote locations. However, the authors also discuss the challenges their program faced, including power outages during the workshop, as well as a lack of ease of some users with the technology, which hindered the program's success.

Ellen Clay and Michel Miller (Chapter 7) also describe using distance learning to improve credentials of teachers in remote areas of Pennsylvania, US. Although Pennsylvania state regulations require certification for teachers of mathematics, many special education teachers who must teach mathematics do not meet state requirements for the subject. Teachers living in rural areas often do not have easy access to the necessary professional development programs to gain the credentials they need. To address this issue, Clay and Miller developed a state-funded, online, asynchronous professional development program to train in-service special education teachers to teach mathematics. Similar to the strategy employed in South Africa, Clay and Miller's approach was aimed at scaling up instructional support to reach a maximum number of teachers requiring in-service education, without sacrificing educational quality or teaching efficiency.

The next set of chapters focuses on formal and nonformal uses of ICT to enhance educational opportunities for other underserved populations.

In Chapter 8, Rosalind Latiner Raby, Joyce P. Kaufman, and Greg Rabb describe the International Negotiation Modules Project (INMP), an online simulation for enhancing the learning and teaching of international issues across the US community college curriculum in places where many US students have had limited opportunities or exposure to international experiences. Raby and her colleagues discuss the challenges of internationalization at community colleges and promote INMP as a viable model for an innovative approach to internationalization of the curriculum, teaching, learning, and faculty development.

Dorothy Ettling and Maria Marquise (Chapter 9) also facilitate internationalization and cross-cultural exchange in their description of a six-year, web-based dialogue among rural women in the Bukoba region of Tanzania, Mongu, Zambia, and San Antonio, TX, US. The dialogue was initiated as a means of cross-cultural exchange and expanding leadership capacities. It grew over the years into a significant opportunity, not only for the sharing of ideas but also as evidence of personal and social empowerment in the women's lives, utilizing web-based technology was a major source of new education and insider knowledge for the participants. Ettling and Marquise's chapter documents the evolving learning process of the women, utilizing frameworks of women's empowerment, and technology innovation.

Rana Tamim's Chapter 10 also looks at the use of technology to enhance women's empowerment. Her case study focuses on a group of young women in the United Arab Emirates (UAE) who are able to go beyond the roles dictated for women by local religious, social, and cultural norms and pursue higher education through a blended face-to-face and online delivery format offered at a new e-Learning university. The educational opportunity she describes empowers mature female learners and allows them to achieve their personal goals and academic development while meeting their professional commitments and family obligations. Finally, Safary Wa-Mbaleka (Chapter 11) discusses the potential ICT may hold for addressing the unique needs and challenges of refugees and internally displaced people in Sub-Saharan Africa.

Reflection

ICT is not a magic bullet that easily transcends existing inequalities related to poverty, class, ethnicity, nationality, locale, or other issues. Nevertheless, it does provide some possibilities, and there are developing trends that suggest positive change for the future.

Capitalizing on the technologies that are already commonly in use in local communities is imperative. Most nations do not have the financial means to construct US$95 million worth of fiber optic cable to make Internet access widely available as was done in Rwanda. Even if they did, it would still be necessary to train individuals to use it before educational programming via the new technology could be introduced, and there would be no guarantee the new technology would be accepted within the target community.

In addition, as student populations become more diverse, ICT must be utilized creatively to maintain respect for diverse virtual classroom communities, and to build on unique cultural customs and strengths (Wellburn and Claeys 2004; Latchem 2005). Collaborative efforts between diverse communities in designing and implementing educational programming allows diverse global populations to learn from each other and maximize their respective strengths. More efforts are being made to produce web-based educational materials in multiple languages, and more languages are also becoming available through Internet-based translation software. If these trends continue, ICT can promote some greater opportunities for educational access and for international exchange.

However, continuing to find ways to maximize the potential of ICT to benefit all users will remain a challenge in the twenty-first century. It is our hope that this volume will provide an avenue for scholars and practitioners to gain new perspectives on the opportunities and challenges of implementing such programs that are both practical and thought-provoking. On the whole, as editors, we found the projects and people we encountered through this volume to be both inspiring and critical in the quest to bring higher education of good quality to diverse and underserved populations.

REFERENCES

Altbach, Philip, Liz Reisberg, and Laura Rumbley. 2009. "Executive Summary." *Trends in Global Higher Education: Tracking an Academic Revolution.* Paris: UNESCO. Available online at: http://www.unesco.org.

Arnoldy, Ben. 2012. "In India, the Challenge of Building 50,000 Colleges." *The Christian Science Monitor,* January 16, no page. Available online at: http://www.csmonitor.com.

Baum, Sandy, Jennifer Ma, and Kathleen Payea. 2010. *Education Pays: 2010: The Benefits of Higher Education for Individuals and Society.* Princeton, NJ: The College Board Advocacy and Policy Center. Available online at: http://trends.collegeboard.org.

Bjarnason, Svava. 2007. "Rhetoric or Reality? Technology in Borderless Higher Education." In *International Handbook of Higher Education*, ed. James J. F. Forest and Philip G. Altbach, 377–391. Dordrecht, The Netherlands: Springer.

Bonk, Curtis. 2009. *The World is Open: How Web Technology is Revolutionizing Education*. San Francisco, CA: Jossey-Bass.

Chandrasekhar, C. P., Simran Kumar, and Kiran Karnik. 2004. *Regional Human Development Report. Promoting ICT for Human Development in Asia: Realising the Millennium Development Goals (India)*. New Delhi, India: National Association of Software and Service Companies / United Nations Development Programme. Available online at: http://www.unapcict.org.

Clothey, Rebecca. 2005. "China's Policies for Ethnic Minority Studies: Negotiating National Values and Ethnic Identities." *Comparative Education Review* 49 (3): 389–409.

Clothey, Rebecca. 2008. "Education for Everyone: Expanding Opportunities through Distance Education." *Journal of the World Universities Forum* 1 (4): 81–87.

Clothey, Rebecca. 2010. "Expanding Access Through Technology: The Drexel Virtual Symposium." *Educational Technology* 50 (6): 50–52.

Clothey, Rebecca, and Stacy Austin-Li. 2009. "Building a Sense of Community through Online Video." *International Journal of Web-Based Communities* 6 (3): 303–316.

Dutta, Soumitra, and Irene Mia. 2011. *The Global Information Technology Report 2011*. Geneva: The World Economic Forum. Available online at: http://reports.weforum.org.

Fantognon, Xavier, Yoshiki Mikami, John Paolillo, Daniel Pimienta, and Daniel Prado. 2005. *Measuring Linguistic Diversity on the Internet*. Paris: UNESCO. Available online at: http://www.unesco.org.

Fiber Optic Mania. 2011. "Rwanda Completes 2300km Fiber Optic Cable Network." *Fiber Optic Mania,* March 28. Available online at: http://www.fiberopticmania.com.

Harris, Roger W. 2004. *Information and Communications Technologies for Poverty Alleviation*. Kuala Lumpur, Malaysia: UNDP-Asia-Pacific Development Information Programme (APDIP). Available online at: http://www.apdip.net.

IWS (Internet World Stats). 2011. *Internet World Stats' Website*. Bogota, Columbia: Miniwatts Marketing Group. Available online at: http://www.internetworld-stats.com.

Kan, Michael. 2012. *China's Internet Users Cross 500 Million*. San Francisco: PCWorld Communications. Available online at: http://www.pcworld.com.

Latchem, Colin. 2005. "Towards Borderless Virtual Learning in Higher Education." In *Global Perspectives on e-Learning: Rhetoric and Reality,* ed. Alison A. Carr-Chellman. Thousand Oaks, CA: SAGE Publications.

Latchem, Colin, and Insung Jung. 2010. *Distance and Blended Learning in Asia*. New York: Routledge.

McQuaide, Shiling. 2009. "Making Education Equitable in Rural China through Distance Learning." *The International Review of Research in Open and Distance Learning* 10 (1): 1–21.

Remme, Uwe, Nathalie Trudeau, Dagmar Graczyk, and Peter Taylor. 2011. *Technology Development Prospects For The Indian Power Sector.* Paris: International Energy Agency.

Richardson, Jayson. 2009. "Providing ICT Skills to Teacher Trainers in Cambodia: Summary of Project Outputs and Achievements." *Journal of Education for International Development* 4 (2): 1–12.

Selwyn, Neil, Gorard Stephen, and Williams Sara. 2001. "Digital Divide or Digital Opportunity? The Role of Technology in Overcoming Social Exclusion in U.S. Education." *Educational Policy* 15 (2): 258–277.

Snyder, Thomas D. 2011. *Mini-Digest of Education Statistics, 2010.* U.S. Department of Education National Center for Education Statistics (NCES) Report No. NCES 2011–016. Washington, DC: NCES. Available online at: http://nces.ed.gov.

UNESCO. 2011. *Transforming Education: The Power of ICT Policies.* Paris: UNESCO. Available online at: http://www.unesco.org.

UIS (UNESCO Institute of Statistics) 2010. *Trends in Tertiary Education: Sub-Saharan Africa.* UIS Fact Sheet, December 2010, No. 10. Montreal: UIS. Available online at: http://unesdoc.unesco.org.

US Department of State. 2011. *Background Note: Rwanda.* Washington, DC: US Department of State. Available online at: http://www.state.gov.

Uzuner, Sedef. 2009. "Questions of Culture in Distance Learning: A Research Review." *International Review of Research in Open and Distance Learning* (10) 3: 1–19.

Wellburn, Elizabeth, and Gregory Claeys. 2004. "Community-Based Distributed Learning in a Globalized World." In *Distance Learning and University Effectiveness: Changing Educational Paradigms for Online Learning,* ed. Caroline Howard, Karen Schenk, and Richard Discenza. Hershey, PA: Idea Group.

Young, Patricia. 2008. "The Culture Based Model: Constructing a Model of Culture." *Educational Technology & Society* 11 (2): 107–118.

Part I

Policy Debates

Chapter 1

ICT in Education Policies and National Development
Why the "Twain" Should Meet (But Could Not)

Mercedes del Rosario

Oh, East is East, and West is West, and never the twain shall meet.

–Rudyard Kipling 1892

Lured by the promise of progress brought about by information and communication technology (ICT), developing countries leave no stone unturned to turn the promise to reality. The lure is strong because of the acknowledged potential of ICTs, which is recognized by technologists and economists alike, to be drivers of economic growth, productivity, and competitiveness. Because of this, ICTs are widely deployed and utilized by developing countries to improve their intellectual capital, workforce skills, productivity, market access, and social structures, and enable them to become more competitive, both regionally and globally (USAID 2003). One strategic area of deployment is the education sector. The deployment raises several implications, one of which is the reconfiguration of education, and particularly higher education, as the producer of teachers and learners who will supply the human resource base of a country aiming to develop through ICT. The reconfiguration invites more than a cursory look into how ICT is used in education, especially given the more recent role ascribed to ICTs as knowledge enablers, that is, as drivers of knowledge generation, transfer, codification, and storage (Lopez et al. 2007). Given the cost of ICT and the acknowledged scarcity of resources in developing countries, the judicious enactment and application of ICT policies in education is not only wise but also necessary. If only for this fact, not to mention the ever-increasing influence of and reliance on ICT in education, and how education is in turn deemed as the road to redemption of developing countries, there is no doubt that the "twain" between policy goals and implementation should meet.

Using the experience of selected Asian countries as a case in point, I argue in this chapter that the "twain" between policy goals on ICT, particularly ICT in education, and their implementation do not always meet, regardless of how such policies are widespread, transferred, borrowed, or adopted from developed to developing countries. The essay draws from the experience of selected Asian countries, particularly in East Asia, since East Asia is not only a major ICT production center, but also most regional governments in the area actively support the ICT industry and foster the use of new technology (DFAT 2002). The primacy of East Asia in the ICT market has continued to grow as indicated by the region's ICT goods and services spending. Recent data by the United Nations Conference on Trade and Development (UNCTAD 2011) show that Asian economies in 2009 accounted for 66.3 percent of global exports of information (ICT) goods, up from 63.8 percent in 2008. The data also reveal that global ICT exports, representing 12 percent of world merchandise trade in 2009, are increasingly dominated by Asia. Seven of the top ten exporters are Asian economies–China is the largest, with ICT goods exports totaling US$356 billion in 2009; next is Hong Kong (China), with US$142 billion; and then the United States, at US$113 billion (UNCTAD 2011).

In many developing economies ICT goods are of great significance. In Asia, as in the case of Hong Kong, reliance on ICT products is very evident as such items represent more than 43 percent of all merchandise exports. Other Asian economies where ICT goods comprise 30 per cent or more of exports include China, Singapore, the Republic of Korea, Taiwan, and the Philippines (UNCTAD 2011). Over the past two decades, East Asian countries enjoyed a tremendous rise in the global economy caused by a rapid increase in exports. The combined share of East Asian countries in world non-oil exports recorded a threefold increase, from 11 percent to 33 percent, between 1969–1970 and 2006–2007. By 2006–2007, over 58 percent of total world ICT exports originated from Asia, with China alone accounting for 23 percent. Export dynamism in these product lines has been driven by the ongoing process of global production sharing, and the increasingly deep integration of East Asian countries into global production networks (Athukorala 2010). To accelerate ICT and e-commerce, East Asian governments are committed to strengthening their relevant infrastructure, regulatory regimes, and education systems (DFAT 2002).

This chapter provides a comparison of ICT policies of selected Asian countries, the policy proliferation and the role of international organizations, and a discussion on why there is a gap between policy and implementation. It concludes with a brief recap and final remarks.

Comparison of ICT Policies of Selected Asian Countries

This comparative narrative on the countries' ICT in education policies is meant to provide a lens from which one can situate ICT in education vis-à-vis the countries' overall ICT policies and developmental goals; also, to provide the necessary contextual framework on the succeeding discussion on the gap between policy and implementation.

In terms of ICT use in education in the Asia-Pacific region, countries in the area are roughly categorized into three types: those which are already integrating the use of ICT into the education systems (Australia, South Korea, and Singapore); those with policies and plans and which are starting to apply and test various strategies (China, India, Japan, Malaysia, Philippines, and Thailand); and those which have just begun and are more concerned with ICT infrastructure and connectivity installation, or countries which have not started at all (Myanmar, Lao PDR, Vietnam, Cambodia, Bangladesh, Maldives, Bhutan, and the Pacific Islands, among others) (UNESCO 2003a, 2003–2004a). As noted, among the governments with national ICT policies and master plans in education, although not yet fully integrating ICT within their education systems are China, India, Japan, Malaysia, Philippines, and Thailand (UNESCO 2003a, 2003–2004a). Although India is in South Asia, it is included in this analysis because of the major role it plays in the ICT industry not only in Asia but also in the whole world.

A closer look at the ICT policies of the said countries reveals that they all share the same features: they have both developed national ICT policies in education and established goals and objectives in introducing ICT in various aspects of education, from teacher training to teaching/learning. Their specific goals deal with the improvement of the teaching and learning process—to produce students who are confident, creative, and productive users of new technologies; to learn how to use ICTs as enabling tools to access information and gain knowledge; to link all educational institutions to the wealth of resources that are online; and to use ICT for distance education for all citizens, regardless of age, profession, distance, or geography. Their policy goals are linked with overall national ICT policies–that is, to introduce ICT in education to contribute to the knowledge society for economic development; foster creative industrial manpower; and construct a performance support system, bridge the digital divide, and promote equity in access (UNESCO 2003a). The ICT in education policies of these nations are summarized below.

China

The Chinese government believes that modernization of education by applying information technology, a process it refers to as *educational "informationisation,"* is imperative in transforming its enormous population burden into valuable human resources. Its overall ICT policy aimed at meeting these goals by 2010:

- ICT-based infrastructure that covers the whole country will be setup.
- ICT education will be popularized in most places.
- The competence of ICT application for all Chinese citizens will be improved.
- There will be enough ICT specialists to meet social development needs.
- A lifelong education system will be in place.
- Software producing centers and ICT corporations will be operational.
- The general level of infrastructure development and ICT application in education will rank at the top level among developing countries (UNESCO 2003a).

China's educational "informationisation," as with any other country, can be classified into three steps: the first is information infrastructure construction, the second is integrating ICT into all aspects of education, and the last step is to improve all aspects of the education system, particularly the education environment, educational content, pedagogy, and administration methods. At this point, China has almost finished part of step one in major cities, but not in villages. Two kinds of effort are still necessary for China to complete its educational "informationisation": one is to support village schools to complete step one and the other is to push other schools to pass the second and the third steps as soon as possible (UNESCO 2003b).

India

India's National Council for Educational Research and Training (NCERT) released the National Curriculum Framework for School Education in India in November 2000, providing guiding principles for reshaping the curriculum for schools. It recognizes that the process of education can no longer ignore the social and psychological impacts of ICTs. The framework also acknowledges the potential that global information sharing enables identifying the need to provide access to global information sources as a priority goal (UNESCO 2003a).

India's ICT policies include the formulation of plans for the integration of computers into the curriculum, the creation of a framework for enhancing learning opportunities using ICTs across the curriculum, designing a flexible curricular model that would embrace interdisciplinary and cross-disciplinary thinking, and the development of attitudes that are value driven, rather than technology driven. Further, India deems it vital to the success of its ICT implementation to provide professional development opportunities for teachers, enabling them to act as facilitators of learning, helping the students to become their own teachers and to think for themselves (UNESCO 2003a).

Japan

Japan's ICT potential, notwithstanding the fact that it is especially advanced in terms of technology and ICT infrastructure, has not yet been fully explored. Its use of ICT at the institutional level remains comparatively low, and ICT is not regarded as a priority in national education policy. However, it recognizes that if ICTs are used appropriately, they have great potential to be effective tools not only to enrich its existing programs but also to deliver education to rural areas.

Japan's Science and Technology Basic Plan (2001–2005), which covers its ICT policies, aims to establish Japan as a nation based on the creativity of science and technology. In the area of education, the plan achieves to

- improve science and technology education through the provision of better teacher training,
- supply adequate equipment as well as improved facilities for science and industrial education and introduction of educational computers,
- conduct practical research on Internet use in education, and
- promote educational software development and establish an Educational Software Library Centre (UNESCO 2003a).

In the last few years, most national policy targets for ICT use in classrooms have been fulfilled. The infrastructure is largely in place, and it is no longer uncommon for a student to access the Internet at home as well as at school. The issue remains how to successfully incorporate ICT into the teaching process. It is not at all easy for teachers to obtain the training they need. In addition to providing training opportunities, it is critical to build an environment that facilitates such training (UNESCO 2003b).

Malaysia

Malaysia is making every effort to steer its economy toward a knowledge-based one. "Vision 2020," Malaysia's long-term plan, calls for sustained, productivity-driven growth, possible only with a technologically literate, critically thinking workforce, which is prepared to participate fully in the global economy of the twenty-first century. Malaysia's National Philosophy of Education also calls for "developing the potential of individuals in a holistic and integrated manner, so as to produce individuals who are intellectually, spiritually, emotionally and physically balanced and harmonious" (UNESCO 2003b, 107).

The Ministry of Education sees ICT as a tool to revolutionize learning, to produce richer curricula, enhanced pedagogies, more effective organizational structures in schools, stronger links between schools and society, and the empowerment of learners. The concept of ICT in education, as seen by the Ministry of Education, includes three main policies:

- ICT for all students, meaning that ICT is used as an enabler to reduce the digital gap between the schools.
- The role and function of ICT in education as a teaching and learning tool, as part of a subject, and as a subject in its own right.
- Using ICT to increase productivity, efficiency, and effectiveness of the management system (UNESCO 2003a).

Although the Malaysian government has concentrated its efforts to enhance the use of ICT in schools, its impact in actual classroom teaching and learning continues to be insignificant. The Malaysian Ministry of Education is faced with the challenge of convincing teachers who still use traditional methods of teaching and learning to embrace change and to incorporate ICT into their instruction. Malaysia also struggles with problems related to the digital divide: the inequality between the haves and the have-nots is evident by the fact that students in more advantaged schools have acquired computer/ICT skills beyond the basic, while others in less advantaged schools have never even used a PC (UNESCO 2003b).

The Philippines

The Philippines has begun to reconceptualize its policies and strategies of ICT in education toward lifelong learning in its ICT Plan. It integrates ICT in education as an enabling and productivity tool to enhance learner performance, and rechannel educational efforts to meet the requirements of the learners and the job market through ICT (UNESCO 2003c). The Department of Education's initiatives on the use of ICT in education were embedded in the Department's Modernization Program begun in 1996, which introduced the use of modern technology to improve the teaching and learning process, educational management, and support operations in the educational system. The 1996 General Appropriations Act (GAA) laid the grounds for the provision of IT equipment in public secondary schools, providing the necessary funds for the procurement of hardware and software, teacher training, and courseware development (UNESCO 2003b). In August 2007, the Department of Education issued a Five-Year Information and Communication Technology for Education Strategic Plan (DepEd ICT4E Strategic Plan), which details a description of knowledge, understanding, skills, capacities, and values related to ICT that all learners in the Philippines should have:

• Abilities to seek, evaluate, organize, and present information.
• Higher-order thinking skills.
• Habits of lifelong learning to fully participate in the information age.
• An understanding of the pervasive impact of ICT on their daily lives and the society.

Designed as a policy measure, the ICT4E Strategic Plan is aimed to provide the direction needed to integrate ICT within the Philippine education system, and help move the country forward (DepEd 2007).

Thailand

Thailand's education is going through a reform process led by the Education Reform Act adopted in 1999. In the context of this reform, a national policy was formulated by the newly established National Institute for Technology for Education (NICTE). The Thailand government recognizes that ICT is vital and must be viewed as a tool for achieving broader national objectives, both social and economic, rather than regarding ICT as merely an end in itself. The policy is formulated in recognition of the vast potential of ICT to spread economic activity, democratic principle, wealth distribution, and social benefit provision such as education across every region of the country (UNESCO 2003a).

Policy Proliferation: The Role of International Organizations

It is widely acknowledged that policies for ICT in education have been developed and targeted for implementation within the context of the fast emerging globalized information society and economy. The conjunction of globalization, advances in ICTs and the resulting shifts in the labor market, and the conduct of business enterprises have led to basic changes in the economy and the society. This also has major implications for the role of education and training (Kearns 2002). One of such implications is the new conception of the relationship between knowledge and society, where knowledge is deemed both as the engine and product of social and economic development. Consequently, the production of knowledge, which is the essence of a knowledge-based society, has become more valuable than the mere acquisition of knowledge per se (Kearns 2002; OECD 2004). As the Organisation for Economic Co-Operation and Development (OECD) explains, knowledge is now recognized as the driver of productivity and economic growth. As a result, there is much attention and recognition given to the role of information, technology, and learning in economic performance. A "knowledge-based economy" or "knowledge-based society" becomes more significant from the fuller acknowledgement of the place of knowledge and technology, especially in modern OECD economies (OECD 1996).

In assessing globalization's true relationship to educational change, it is imperative "to know how globalization and its ideological packaging affect the overall delivery of schooling, from transnational paradigms, to national policies to local practices" (Carnoy and Rhoten 2002, 2). Among the areas where such a relationship becomes manifest is in finance, labor market, quality of national educational systems, information technology, and globalized information networks (Carnoy and Rhoten 2002).

In financial terms, most governments are pressured to reduce public spending on education and instead find other means to fund expansion of their educational systems. In labor terms, governments are further under pressure to attract foreign capital and provide a ready supply of skilled labor. This means more pressure to increase the average level of education in the labor force resulting, in turn, to more pressure to increase the average level of production in the labor force. In educational terms, the quality of national educational systems is consistently being compared internationally, and there is more emphasis on math and science curriculum, standards and testing, and on meeting standards through a change in the delivery system (Carnoy and Rhoten 2002). According to Roger Dale and Susan Robertson (2002) regional organizations, in particular, the North American Free Trade Agreement (NAFTA), the European Union (EU), and the Asia-Pacific Economic Cooperation (APEC), are as much as instrumental in steering the forces behind global capitalism and globalization as they are in the areas of social infrastructure and the formation of human capital, and directly or indirectly, on the shaping of regional educational policies.

Dale and Robertson (2002) note that countries in the Asia-Pacific region follow the philosophy of "concerted unilateralism" and "individual action plans," that is, the majority of the members of APEC assign a critical role to education and human capital formation in economic development and adopt this as a core of their overall policy, but they all achieve this in their own ways (Dale and Robertson 2002). DFAT shares the same observation and notes that most regional governments actively support the ICT industry and foster the use of new technology, although ICT and e-commerce regulation and policies vary considerably throughout the region. As an example, in 2000, APEC leaders committed to tripling their populations' Internet access by 2005. To accelerate the use of ICT and e-commerce, East Asian governments further seek to strengthen relevant infrastructure, regulatory regimes, and education systems while also seeking to develop their own populations' education and ICT skill levels (DFAT 2002).

Evidently, regional organizations such as APEC exert some influence in the diffusion of ICT in East Asian countries. The same could be arguably said on the role of international organizations such as the World Trade Organization (WTO) in brokering technology transfer in developing countries and least-developed countries. The proliferation of ICT in such countries is the result of a concerted effort by developed countries to transfer technology to least-developed countries (Hoekman et al. 2004). A 2004 World Bank Policy Research Working Paper cites the following articles of the World Trade Organization Agreement on Trade-Related Aspects of Intellectual Property Rights (TRIPS), a document that promotes the transfer of technology from developed countries to developing countries and least-developed countries: Article 7 provides for the promotion of technological innovation and the transfer and dissemination of technology and Article 66.2 calls on developed WTO members to provide incentives to their enterprises and institutions to promote technology transfer to the least-developed countries (Hoekman et al. 2004). The said provisions were reflections of the WTO's overall efforts to enhance its role in development.

Policy strategies to implement the provisions include the exploration of various channels of technology transfer; for example, trade in goods and services–all exports have the innate potential to transmit technology information, imported goods, and technological inputs; however, they can also directly improve productivity as they are used in the production process; foreign direct investments (FDIs)–technological information is generally transferred from multinational enterprises (MNEs) to their local subsidiaries, which later seeps through the local host economy; and *direct trade in knowledge via technology licensing*–this may transpire within firms, among joint ventures or between unrelated firms. Patents, trade secrets, copyright, and trademarks can act as facilitators of knowledge transfers (Hoekman et al. 2004).

ICTs and National Development: What's Behind the Policies?

Indeed, why ICT for development? Why ICT in education? Why all these policies with such lofty goals, to wit: "employ the use of technology as the foundation of the country's future economic development and ... leapfrog into the new economy by enhancing its competitive edge in ICT" (NEDA 2004, 1)? I offer two sets of answers to these questions. First, from the perspectives of modernization and human capital theories and second, the practical realities of the role of international organizations such as the World Bank and the World Trade Organization in pushing technology transfer from OECD countries to developing countries.

Modernization Theory

Popular in the 1950s through 1960s, modernization theory, posited by among others, Walt W. Rostow (1960), James Coleman (1968), Alex Inkeles and David Smith (1974), and Nell Smelser (1964), maintains that the only way for traditional societies to develop is to follow the ways of Western modernization. It claims further that the reason why traditional societies continue to be undeveloped is because they do not subscribe to the modernization processes of the West. It argues that there is a polarized and a linear relationship between the developed and nondeveloped countries or traditional societies, and the only method to bridge such polarity is through modernization. The theory also posits that

- Western countries are the most developed while other countries, particularly former colonies, are in the earlier stages of development; these countries will eventually reach the same level as the Western world if they follow the Western model of modernization,
- the development stages start from the traditional societies to developed ones, and
- Third World countries lag behind in their development and must follow the Western model to become developed.

Rostow (1960) offers a framework on the stages of modernization: traditional society, conditions for takeoff, takeoff, maturation, and mass consumption. The way for traditional societies to progress from one stage to the other is through education. Education is deemed to lead to economic growth, and economic growth is seen to provide more human services, choices, luxury, and opportunities for humanitarianism. Necessarily, in progressing from one stage to the other, there is some tension created. To avoid such tension, modernization should be accelerated (Lewis 1965).

Human Capital Theory

A related concept underpinning modernization is the human capital theory developed by among others, Theodore Schultz (1961), Edward Denison (1962), and Gary Becker (1964). Human capital theory promotes and supports the idea that education, and particularly higher education, enhances skills, values, and dispositions that advance the productive capability of the individual. Note is further made of the importance of education in transitioning from the traditional society to modernization. Both modernization and human capital theories promote the idea that education provides an individual with more skills and posit that an individual with more skills is rewarded with higher earning. The collective productivity of individuals, therefore, translates to greater productivity at the national level.

Reflecting on this overview, one could argue that the tenets of modernization picture underdeveloped and developing countries as not capable of breaking away from the molds of traditional societies and outdated systems of production, since they do not have the knowledge or resources to do so. To enable them to develop, they must emulate the developed nations of the West, which supposedly, have the modes of production, the know-how, the availability of capital, a skilled workforce, and an entrepreneurial class to achieve growth (Rostow 1960). As advanced by the modernization and the human capital theories, the key to breaking from the mold of traditional society and its traditional modes of production is through education based on a western model.

According to Renee Houston and Michelle Jackson (2003), the model of change posited by modernization is that technology is an important causal element for development. The model is based on the idea that there is a causal link between five sets of variables: modernizing institutions, modern values, modern behavior, modern society, and economic development (Houston and Jackson 2003). Thus, modernization operates on the belief that in transferring ICTs to "traditional" societies not only does a technology transfer occur but also the sociopolitical culture of modernity. The acceptance of this argument also gave rise to the position that technology or ICTs contribute to literacy, urbanization, and industrialization (Houston and Jackson 2003).

Drawing upon the intertwined perspectives of modernization and human capital theories therefore, and Houston and Jackson's (2003) explanation of ICT's role and place in the modernization paradigm, a case could be made that the reason why the developing countries employ ICT as tools for development is because they emulate developed countries in their effort to be modern and developed. Aware of how ICTs contribute to the further development of the developed countries, they also want to taste the benefits of ICTs that these countries have experienced from the employment of ICTs.

Maung Sein and G. Harindranath (2004) argue that ICTs could actually serve as a catalyst for development and even help poorer countries to leapfrog stages of development. Since they could learn from the experience of developed countries, they do not have to go through the growing pains of discovering and creating new technological innovations and, in the process, save investments and resources while learning what works and what does not. An example of this is in Africa, which in the last decade saw a rapid growth in its ICT sector that resulted in the major transformation on Africa's business operations and processes (Kimenyi and Moyo 2011). Sein and Harindranath (2004), however, contest the perspective that equates development with Western modernization, pointing out that such perspective has been discredited, because it does not take cultural and local contexts into account and only focuses on the ethnocentric point of view of the West–a common criticism lodged against modernization.

Attention is also called to what, I argue, are symbolic values ascribed to ICT, which, from all indications, are today's most ubiquitous symbols of modernization. From the way different international organizations keep a yearly track of network readiness, Internet connectivity, and computer penetration of both developing and developed countries, one could posit that these values include the prestige and political economy of being high tech, or on the cutting edge of the latest technology, and therefore up-to-date with the latest innovation.

One may cite the case of Latin America, a region reputed to be a developmental laggard, which has fast become one of the most dynamic areas for the implementation and use of new technologies through the expansion of mobile technology. Mobile phone technology has contributed to tapering the Latin American digital divide, reaching a penetration rate of more than 80 percent of the population (World Economic Forum 2011). Being regarded as high tech and network ready is, I argue, a symbolic value ascribed to ICT, since it indicates a country's ability to join the information society. As such, developing countries join the bandwagon in using ICT for national development. Being high tech and network ready is thus construed as concrete expressions of being "modern," as signals to the global ICT industry that a country is ready to participate in the ICT market.

The assertion about the symbolic values of ICT coincides with the socioanthropological views about the purported function of ICT as a mythic symbol of economic optimism and of power for politicians and the general public (Robertson 2003). Theodore Roszak (1986) is known to have advanced the popular conception that "access to computers was something we owe to our children, but which also relates to the myth of national prestige and power" (Roszak cited by Robertson 2003, 328). This articulation is rooted on the widely and long-held expectation about technological innovation revolutionizing education in the United States since the mid-1800s, beginning with the introduction of text books through the use of technologies such as film, radio, television, and computers (Twining 2002). Since then the mythology of political power and elitism and prestige has been ascribed to ICT.

One could argue that ICTs, therefore, thrive in the powerful mythologies of political power and prestige and, as already pointed out, from economic optimism. As John Robertson (2003) relates however, the mythology fails to extend to ICT in education, since ICT in education has no narrative outside purported economic benefits. ICT in education is bereft of a mythology of learning at its heart and "requires a theory about its purpose and meaning" if it is to win the hearts of teachers (Robertson 2003, 328).

Policy Formulation and Failure

Sein and Harindranath (2004) offer an explanation on why government policies on ICT often fail to achieve their intended objectives. They note the standard "tool" model of ICT often tends to underestimate the costs and complexities of computerization. The tool view focuses on ICT as "tools," and thus has emphasized policies that aim to develop and cultivate ICT production facilities. Kenneth Kraemer and Jason Dedrick (1994) cite studies of various countries, including Brazil, India, Mexico, the Philippines, and Vietnam, where the policies for ICT development were mainly directed toward an increase in "numbers" of ICT artifacts, such as an increase in the number of Internet connections. The problem with this is that the potential of ICTs in the entire developing world, taken as a whole, is limited.

Lars Soeftestad and Maung Sein (2003) observe that not all countries can become chip manufacturers or software producers. A case in point is the software industry in India; although it has proved to be a success, its impact on the economy is debatable. India's software industry, mainly centered in India's IT hub Bangalore, is held up as a model success story. However, UNDP's Technology Achievement Index shows that India is still listed as a "Dynamic Adopter," the third of four levels on. India ranks fairly low, because in the other indices, that is, "creating new technology," "diffusing recent innovations," "diffusing existing technologies that are still basic inputs to the industrial and the network age," and "building a human skill base for technological creation and adoption," the statistics are not as impressive (Soeftestad and Sein 2003).

Therefore, instead of viewing ICT as mere tools, public ICT policy formulation should transition from the increased use of ICT, to the emergence of new societal structures and change and finally, to ICT as "knowledge enabler," that is as *drivers* of knowledge generation, transfer, codification, and storage (Lopez et al. 2007). Recalling the specific example of India's software industry, Sein and Harindranath (2004) note how the origins of this industry were viewed from the "tool" view of ICT. However, with time the software industry itself realized that it could not fully develop without addressing what it could do for other economic and developmental activities (Sein and Harindranath 2004).

Echoing the same view, Edward Steinmuller (2001) explains that a technology rarely stands independently; most of the time it relies upon a variety of complementary technologies and capabilities. In other words, most technologies are systemic and include linkages with other industrial sectors. The development of markets for complementary technologies is therefore likely to affect technology transfer and leapfrogging strategies. Furthermore, in industrialized markets the linkages between industries are usually well developed, and markets for intermediate inputs have often become competitive, features that support the effective and rapid supply of needed complementary technologies and components (Steinmuller 2001).

The same observation cannot, however, be said of developing countries (Steinmuller 2001); thus, one can argue that no matter how finely crafted their ICT policies in general, and their ICT in education policies in particular are, achieving the development and leapfrogging objectives the policies stipulate remains a gargantuan challenge if the markets and the linkages between different industrial sectors on which these markets operate are not developed.

The challenge becomes more daunting if the absorptive capacities of developing countries to produce and use ICTs and their access to technology are taken into account. The capacity of people to absorb new technology spells the difference in the successful transfer of technology, and the translation of policy to implementation (Steinmuller 2001). The matter therefore becomes a question of access and human capital. To access and absorb new technology, one has to have a certain degree of education and cognitive performance and ability. As Everett Rogers ((2003) explains, the ultimate adoption and diffusion of an innovation, such as new technology, is not a simple process of instantaneous acceptance or implementation; rather, it requires one to go through a conscious decision-making process to decide whether to adopt an innovation; once an innovation is adopted, it is only then that it is communicated through different channels, over time, by members of a social system.

Thus, if the absorption of new technology is skill-based, then its successful adoption requires a higher level human capital–which, in turn requires education, on one hand, and access to ICT infrastructure and technology, on the other. However, it is also the case that educational attainment and literacy rates, including enrollment ratios, are a lot lower in developing countries than in industrialized ones (Sidorenko and Findlay 2001).

In terms of ICT policies in education, Willem Pelgrum (2001) cites lack of infrastructure, lack of access, and limited deployment in actual classrooms as top obstacles in ICT integration in education in both developing and developed countries. This is exacerbated by the lack of time for teachers to explore and be trained to use both the equipment and the software (BECTA 2003). According to the British Educational Communications and Technology Agency (BECTA) (2003), the barriers in ICT use in teaching can be classified into teacher-level barriers and school-level barriers. Teacher-level barriers encompass lack of self-confidence in using ICT (Pelgrum 2001), negative prior experience using ICT (Snoeyink and Ertmer -(2002), perception that ICT use does not enhance learning (Cox et al. 2000; Yuen and Ma 2002), and lack of motivation to change long-standing pedagogical practices (Snoeyink and Ertmer 2001). The school-level barriers are as follows: obsolescence of software and hardware (Cox et al. 2000); unreliability of equipment (Cuban et al. 2001; Butler and Sellbom 2002); lack of technical support (Cox et al. 1999, 2000); lack of administrative support

(Albaugh 1997; Butler and Sellbom 2002); lack of institutional support through leadership, planning, and the involvement of teachers as well as managers in implementing change (Larner and Timberlake 1995; Cox et al. 1999); lack of training based on teachers' existing ICT skill levels (Veen 1993); and lack of training focusing on integrating technology in the class-room rather than simply teaching basic skills (VanFossen 1999).

A look at the situation in particular developing countries is not promising. The results of System Assessment and Benchmarking for Education Results (SABER), a recent UNESCO Bangkok and World Bank survey on 12 countries in East and Southeast Asia comparing educational policies for improving student learning and system performance, are illustrative of the gap between policy and implementation (UNESCO 2011). The survey used the following indicators in the study:

- Proportion of schools with Internet access.
- Proportion of learners who have access to the Internet at school.
- Proportion of ICT-qualified teachers in primary and secondary schools.
- Proportion of learners enrolled at the post-secondary nontertiary and tertiary level in ICT-related fields.

The results are not encouraging. Of all policy domains surveyed, the ICT domain had the lowest response and completion rates, indicating that there are no systematic efforts to collect even those basic data related to the availability of ICT-related infrastructure in schools. Most countries surveyed reported that such data had not been collected by Ministries of Education and were therefore not available (UNESCO 2011). Survey data collectors also reported that their countries, including those described as having ICT in education policies in place, such as Cambodia, China, Lao PDR, the Philippines, and Thailand, have yet to define ICT-related terms and indicators or felt ill at ease with the questions asked. Examples of areas that raised questions included the categories: "ICT-qualified teach-ers" (e.g., what does it take for teachers to be considered ICT-qualified?) and "learners entitled to use computer labs" (e.g., what does "entitlement" mean at a school level?) (UNESCO 2011).

Another study by the Southeast Asian Ministers of Education Organization on ICT Integration in Education (SEAMEO 2010)places member countries according to one of ten identified dimensions[1] of ICT in education integration. Malaysia and Singapore are well ahead in infus-ing and transforming stages for most of these dimensions, except in two; those are "ICT in the national curriculum" and "assessment dimensions." Indonesia, Philippines, Thailand, and Vietnam are mainly at the infusing stage for most of the dimensions, yet most of them already have devel-oped ICT plans and policies in education. However, due to the rural-urban gap and different levels of access to ICT infrastructure, some of the dimensions are just at the "emerging stage." Other schools in Vietnam and in Indonesia, Philippines, and Thailand are in the infusing and applying stages. Indonesia also has schools in the emerging stage (SEAMEO 2010). It is interesting to note however, that not one of these countries has achieved the lofty goals they have provided in their ICT in education policies.

Perhaps the results of a study on equity in education in Southeast Asia (Sadiman 2004) can explain the disparity between policy and implementation, especially when it comes to access to ICT:

- Lack of available school buildings and classrooms with all required facilities.
- Shortage of teachers, especially in remote areas, resulting in countries such as Thailand and Indonesia having one teacher responsible for many grades.
- Uneven spread of population, which also creates serious disparities in educational opportunity, especially in a big country such as Indonesia.
- Lack of good textbooks and other learning materials, especially in remote schools.
- Lack of budget for building more schools, classrooms, and learning facilities.

In the particular case of India, a country study by the infoDev (2010) of the World Bank cites the following constraints:

- Low literacy level–even those deemed to be literate are perhaps not competent enough to receive IT education. Educational standards would need to be raised before the citizens can become digitally literate.
- Technophobia–teachers are typically wary of technology.
- Monitoring and evaluation–the penetration of hardware (computers) is fairly high in most schools, however the level of usage is unknown because there is no auditing or monitoring system.
- Guidelines for procuring content–identifying quality content is a common constraint for schools looking to use ICT-enabled teaching-learning practices.
- Institutional fragmentation–curriculum decisions, infrastructure decisions, content decisions, policy making, and policy implementation are all taken up by different bodies at different levels.

Other constraints faced by India include linguistic diversity and income disparity. The digital divide in the country is so acute that policy makers find it difficult to frame universal policies to be implemented (infoDev 2010).

Conclusion

Drawing upon the intertwined perspectives of modernization and human capital theories, I argue that the reason why developing countries, as exemplified by the Asian countries described in this paper, employ ICT as tools for development is because they try to emulate developed countries in their effort to be modern and developed. Not only do they want to be modern and developed, but they also want to taste the benefits of ICTs that these countries have experienced from the employment of ICTs. As such, they pattern their developmental goals and strategies after the goals and strategies of developed countries. This is clearly evident with the way developing countries borrow and adopt the ICT policies of developed countries, particularly their ICT in education policies. Note is made on how developed countries, through regional and international trade and financing organizations, facilitate the transfer and borrowing of said policies.

A comparative analysis of the ICT in education policies of selected Asian countries indicates that the transfer and borrowing could only be described as successful. As discussed, these countries have their policies, goals, and objectives well in place, however, when it comes to implementation, the "twain" between policy and actual realization do not meet. The reasons cited are as follows: in developing countries, the market for intermediate inputs and linkages between industries that provide complementary technology to support the ICT industry are not well developed; there is not much capacity, in terms of human capital and access to absorb the new technology; and in terms of ICT in education policies, the barriers to ICT integration include, lack of infrastructure and equipment and access to the equipment, lack of training and exposure of teachers to ICT equipment and software, lack of motivation to change long-held pedagogical practices, and the belief that technology does not enhance learning. The question therefore remains: what could be done to make the "twain" meet? Perhaps, knowing the reasons why the "twain" do not meet, as this chapter has attempted to articulate, is the first step.

NOTE

1. Ten ICT in education dimensions were identified based on the country case studies, where these dimensions are necessary and sufficient conditions that support the integration of ICT in education: (1) national ICT in education vision; (2) national ICT in education plans and policies; (3) complementary national ICT and education policies; (4) ICT infrastructure and resources in schools;

(5) professional development for teachers and school leaders; (6) community/ partnerships; (7) ICT in the national curriculum; (8) teaching and learning pedagogies; (9) assessment; and (10) evaluation and research (SEAMEO 2010).

References

Albaugh, Patti. 1997. "The Role of Skepticism in Preparing Teachers for the Use of Technology." Paper presented at Education for Community: A Town and Gown Discussion Panel, Westerville, OH, 26 January 1997. Available online at: http://www.eric.ed .

Athukorala, Prema-Chandra. 2010. *Production Networks and Trade Patterns in East Asia: Regionalization or Globalization?* Asian Development Bank (ADB) Working Paper Series on Regional Economic Integration No. 56. Manila, Philippines: ADB.

Becker, Gary S. 1964. *Human Capital: A Theoretical and Empirical Analysis, with Special Reference to Education.* Chicago: University of Chicago Press.

BECTA (British Educational Communications and Technology Agency) ICT Research. 2003. *What the Research Says About Barriers to the Use of ICT in Teaching.* Coventry, UK: BECTA. Available online at: http://www.mmiweb.org.uk.

Butler, Darrell, and Martin Sellbom. 2002. "Barriers to Adopting Technology for Teaching and Learning." *Educause Quarterly* 25 (2): 22–28. Available online at: http://net.educause.edu.

Carnoy, Martin, and Diana Rhoten. 2002. "What Does Globalization Mean for Educational Change? A Comparative Approach." *Comparative Education Review* 46 (1): 1–9.

Coleman, James S. 1968. "Modernization: Political Aspects." In *International Encyclopedia of the Social Sciences,* ed. David L. Sills, 395–402. Washington, DC: Free Press.

Cox, Margaret, Christina Preston, and Kate Cox. 1999. "What Factors Support or Prevent Teachers from Using ICT in Their Classrooms?" Paper presented at the British Educational Research Association Annual Conference, University of Sussex at Brighton, UK, September 2–5, 1999.

Cox, Margaret, Christina Preston, and Kate Cox. 2000. *Teachers as Innovators in Learning: What Motivates Teachers to use ICT.* Surrey, UK: MirandaNet. Available online at: http://www.mirandanet.ac.uk.

Cuban, Larry, Heather Kirkpatrick, and Craig Peck. 2001. "High Access and Low Use of Technology in High School Classrooms: Explaining and Apparent Paradox." *American Educational Research Journal* 38 (4): 813–834.

Dale, Roger, and Susan Robertson. 2002. "Regional Organizations as Subjects of Globalization." *Comparative Education Review* 46 (1): 10–38.

Denison, Edward. 1962. "Education, Economic Growth, and Gaps in Information: Investment in Human Beings." *The Journal of Political Economy* 70 (5): 124–128.

DepEd (Department of Education of the Philippines). 2007. *Five-Year Information and Communication Technology for Education Strategic Plan (DepEd ICT4E*

Strategic Plan). Pasig City, Philippines: DepEd. Available online at: http://www.deped.gov.ph.

DFAT (Department of Foreign Affairs and Trade Commonwealth of Australia). 2002. *Connecting with Asia's Tech Future: ICT Export Opportunities.* Barton, ACT: DFAT. Available online at: http://www.dfat.gov.au.

Hoekman, Bernard M., Keith Maskus, and Kamal Saggi. 2004. *Transfer of Technology to Developing Countries.* World Bank Policy Research Working Paper No. 3332. Washington, DC: World Bank. Available online at: http://go.worldbank.org.

Houston, Renee, and Jackson Michelle. 2003. "Technology and Context Within Research on International Development Programs: Positioning an Integrative Perspective." *Communication Theory* 13 (1): 57–77.

infoDev. 2010. *ICT4E in India and South Asia–India Country Study.* Washington, DC: World Bank. Available online at: http://www.infodev.org.

Inkeles, Alex, and David. H. Smith. 1974. *Becoming Modern.* Cambridge: Harvard University Press.

Kearns, Peter. 2002. *Towards the Connected Learning Society: An International Overview of Trends in Policy for Information and Communication Technology in Education.* Canberra, Australia: Commonwealth of Australia. Available online at: http://www.dest.gov.au.

Kimenyi, Mwangi, and Nelifer Moyo. 2011. *Leapfrogging Development Through Technology Adoption.* Washington, DC: Brookings Institution Publications. Available online at: http://www.brookings.edu.

Kraemer, Kenneth, and Dedrick Jason. 1994. "Payoffs from Investments in Information Technology: Lessons from the Asia-Pacific Region." *World Development* 22 (12): 1921–1931.

Larner, David, and Laura Timberlake. 1995. *Teachers with Limited Computer Knowledge: Variables Affecting Use and Hints to Increase Use.* Charlottesville, VA: University of Virginia.

Lewis, Arthur W. 1965. "A Review of Economic Development." *American Economic Review* 55 (1–2): 1–16.

Lopez, Susana, Jose Peon, and Camilo Ordas. 2007. "Information Technology as an Enabler of Knowledge Management." In *Knowledge Management and Organizational Learning: Annals of Information Systems,* ed. William R. King, 111–129. New York: Springer.

NEDA (National Economic Development Authority). 2004. *Medium Term Development Goals 2004–2010.* Pasig City, Philippines: NEDA. Available online at: http://www.neda.gov.ph.

OECD (Organisation for Economic Co-Operation and Development). 1996. *The Knowledge-Based Economy.* Paris: OECD. Available online at: http://www.oecd.org.

OECD. 2004. *Knowledge Management: Innovation in the Knowledge Economy: Implications for Education and Learning.* Paris: OECD.

Pelgrum, Willem J. 2001. "Obstacles to the Integration of ICT in Education: Results from a Worldwide Educational Assessment." *Computers & Education* 37 (2): 163–178.

Robertson, John W. 2003. "Stepping Out of the Box: Rethinking the Failure of ICT to Transform Schools." *Journal of Educational Change* 4 (4): 323–344.

Rogers, Everett. 2003. *Diffusion of Innovations*. 4th ed. New York: The Free Press.

Rostow, Walt Whitman. 1960. *The Stages of Economic Growth: A Non-Communist Manifesto*. Cambridge, MA: Cambridge University Press.

Roszak, Theodore. 1986. *The Cult of Information*. Berkeley, CA: California University Press.

Sadiman, Arief. 2004. "Challenges in Education in Southeast Asia." Paper presented at the International Seminar on Towards Cross Border Cooperation between South and Southeast Asia: The Importance of India's North East Playing Bridge and Buffer Role, Kaziranga, India, 16–19 November 2004. Available online at: http://www.seameo.org .

Schultz, Theodore W. 1961. "Investment in Human Capital." *The American Economic Review* 51 (1): 1–17.

Sein, Maung, and G. Harindranath. 2004. "Conceptualizing the ICT Artifact: Toward Understanding the Role of ICT in National Development." *The Information Society* 20 (1): 15–24.

SEAMEO (Southeast Asian Ministers of Education Organization). 2010. *Report: Status of ICT Integration in Education in Southeast Asian Countries*. Bangkok: SEAMEO. Available online at: http://www.seameo.org.

Sidorenko, Alexandra, and Christopher Findlay. 2001. "The Digital Divide in East Asia." *Asian Pacific Economic Literature* 15 (2): 18–30.

Smelser, Nell. 1964. "Toward a Theory of Modernization." In *Social Change: Sources, Patterns and Consequences*, ed. Amitai Etzioni and Eve Etzioni, 258–274. New York: Basic Books.

Snoeyink, Rick, and Peggy A. Ertmer. 2002. "Thrust into Technology: How Veteran Teachers Respond." *Journal of Educational Technology Systems* 30 (1): 85–111.

Soeftestad, Lars T., and Maung K. Sein. 2003. "ICT and Development: East is East and West Is West and the Twain May Yet Meet." In *The Digital Challenge: Information Technology in the Development Context*, ed. S. Krishna and Shirin Madon. Aldershot, UK: Ashgate.

Steinmuller, Edward W. 2001. "ICTs and the Possibilities for Leapfrogging by Developing Countries." *International Labour Review* 140 (2): 193–210.

Twining, Peter. 2002. *ICT in School: Estimating the Level of Investment*. Report No. 02.01. Milton Keynes, UK: meD8. Available online at: http://www.med8.info.

UNCTAD (United Nations Conference on Trade and Development). 2011. *In Wake of Financial Crisis, Asia's Share of Global ICT Exports Surges to Record High*. Geneva, Switzerland: UNCTAD.

UNESCO. 2003a. *ICT Policies of Asia and the Pacific*. Bangkok: UNESCO. Available online at: http://www.unescobkk.org.

UNESCO. 2003b. *Meta-Survey on the Use of Technologies in Education in Asia and the Pacific: Malaysia*. Bangkok: UNESCO.

UNESCO. 2003c. *ICT Policies of Asia and the Pacific: The Philippines*. Bangkok: UNESCO.

UNESCO. 2003–2004a. *Meta-Survey on the Use of Technologies in Education in Asia and the Pacific.* CD-ROM. Bangkok: UNESCO.

UNESCO. 2011. *Measuring ICT Application in Education: Feedback and Lessons from the SABER East Asia Pilot.* Bangkok: UNESCO.

USAID (United States Agency for International Development). 2003. *Digital Opportunity Through Technology and Communication (DOT-COM) Project, dot-gov Component.* Washington, DC: USAID.

VanFossen, Phillip J. 1999. "Teachers Would Have to Be Crazy Not to Use the Internet." Paper presented at the annual meeting of the College and University Faculty Assembly of the National Council for the Social Studies, Orlando, Florida, 19 November 1999.

Veen, Wim. 1993. "The Role of Beliefs in the Use of Information Technology: Implications for Teachers Education or Teaching the Right Thing at the Right Time." *Journal of Information Technology for Teacher Education* 2 (2): 139–153.

World Bank. 2005. *Monitoring and Evaluation of ICT in Education Projects: A Handbook for Developing Countries.* Washington, DC: World Bank.

World Economic Forum. 2011. *The Global Information Technology Report 2010–2011. Transformations 2.0.* Geneva, Switzerland: World Economic Forum. Available online at: http://www3.weforum.org.

Yuen, Allan H. K., and Will W. K. Ma. 2002. "Gender Differences in Teacher Computer Acceptance." *Journal of Technology and Teacher Education* 10 (3): 365–382.

Chapter 2

Rich Media Technologies
Opportunities in Australian Higher Education

Robyn Smyth, Trish Andrews, Richard Caladine, and Jason Bordujenko

Introduction

This chapter reports the outcomes of a two-year project investigating the implementation of rich media technologies in higher education in Australian universities. Rich media technologies are described as the range of synchronous and asynchronous videoconferencing technologies that facilitate interactive communication between users who can see, hear, and interact with multiple communication streams. The investigation used a taxonomic approach to define which technologies could be included in the "rich media" category and established a website providing access to professional development resources and case studies demonstrating effective practice as well as scanning the higher education sector nationally and internationally for exemplars of policy and practice that could inform future implementations. It found that rich media technologies have the potential to be lighthouse technologies for reducing costs and environmental footprints across the higher education sector while improving the efficiency of administration and research as innovations in pedagogy for learning and teaching emerge. Surprisingly however, our research indicated that rich media technologies are sinking into the wash of the e-learning tide in Australian higher education, rather than cresting the wave of the social communication software swell, primarily due to lack of coherent policy and planning within the sector. They have not maintained their status as lighthouse technologies because their capability in a digital world is not well understood by managers and others beyond a small number of videoconferencing enthusiasts.

The Project and Its Relevance

The Leading Rich Media Technologies Collaboratively[1] project began late in 2007 with the aim of improving teaching and learning outcomes and increasing institutional efficiency and effectiveness by providing frameworks for decision-making about the use of rich media technologies. Across the sector these technologies are well supported by the online academic network provided by the Australian Academic and Research Network (AARNet), so they are able to be used for learning, teaching, administration, and research. The project set out to investigate, provide, and promote sustainable, scalable frameworks for strengthening learning and teaching when engaging with and using rich media technologies. Drawing from survey data collected from 22 out of 39 Australian universities on their use of rich media technologies, the findings indicate that the project has largely succeeded in this intent (Smyth and Vale 2011). Our findings also show that in higher education institutions where rich media technologies are embedded, their use provides opportunities for equality of access to learning among students, whether they reside in metropolitan, regional, or rural settings. However, the other primary focus of the project was the evaluation of policy development around technology use in higher education institutions, an area where institutions have been much less successful. This theme is discussed extensively in the second part of this chapter.

Project Approach and Methodology

By using a theoretical framework based on extensive body of work on educational change of Thomas Sergiovanni (1998), operationalized through the integrated competing values framework from organizational development theory (Vilkinas and Cartan 2006), the project team was able to manage the project effectively as a videoconference collaboration in line with our desire to "practice what we preach" and to use rich media technologies to facilitate the collaborative effort of the project. The vectors from the competing values framework (that demonstrate human commitment, adaptation, maximization of output, and expansion) synergized well with the conceptual ideals of Sergiovanni's "professional community" model, which encapsulate the values required for success to leverage deep and enduring change including expertise, collegiality, professional obligations, norms, and conduct (Sergiovanni 1998), occurring in circumstances of respect, collaboration, and consensus about directions for change. The intent here was to use two approaches in combination to act as the conceptual framework for the project. We used the lens of educational change theory to explore the use of rich media technologies in Australian universities and the lens of organizational behavior to analyze how and why technologies are implemented.

The team carried out the investigation in two stages over 24 months, meeting regularly by videoconference. In stage 1, the project team established management protocols including publication plans, meeting schedules, and work responsibilities. The first task was literature review and the gathering of gray data–to update and extend the AARNet sector survey (AARNet Pty. Ltd. 2006) and an earlier informal collection of gray data concerning management and use of rich media technologies over recent years. The outcome of this stage was the identification of theory and practice in relation to current implementation of rich media technologies and codification of data.

The AARNet 2006 sector-wide survey highlighted five major recommendations in interoperability, user support and training, policy and best practice development, as well as broader industry support for embracing education use of videoconferencing technologies. Due to the evolving nature of the videoconferencing market, a watching brief was kept on the technology adoption via the AARNet National Video Conferencing Service, which had been set up to put the findings of this report into action. The AARNet Group became our reference group for the project.

This information was then used by the team in stage 2 to formulate the questions for the survey of Australian higher education institutions on their policy making about and the use of rich media technologies. The project team was very pleased with the number of institutions represented in the data collection—a total of 40 respondents representing 22 out of 39 Australian universities—and felt that this gave a good overview of the state of implementation of rich media technologies in Australian universities. For purposes of comparison beyond the Australian higher education sector, a consultant from Wainhouse Research in the United States was engaged to provide a report on the state of rich media technologies worldwide (Greenberg 2009b). This resulted in an extensive report focusing on the "big picture" view of rich media technologies internationally, and a review of the technologies expected to impact on higher education in the near future. In addition, an Australian consultant with extensive experience in videoconference management was employed to compare our data with government and corporate implementations (Berriman 2007; 2010). Once the literature review was completed and reports presented, we sought an expert opinion about the efficacy of the data gathered from our European counterparts at SurfNet, the equivalent of AARNet in the Netherlands and from our extensive national network of Australian videoconference managers who acted as technical and operational experts. In this way we believe that our findings do represent an accurate picture of rich media technologies policy making and implementation prior to 2011.

Literature Review

The review of literature for the Leading Rich Media Technologies project proved more challenging than first expected. First, the technology is changing at a rapid pace with new technologies appearing constantly for early adopting individuals to assess, while the use of "older" technology has barely come into general use by tertiary institutions. There is a lot of overlap in the technologies being used or experimented with by staff in universities, but scholarly review and research of the effectiveness of a particular media may appear well after individuals and institutions have moved to newer technologies and applications. To gain a broad overview of the state of play in the use of rich media technologies by higher education institutions, we constructed an annotated bibliography in chronological order. This form of literature review provided details of and comments on the publications for 2002–2010, while highlighting the rapid change in technology over a quite short period of time. The chronology provided an extra dimension to the research that may not have been as easily seen in the standard literature review format.

The literature review revealed many papers on specific uses of technologies such as videoconferencing and an almost never-ending stream of press releases about equipment available for purchase. It was difficult to obtain some of the more scholarly reports as the most recent are not offered online in journals but have to be purchased from commercial sources.

After completing the literature review the team concluded that there was a paucity of scholarly work to add to their combined knowledge, leaving them little better placed to answer the question, "How will institutions make decisions on which technologies to use to aid student teaching and learning?" The team's broad personal experience and knowledge of the field spanned from technical to pedagogical and beyond, so we were confident that we could effectively evaluate what we had found and determine what was lacking. However, a scan of the field internationally did add to the team's knowledge (Greenberg 2009b). The complete chronological annotated bibliography can be found on the project's website: www.richmedia.edu.au.

A Taxonomy Defining Technologies and Media

One of the project goals was to bring some clarity to terminology surrounding synchronous communications or rich media technologies. Technology is usually defined as applied knowledge, particularly in the areas of engineering and science (Caladine 2008a). However, often the term "technology" is used to refer to pieces of machinery or equipment (notably in the case of electronic or computer equipment). In yet other instances the same term is used to define systems of human and nonhuman components, for example a manual telephone system consisting of handsets, operators, exchanges, and wires.

The term "educational technology" has been used to refer to all manner of devices and applications that are used in teaching and learning. In the past they included record players and slide projectors, among others. Or using the systemic definition, record players and records, slide projectors, screens, slides, and often blinds and dimmers to control the light in the room. Modern examples of educational technology (sometimes referred to as "learning technology") include Learning Management Systems (LMS).

For clarity, in this project we have adopted the popular usage of the term "technology" to mean devices or applications. Thus, for this project, videoconference, podcasting, telephony, and email are examples of technologies. However, as technologies converge some are more adequately defined as collections of technologies or collections of technological elements. In this way web collaboration can be viewed as the convergence of videoconference, a shared digital canvas and other functions. Also an LMS can be a collection of two-way technological elements for communications and one-way elements for the delivery of content.

This project is concerned with the subset of communications technologies shown in the last column of Table 2.1. They are rich media technologies as they afford communication by audio or by audio and video. They are two-way and synchronous.

Rich media technologies are described as the range of synchronous and asynchronous videoconferencing technologies now becoming "as simply

Table 2.1 Subset of Communications Technologies

	One-Way		Two-Way	
	Asynchronous	Synchronous	Asynchronous	Synchronous
Rich Media	Podcasts Vodcasts Video Video can be recorded to media such as DVD, Blu-Ray, or tape. Video can also be hosted on a website. Recorded Presentations Several products are available for the automated recording of presentations or lectures. These include Lectopia (previously known as iLectures).	Broadcasts. For example television and radio (satellite or terrestrial). Webcasts	Voicemail (when two-way)	This Project iVC or Internet Visual Communications. For example Skype (video), MSN messenger, Windows Live Messenger, Apple iChatAV Videoconference. For example appliance-based systems such as Tandberg, Polycom, and Lifesize etc. Web Collaboration. For example Webex, Ellunimate, Marratech, Cisco Meetingplace, and Adobe Connect (Breeze) Access Grid Telephony. The plain old telephone system. Teleconference. For example a telephone conference call.
Text	Email (electronic mail) Letter (print or snail mail)		Wiki Email (exchanges) CMC Letters (exchanges) (print or snail mail)	IM (Instant Messaging) Text based. Also known as Chat. For example IRC (Internet Relay Chat) SMS exchanges (Short Message Service)

and easily accessible as the telephone" (Berriman 2007, 4). This description encompasses those videoconferencing technologies that facilitate interactive communication between users, who can see, hear, and interact with multiple communication streams synchronously or access them asynchronously (AARNet Pty. Ltd. 2006). Rich media is further defined as media that approximates the immediacy of face-to-face communication where participants read nonverbal cues such as vocal inflection and body language (93 percent of all communication) to increase understanding and obtain rapid feedback (Daft and Lengel 1986 as cited in Baecker 2003). One-way technologies such as i-Lecture (Lectopia) and other such software were not intended as a focus of this project.

Surveying Australian Universities

Our project team for this research was small but widely distributed geographically. It comprised three academics, the project officer, and an AARNet representative. The project leaders sought to gain insight into practice and to move toward the goal of investigating and providing frameworks for strengthening learning and teaching when engaging with and using rich media technologies. To reach this goal the project team needed information from the Australian university community on practice and policies underpinning implementation of rich media technologies within institutions and across the sector. We therefore collected data by surveying all Australian universities. An initial large survey was set up using the online Survey Monkey tool and upper level managers (deputy/pro vice-chancellors, Information Technology Departments, ITD/Teaching and Learning Centre, TLC, directors, etc.) from all 40 institutions were invited to respond or to pass the survey link on to more appropriate staff. Both quantitative and qualitative data were gathered, the latter being analyzed using the NVivo software platform. Follow-up reminders were sent on three occasions to increase the response rate. Interviews were conducted to gather case study data of exemplar programs nominated by surveyed institutions or known to the researchers. All data was presented to the project's national and international evaluators to test its efficacy. Case study data was the report in detail along with the Wainhouse Research Consultant's report and a comparative report from the Commercial Sector (Berriman 2010).

Our survey of Australian higher educational institutions resulted in 22 of the 39 universities in Australia responding to the call for information about their policy for and use of rich media technologies in their institution. A total of 40 responses were received covering a wide range of topics on how the technologies are being used and planned for. The highlights of the survey results are summarized below with analysis in subsequent sections.

- Eleven (50 percent) of the responding institutions spoke of rich media technologies being aligned with their institutional strategic plan through supporting teaching and learning, and eight (36 percent) of the institutions said it aligned with their plan for research.
- Six (27 percent) of the institutions cited flexibility in the delivery of teaching programs, and five (23 percent) supported multicampus and/or distance education as being a part of their strategic plan and said that rich media technologies enhanced these aims.
- Four (18 percent) of the institutions said that it was an aim of their strategic plan to be more responsive to students' needs, and two (9 percent) thought that the use of rich media technologies aligned with their desire to form a community of learning.

Possibly some of the preconditions that needed to be met before implementing rich media technologies were concerned with policy and legislation. Respondents stated that more policies would need to be developed for the implementation of the technology—specifically for issues such as ethics, privacy, and copyright.

One of the interesting conclusions from this analysis is that none of the directors of the ITD departments believed that the sole responsibility for policy development regarding rich media technologies should reside in their own departments.

Respondent and Institutional Details

Twenty-two of thirty-nine institutions are represented in the survey results with forty individual responses. All Australian states are represented. We did not get any responses from the Australian Capital Territory or the Northern Territory (representing 4/39 universities).

Respondents included deputy and pro vice-chancellors, directors of IT departments, directors of Teaching and Learning Units, staff involved with media and communications and videoconferencing managers, others involved with instructional technology and academic development, a program manager for learning environments, a visualization officer, and those involved with media and communications and venues and events.

The majority of respondents came from institutions with multiple campuses (86 percent), and 36 percent of respondents represented institutions involved in distance education. Four institutions had international campuses and two dual sector institutions (university and technical college).

This variety of respondents gives the project much scope to investigate how rich media technologies are being used in Australian universities.

Rich Media Technologies in Use or Planned for Adoption

Respondents were asked to select all of the technologies in use at their institution from a list provided. Videoconferencing was the most common technology in use–all of the universities responding to the survey used videoconferencing. Access Grid was the least used technology with 14 of the institutions reporting its use. The use of personal videoconferencing (18 universities) and capture/desktop technologies (20 universities) reflects the changing nature of rich media within higher education institutions. Greenberg (2008, 2009b) predicted that the desktop type of rich media technologies will overtake the use of videoconferencing within the next few years, and our experience since the end of the project supports this trend.

Although 14 of the institutions were planning to increase their use of videoconferencing and 13 their use of Access Grid, the greatest increase in rich media technology use was in personal web conferencing (77 percent) and streaming, both asynchronous and synchronous (73 percent). These responses are in keeping with the research by the Wainhouse Research group that predict that the use of web conferencing and video streaming would increase greatly in the next three years (Greenberg 2008, 2009a).

Uses of Rich Media Technologies

The project team sought to ascertain all of the ways in which rich media technologies are being used by Australian universities. The most common uses for the technologies were for learning and teaching (100 percent) and as a personal communication tool (86 percent). The respondents identified uses in administration (73 percent) and research (77 percent), and three of the institutions reported that rich media technologies were being used in widely ranging fields such as event recording, webcasting, training, and for engaging with prospective students and community outreach projects. Nineteen of the institutions (86 percent) had tested pedagogical models for using rich media technology, and twelve of the institutions (59 percent) participating in the survey had implemented pedagogical models.

Institutions seem to be unanimous in recognizing the value in using rich media. All of the institutions where rich media technologies are embedded state that the use of rich media technology provides opportunities for equality of access to learning amongst their students, whether they reside in metropolitan, regional, or rural situations. They believe that it is the distance between students, teachers, and researchers coupled with a desire to bring them together for interaction that drives the use of the technology. A bonus is that costs can be constrained when staff does not have to travel great distances to carry out their work.

Additional studies that we reviewed or data collected in our case studies also supported the value proposition of rich media technologies:

> Technical And Further Education South Australia (TAFESA) has found that class sizes become viable when they can aggregate metropolitan and rural students into one class—making the ranges of subjects more extensive than if they had to rely on student numbers from one geographical area. TAFESA managers believe that the benefits of their extensive use of technology include connections with other staff and students that provide more realism and sense of quality of engagement. Both staff and students report dealing with real people, no matter where they are located, as being highly valuable. Staff particularly report that students feel more connected, and thus are more willing to seek help where necessary. (Smyth 2009)

There was a similar response in another case study we compiled of the National Centre of Science, Information and Communication Technology and Mathematics Education for Rural and Regional Australia (SiMERR) (Smyth and Vale 2011). Participants and instructors found that the greatest benefits of the use of rich media technologies were as follows:

- cost savings
- convenience
- improved collaboration, because it is easier than travelling
- richer thinking, because the technology enables deeper discussion
- easier management and progress tracking with remote projects.

This data from our case studies reflects the benefits of rich media technologies that have the potential to be generalized throughout universities. Analysis of policy and responsibility that follows provides some clues about why technologies were not usually generalized.

Responsibility for Rich Media Technologies

One of the survey questions required the participants to check a box indicating who was responsible for maintenance, bookings, policy, and facilities at their institution. They were given choices for indicating the areas of responsibility–ITD, TLC, library, or faculties, and also given the option of checking a box headed "none" or "various." The project researchers wished to ascertain if there were any consistencies across the institutions represented, and how rich media technologies are managed by the universities.

The different categories of responsibility included in the question were based on our experience that the responsibility for rich media management fell to multiple departments in most of the universities responding to the survey. The graphics below summarize the responses.

As reflected in Figure 2.1, the responsibility for maintenance fell solely upon ITD departments in 10 of the institutions, though over half (12) said that various departments were responsible for maintenance. When it came to booking the use of the equipment only six institutions nominated ITD departments as the sole provider of bookings, and three said that their TLC had sole responsibility. The other 13 institutions nominated various or multiple responsibilities for booking the use of rich media equipment.

The responsibility for policy and facilities were even less clear according to the respondents to the survey. Twenty of the institutions nominated multiple or various divisions as being responsible for policy on rich media technologies, while only one said it was the purview of the ITD departments. One institution said that no one was responsible. The ITD department of 4 institutions claimed sole responsibility for the management of facilities in the institutions responding to the survey, and the remaining 18 institutions reported multiple or various departments claiming responsibility. It would appear from these responses that the use, maintenance, and policy for videoconferencing and other rich media technologies is not limited to a central department overseeing these technologies. This is in line with other evidence gathered in data and through the literature review

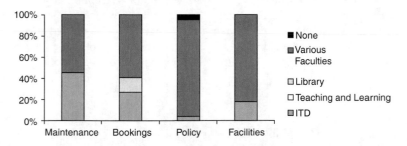

Figure 2.1 Departmental Responsibility for Rich Media Technologies by Task.
Source: Created by the authors.

into implementation of e-learning and rich media technologies (Keegan et al. 2009). Responsibility for rich media services is clearly distributed across a number of departments in the universities, indicating a need for coordination among several groups to achieve usage and strategic goals.

Additional data from a survey conducted by one of the project partners (Caladine 2008b), indicated that the ownership of rich media technologies within higher education institutions is often by an audiovisual department, which in the past has managed learning technology. However, the researcher asks the question: *Now that most videoconference equipment uses the Internet does it make sense to change who "owns" it?* This study raises questions in this regard that will need to be addressed by universities sooner or later.

Policies in Action

When respondents were asked to provide the URL to their policies governing use of rich media technologies at their institution, responses were as follows:

- Eleven of twenty-two did not supply a URL. Three specifically stated that there is no such policy.
- Eleven of the twenty-two did supply a URL. However, three of these were not accessible.

Of the eight that were reviewed, we noticed that the majority were generalized ITD policies not particularly aimed at the use of videoconferencing or other real-time technologies and/or caveats regarding the use of technologies such as "Skype" and limitations of their use. This would appear to confirm Caladine's findings that the use of peer-to-peer real-time communications systems was not being encouraged in the university environment, regardless of the general trends identified by industry studies (Caladine 2008a). We speculate that rich media technologies and their different uses are proliferating faster than policy makers have the time to draft policies for governance of the technologies in the universities. The lack of a coherent policy may also be connected to the lack of clarity surrounding who is responsible for policy.

Responsibility for Policy

Another way of examining the institutional view on policy for emerging technologies was to examine the answers given by position in the university represented by the survey participants. The survey participants were

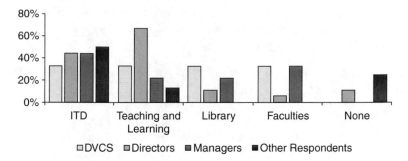

Figure 2.2 Responsibility for Policy.
Source: Smyth and Vale (2011).

divided into groups by position in the organization, as stated on their answers to the survey. They were divided into four categories: deputy vice-chancellors (three), directors (eighteen), managers (nine), and others, which included lecturers and academic developers (eight).

As shown in Figure 2.2, eleven of these felt that responsibility for policy was spread across a number of areas of their institution, six of these being ITD directors and five being directors in the other category. Two of the directors of ITD departments felt that there was not any specific area responsible for policy development, and one ITD director believed that the responsibility for policy should be in the TLC. One representative of directors of TLCs believed that the responsibility for policy development regarding the use of rich media technologies resided in the TLC. Three directors from the "Other" category also felt that the responsibility for policy should sit in the TLC.

One of the interesting conclusions from this level of analysis is that none of the directors of the ITD departments believed that the sole responsibility for policy development regarding rich media technologies should reside in their own departments. All of the ITD directors who chose numerous institutional departments for the responsibility included the ITD department as part of a group of policy makers, but none felt it was their sole responsibility at present.

Strategic Planning and Rich Media Technologies

We also asked the respondents to describe how the implementation and use of rich media technologies aligned to their institution's strategic plan. Two of the universities did not comment on this question. Key areas of institutional strategic plans that aligned with the use of rich media technologies included

- teaching and learning: 11/22 (50 percent),
- research: 8/22 (36 percent),
- flexibility in the delivery of teaching programs: 6/22 (27 percent),
- multicampus and/or distance education: 5/22 (23 percent),
- increased responsiveness to student needs: 4/22 (18 percent), and
- formation of a community of learning: 2/22 (9 percent).

Some of the more innovative uses of rich media technologies taken from the universities' strategic plans were

- encouraging community participation in university events (regional university),
- maximizing access to scholarly expertise and cultural collections (metropolitan university), and
- to foster community outreach (metropolitan university).

Such data provide insight into the broader benefits of rich media technologies for universities wishing to engage with their communities but were found not to be strong enough drivers for adoption of the technology as a strategic priority or a university-wide policy direction.

Drivers for Adoption

Most of the respondents believed that the adoption of rich media technologies was being driven by student demand (83 percent), followed closely by demand from the staff at their university (78 percent). Reducing travel budgets was also seen as a driver by 28 of the respondents (70 percent). Interestingly, no respondents cited actual policies as drivers of rich media technologies implementations, a key finding given the intent to investigate the impact of policy development.

As shown in Figure 2.3., other reasons given for driving the adoption of rich media technologies were

- pedagogy to enhance the student experience, advance teaching, and support learning;
- support and enhance communication at a distance;

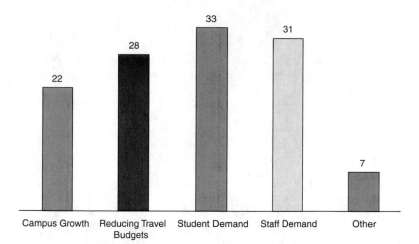

Figure 2.3 Drivers for Adoption.

- reducing stress and environmental impact of staff travel, rather than costs savings;
- reduced intercampus travel;
- Flexibility in teaching and learning delivery. Working in partnership to bridge the divide between pure and applied research;
- increased number of remote sites requiring increased levels of communication between sites;
- external student base, flexibility for remote learning, and accessibility;
- strategic planning, in particular the drive for curriculum renewal;
- international and distance teaching such as remote health clinics and hospitals;
- enhancing teaching, learning, scholarship, and research;
- e-research or e-learning initiatives;
- establishment of access centers as initial impetus;
- social shifts and contemporary media demands;
- technology enabled pedagogy;
- innovation, market share, enhanced student learning outcomes, and experiences; and
- support for the university's vision and objectives.

This final point captures the situation well. Rich media technologies are regarded as "support" rather than "core" technologies.

Sources of Funding

Figure 2. 4 shows another question, which we hoped might point toward a policy impetus, in which we asked the respondents to identify the sources of funding for

- the initial purchase of rich media equipment,
- the upgrade and replacement of equipment,
- the operational costs of using rich media technologies, and
- the maintenance of the equipment.

The source of funding for initial purchase of the equipment was most likely to be a project specific grant or source of funding, as well as capital pool development funding (government grants) or the purchase being funded from central university funds. For all of the other categories–upgrade or replacement, operational costs, and maintenance–the respondents thought that the funds for these, on the whole, were sourced from central funding from university funds. A second key finding was that there was little evidence of proactive policy development about funding with purchases tied to one-off funding. No one indicated that ongoing support for staff was included as a budgeted item.

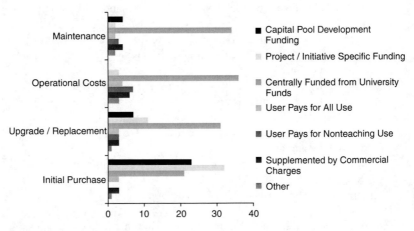

Figure 2.4 Funding Sources.

Source: Smyth and Vale (2011).

Barriers to Adoption

Respondents were also asked to rate four different barriers to the adoption of rich media technology at their university from highest to lowest and this is the order that resulted:

- security policies
- financial support
- staff expertise
- network capacity.

These findings align well with the results of the survey carried out by Greenberg (2009b) who asked respondents to rate ten barriers to the adoption of rich media technologies. The greatest barrier in this survey was also funding, although network/bandwidth capacity rated ninth. The barriers are illustrated in Figure 2.5.

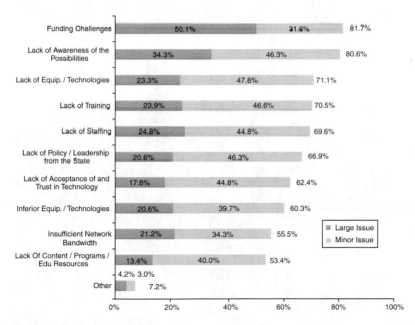

Figure 2.5 Barriers to Adoption.

Source: Smyth and Vale (2011).

Preconditions to Implementation

The following question was asked: *Will any preconditions to the implementation of rich media technology be required at your institution?* The responses gave more details of issues that need to be addressed before rich media technology can synchronize with the everyday business of an Australian university. Interestingly, five respondents stated that there were no preconditions. The most numerous responses were as follows:

- more training and professional development for staff: 7 (32 percent)
- none: 5 (23 percent)
- ensure the technology enhances teaching and learning: 5 (23 percent)
- increased funding: 4 (18 percent).

The rest of the preconditions cited fell into three main groups: the lack of thought about policy and strategy across universities and the sector; the need for more legislation around the implementation of the technology, specific issues being ethics, privacy, and copyright; and technical concerns including coordination and uniformity across all of their campuses in addition to infrastructure and network upgrades.

Conclusions from Survey Data

The Leading Rich Media Technologies survey has provided the project with some very useful information, which will be used to further the project research into the viability, scalability, and sustainability of the uses of rich media technologies and to make recommendations to the participating universities. However, the silences in the data about policy and the evident confusion of information may reflect the state of thinking about the use of rich media technologies in Australian universities. For insight, we looked to the Megatrends Report (Keegan et al. 2009). After studying why some e-learning programs in Europe had failed, the Megatrends authors made five major conclusions and recommendations that are characteristic of all or nearly all of the initiatives that had ceased, because they failed to reach the targeted goals (Keegan et al. 2009; Weinstein et al. 2010). Their recommendations should be considered by the Australian higher education sector, which could benefit from the European experience. As the Megatrends Report states:

- Hard-nosed market research is essential for the success of any e-learning initiative;

- E-learning initiatives should plan carefully for and control carefully their revenue and expenses. Seeding funding dries up quickly;
- Choice of courses and its accreditation is crucial;
- It is important that those planning e-learning initiatives should define precisely the relationships of their initiative to existing providers and define precisely the institutional model they will adopt;
- E-learning initiatives should plan carefully to manage both their educational and business activities. (Keegan et al. 2009, 96)

These recommendations point to the need for planning and policy in the purchasing and use of rich media technologies. As can be seen from some of the sections of this report, policy on the use of rich media technologies is lagging behind the use of the technology, and many institutions rely on grant types of funding to provide the infrastructure for the technology. The e-learning scene is changing very rapidly, and all of the institutions participating in this survey are endeavoring to provide their students with the best possible means of enhancing their teaching and learning experience. They may, however, need to allow more time for the development and implementation of policy regarding the use of rich media technologies. Institutions may also need to allow time to examine how these technologies rate in the importance of enhancing teaching and learning in their institutions and plan for their continued use and upgrade of equipment. In these ways, viability, sustainability, scalability, and pedagogical concerns may be discussed during planning processes, therefore, reducing risk of inappropriate implementation and failure to leverage sustained change.

Usefulness of Findings to Institutions and the Sector

We began our work with a vision that rich media technologies should become viable and sustainable technologies contributing to institutional and sector growth, and development in an increasingly visual digital world where reduction of environmental consequences of travel is seen as desirable. Our findings and the approach used to derive them should have applicability across the sector and possibly internationally. From these findings, individual institutions should be able to distil cues for work in their own contexts, especially in regard to policy development. We forecast the following for individual institutions and the sector:

- Rich media technologies will become integrated into virtual learning and work environments within the sector, because they will have a positive impact on teaching and learning outcomes but will require new policy development.

- User support will be a policy necessity, costed into purchase and maintenance planning and provided by appropriately experienced educational technologists and videoconference technicians rather than generic IT staff.
- Desktop applications will become the norm for person-to-person linkages but will require user support to be embedded in implementation and supported by policy.
- Room systems will be essential for group meetings and some learning situations so should remain as core technologies embedded in institutional policy making.
- Behavioral change such as strategies aimed at encouraging the use of rich media technologies as a low-cost alternative for regular intra-interstate, national, and international travel will support the growth of one-to-one and one-to-some uses of rich media technologies in administration, research, and higher degree research supervision if they are required by institutional procedures.
- Organizational champions will stimulate sector partnerships and institutional management to develop appropriate policies and practices.
- The scholarly research void will encourage further research in the sector and individual institutions, so that the sector is not reliant on vendor information to inform policy and practice.

Our research indicates that rich media technologies are at risk of sinking into the wash of the e-learning tide in Australian higher education rather than being on the crest of the wave breaking into the social communication software swell. It is our intention that this study and our predictions will focus attention on adoption of rich media technologies, moving them some way toward their place as lighthouse technologies for administration and research, while innovations in pedagogy for learning and teaching emerge. We similarly hope that others will follow our direction and build on this work.

Our concern is that the needs of the technologies, their defining characteristics, and appropriate uses are not well understood, and so they are equated with other digital applications and social media, which cannot offer the richness of synchronous communication possible with high-quality videoconferencing. Synchronous communications technologies have characteristics that provide them with potential beyond digital, asynchronous interaction. From our data, it is our belief that this potential is underutilized, because planners and policy makers have not demonstrated adequate understanding of the capacity for such technologies to enhance or replace core functions in ways that asynchronous technologies cannot. For example, simulation laboratories or use of Second Life does not replace live observation of heart surgery. However, observation of live surgery from classrooms or students' laptops comes a close second when it is from a well-designed and equipped videoconference enhanced operating theatre on the other side of the world. Similarly, phone conferencing meetings is seen as less than ideal, so geographically disparate managers feel the need to meet face-to-face and travel long distances at great expense. As the *TAFE@ Your PC* case study showed, synchronous meetings using high-quality video-conferencing systems can make face-to-face meetings only necessary for essential meetings, thus reducing travel budgets enormously (Smyth 2009). If they were regarded as lighthouse technologies, rich media technologies would be a core technology underpinning strategic plans across the sector, because they do offer cost savings, more effective communication, and opportunities for broadening reach. These are all characteristics, which are limited in other e-learning modes.

Conclusion

The review of the literature for this project appears to highlight the question, not of whether rich media technologies are of benefit to higher education students, but of how institutions will make decisions on which technologies to support in the improvement of teaching and learning for their students. Most of the respondents to the university survey, who covered a wide range of positions within their institutions, were very positive about the use of rich media technologies. They believed that staff demand for the technology was nearly as high as the student demand, and that rich media technologies could help alleviate the cost of funding travel, both in monetary terms and stress, and give staff more flexibility in teaching, especially in multicampus institutions.

However, the data from our survey of the Australian universities sector revealed that most institutions had no obvious strategy or policy frame-work underpinning purchase, implementation, or support for rich media technologies as an institutional focus. It appeared that planning for the use of sophisticated technology fell to whoever within the institution could afford to purchase the equipment. The Wainhouse Research report concluded that the best way to effectively utilize rich media technologies within the higher education sector, is to "embed them as part of the organisations' DNA" (Greenberg 2009b). Policy is required to achieve this level of sustainability within institutions and scalability across the sector. Three respondents acknowledged that they had a master plan for campus-wide implementation of rich media technologies, and there was a strong correlation between this group and the maturity and integration of the business planning processes that directly link to their university's strategic goals for teaching and learning. Unfortunately, there was little evidence that master plans or strategic goals had been achieved, since evidence of coherent policy development was minimal.

Rich media technologies have potential to contribute to virtual learning environments and are not adequately utilized for administration and research where efficiency gains and cost savings could have significant impact on organizational viability and staff sustainability that is being eroded by travel burnout. Nevertheless, the case studies documented within the study reveal some well executed implementations within organizations committed to the use of rich media technologies with a belief in a corresponding improvement in learning and teaching and a great opportunity for geographically diverse staff and students to communicate with one another. Our conclusion is that rich media technologies are generally not well enough defined within organizational plans, tend to be seen as interesting add-ons rather than core systems within the organization, and are not exploited for their potential to provide significant reductions in travel budgets and environmental footprints. The primary remedy for this malaise is explicit strategy and policy development.

NOTE

1. We acknowledge with gratitude the support for this project from the Australian Learning and Teaching Council, an initiative of the Australian Government Department of Education, Employment and Workplace Relations.

REFERENCES

AARNet Pty. Ltd. and AARNet's Video Working Group, eds. 2006. *The Results of the AARNet Survey on Video over IP in the Australian Academic & Research Sector.* Canberra: AARNet.

Baecker, Ron. 2003. "A Principled Design for Scalable Internet Visual Communications with Rich Media, Interactivity, and Structured Archives." Paper presented at the 2003 Conference of the Centre for Advanced Studies on Collaborative Research, Toronto, Canada, 6–9 October 2003.

Berriman, Andrew. 2007. "." Paper presented at Wainhouse Research Collaboration Summit, Sydney, Australia, 14 February 2007.

Berriman, Andrew. 2010. *Report on the Survey of Business Modelling Practices for Large Scale Acquisition and Implementation of Rich Media Technologies in Higher Education.* Hervey Bay, Queensland, Australia: Durak Consulting.

Caladine, Richard. 2008a. *Enhancing E-Learning with Media-Rich Content and Interactions.* London: Information Science Publishing.

Caladine, Richard. 2008b. *An Evaluation of the Use of Peer to Peer Real Time Communications Applications within the Australian Academic and Research Community.* Wollongong, Australia: Australian Academic and Research Network (AARNet).

Greenberg, Alan. 2008. *The Distance Education and E-Learning Landscape. Volume 2: Videoconferencing, Streaming and Capture Systems for Learning.* Brookline, MA: Wainhouse Research.

Greenberg, Alan. 2009a. *The Distance Education and E-Learning Landscape. Volume 3: Interactive Whiteboards, Web Conferencing, and Synchronous Web Tools.* Brookline, MA: Wainhouse Research.

Greenberg, Alan. 2009b. *The Leading Rich Media Project.* Brookline, MA: Wainhouse Research.

Keegan, Desmond, Jüri Lõssenko, Ildikó Mázár, Pedro Fernández Michels, Morten Flate Paulsen, Torstein Rekkedal, Jan Atle Toska, and Dénes Zarka. 2009. *E-Learning Initiatives That Did Not Reach Targeted Goals.* Bekkestua, Norway: Megatrends Project 2007.

Sergiovanni, Thomas. 1998. "Market and Community as Strategies for Change." In *International Handbook of Educational Change,* ed. Andy Hargreaves, Anne Lieberman, Michael Fullan and David Hopkins, 576–595. Dordrecht, Netherlands: Kluwer Academic Publishers.

Smyth, Robyn. 2009. Evaluation Report: The TAFE@ Your PC CleverNetworks Project of the Regional Institute of TAFE SA. Armidale: Technical and Further Education South Australia.

Smyth, Robyn, and Deborah Vale. 2011. *Leading Rich Media Implementation Collaboratively: Mobilising International, National and Business Expertise.* Canberra: Australian Learning and Teaching Council.

Vilkinas, Tricia, and Greg Cartan. 2006. "The Integrated Competing Values Framework: Its Spatial Configuration." *Journal of Management Development* 25 (6): 505–521.

Weinstein, Ira, Andrew Davis, and David Maldow. 2010. Benchmarking Videoconferencing Success. Brookline, MA: Wainhouse Research.

Chapter 3

A Learning Center-Based Community College Model Separating Educational Infrastructure and Program Providers

Minghua Li

Introduction

From early 2005 through 2008 as the principle investigator, I led a team of researchers from East China Normal University, Peking University, and Columbia University on a Ford Foundation–sponsored project on migrant worker education in China. The project team ran education experiments in manufacturing areas in Shanghai for two years to create an education model for migrant factory workers in China. With a community participation model, the team ran eight courses in one site, and a telelearning center where migrant factory workers could utilize facilities to study. In another manufacturing area, a few other experimental courses were run with a for-profit education provider and an Internet bar business. After a brief introduction of our project experience, this chapter posits a new community education model and focuses on addressing some of the issues that need to be addressed before implementing.

In this chapter, I propose an innovative institutional design: a learning center–based community college model that separates the functions of providing education infrastructure and education programs. This chapter will also cover issues in social recognition systems of learning achievements (education credentials and accreditation) to accommodate the new education institutions and organizations. I believe that this model could make a significant difference among populations that currently do not have access to education by building up networks of community education infrastructure using information and communication technology (ICT). Underserved populations include migrant populations, residents from rural and remote villages, and slum areas in many developing countries. Providing a low-cost and innovative model of community education can boost social and economic development in many of the world's less developed countries.

Lessons Learned from Community Participation Education Model

After three and a half years of running the project on migrant worker education in China, the team took away some important lessons. Migrant workers in China need a very broad range of education and training for their personal and career development including, but not restricted to, remedial adult education, both general and technical/vocational education, both casual lectures/activities and formal certificate/degree programs, and higher education with a combination of technical and degree programs at the associate degree level and an open university scheme. The cornerstone should be something like evening associate degree programs that lead to a ladder of unlimited education achievements.

They also need social support so that they can gradually develop lifelong learning attitudes and habits. Effective learning for the academically less-prepared working students can take place when a social learning incubator is established along with the learning center. A learning incubator is an organized learning environment with features such as a learning team with common goals, rotating learning leadership among the students themselves, implementation of learning plans, emotional peer support, and a time control mechanism. The experiments show clearly that the physical learning center itself does not create learning, but the social learning incubator does.

The project also revealed that the migrant workers prefer mixed methods or blended approaches to learning rather than a single method such as a traditional classroom face-to-face or online learning. We suggest a blended learning model with more innovative teaching and learning pedagogies that will work with academically less well-prepared nontraditional students with full-time jobs.

Many migrants in China are interested in pursuing higher education while working and are willing to pay some portion of the educational cost. In addition, as workers benefit from education and their incomes increase, they are willing to spend more on their own development through education.

Although migrant workers show an interest in learning, we did not observe a high degree of active learning involvement with them. The project team identified seven factors that limit access to learning engagement. These are (1) inadequate transportation, (2) very long work days and weeks, and irregular shifts, (3) difficult living conditions, (4) restricted computer and Internet access, (5) inaccessibility of information, (6) unsupportive social environment, and (7) lack of educational infrastructure. These seven obstacles indicate that education infrastructure and new program models will be required to fully address migrant worker needs for continuing education.

As a result of these findings, our team suggested the establishment of a cluster of learning centers located within 5–15 minutes from where the migrant workers work or live. These centers can, in some situations, form a physical base for building a community college with linked branch campuses. The learning center has the advantages of proximity to the users and shared computing, the same as a telecenter. In addition, I have reached the conclusion that ICT provides a technological basis for establishing networks of telecenter-based community colleges that have the potential to provide access to post-secondary education for millions of educationally disadvantaged people. However, key issues related to a telecenter-based community college model that remain unaddressed include the following:

- How can a community college be formed on a cluster of telelearning centers spread over an area of prospective learners?
- Who will have the incentives to establish the cluster of telelearning centers that are the infrastructure of such a community college?
- Who should be qualified and be allowed to deliver education to this cluster? Can education providers compete on a cluster of such an education infrastructure, or does the builder of the cluster simply monopolize the education market there? Should the education providers be accredited and who and how should accreditation be done on the telecenter-based community college system?

I have made an attempt in this chapter to address these issues in the hope that it will make possible a full-fledged experiment based on the telecenter-based community college model.

Historical Perspectives and the Economics of Transaction Cost

For quite a long time, an institution of higher learning has included a campus with all sorts of facilities and education programs run by a single authority. However, it has not always been like this. Modern universities originated from European universities in the Middle Ages, as widely known from early universities such as the University of Bologna and the University of Paris (Rashdall 1987). University historian Hastings Rashdall (1987, 5) states, "A glance into any collection of medieval documents reveals the fact that the word 'university' means merely a number, a plurality, an aggregate of persons." "University" thus represented more of a community where there was a concentration of scholars (masters) and students from different parts of the world who were involved in higher learning—theology, law, medicine, and such subjects were taught by a considerable number of masters.

In their early days universities did not even have their own buildings, which can be interpreted that there was no such thing as a campus like today's universities have. "In the earliest days of the universities, the lecture room or school was simply a hired apartment, or the private house of the doctor (master)" (Rashdall 1987, 187). Most masters were not hired as lecturers by the "university"; instead, the students hired and paid them for their lectures. The universities were students' guilds, and colleges were masters' guilds. At the peak there were about 10,000 students at Bologna, which originated in the eleventh century.

Although it is difficult to find literature to describe what exactly university organizations were, I have inferred this description from various pieces of information: at the time, masters and students concentrated in Bologna on a large scale, and there was no one organization with central authority called a university to organize all the professors and students together. At that time, a master did his "business" on his own and joined a master's guild called a college that made all the rules by which the masters had to abide, including the procedures to confer a degree. A student acted on his own too: selecting lectures to attend and paying the lecturers, finding a place to live, and joining a student guild called a "university." So, Bologna as a place that hosted such academic activities was an academic community or an academic "market" where the students' guilds and masters' guilds made the rules. As such, the earlier universities were indeed completely different from what we have today—there was a separation of "campus" operations from teaching and learning operations. and even the masters were self-employed. Thus in the eleventh and twelfth centuries, the University of Bologna was really a market for higher education.

Our contemporary universities are completely different from their origins in the Middle Ages. Universities have universally emerged into hierarchical organizations so that today each tertiary institution is a unique organization with a central authority that oversees the operations of the campus and facilities, and education programs. Why has this evolution happened? Although there are many different answers to this question, in this chapter I will focus on the economic concept of transaction cost.

A marketplace is where sellers and buyers meet to buy and sell certain products or services such as an education program. When sellers and buyers do transactions in a marketplace, an associated transaction cost occurs. As Ronald H. Coase, a Nobel Prize winner in Economics, argued in 1937, firm organization occurs as a result of transaction costs. Without transaction cost, all individuals can be sellers of what they have and buyers of what they want; and all the workers and the producers are equal individuals, and the responsibilities and the benefits involved in the transaction are all specified in the contract. However, if a vertical or horizontal merger can reduce the total cost, a firm will emerge and become bigger and that replaces market transactions with internal resource allocation (Coase 1993). This theory explains partially why a Bologna-type university eventually evolved into one that has a "firm" organization format today.

Universities today are still social institutions rather than industrial organizations. A university's budget is constrained by the money it can raise, and it carries out the activities necessary to execute its social mission within that constraint. Historically, there have been a limited number of universities, which educated the social elite—a very small percent of the population. At that level, they kept a balance in which universities served society just as much as the society could provide finance. Today we have reached the epoch of mass higher education, and the time will soon come that higher education will be available for everyone who has an aspiration to learn. But the question of how society will finance mass education remains.

Although it may make people uncomfortable to say there are elite universities and mass universities, in reality, there are two completely different types of institutions of higher learning as evidenced by the tuition structure. For example, for the 2010–2011 school year, undergraduate tuition at Sarah Lawrence College in Bronxville, New York, was US$43,556, Columbia University was US$43,815, and Vanderbilt University was US$40,602 (Wingfield 2010). These three are all private tertiary institutions. By contrast, state universities and community college tuition in the United States averages from US$2,000 to US$10,000 per year; at most research institutions revenues from tuition cover only one-third of the real cost of providing facilities and services. Eventually, the mass universities will have to reform so that they will run more efficiently and serve the public needs for higher education better. The development of a community college system in the United States that produces associate degrees more cost effectively than other institutions of higher learning is one example of an internal tendency within a society to reform higher education institutions to better serve society's needs under the constraints of the public and private financial resources. I would argue that a technological revolution such as through ICT that boosts the productivity of education administration and changes the ways of delivering education could become a major catalyst for the mass universities and colleges to reform by adapting the new technology for both efficiency and quality of service to realize their social missions.

Changes in technology, logistics, and institutions all have implications on transaction costs, which in turn will determine market efficiency. Education operation costs for individual or small program providers used to be and are still very high. These include, for example, the costs associated with recruiting students; billing; class scheduling; paying for the use of education facilities such as classrooms, evaluating students, and keeping records; getting accreditation; and becoming known to the target audience. However, as the Internet has been reshaping the marketplace, many of these operations will be automated, and costs will be reduced to negligible in the years to come. Thus, as a result of the technological change, the opposite evolution of universities, that is, unmerging, could take place so that the overall cost will be lower. Based on the economics of transaction cost and the current technological revolution brought forth by the Internet, I believe that it is likely and would be beneficial for a separation to take place between the operation authorities of a university's physical capital (campus and equipment) and education programs at the lower end of the higher education market to boost both efficiency and quality of education.

Broadening the Definition of Community Colleges

I propose a learning center–based community college model that separates education infrastructures and education program providers. Does this model still fall under the definition of a community college? Or is it a completely new model of higher learning? To answer this question, I need to ask one fundamental question: What makes a college a community college? As Rosalind Raby and Edward Valeau (2009) point out, there is no cohesive definition for community college applied universally around the world, as the local environment varies from place to place. Based on her research of community college models in the United States and many other countries, Raby (2009) identifies similar characteristics of community colleges around the world and provides a comprehensive definition based on those similarities. "Despite the variance, basic similarities exist that define community college models as a unique form of post-secondary education that offers short-term semi- and professional terminal courses as well as an academic curriculum that results in an associate in arts or sciences, and in some cases, the means to transfer to 4-year universities" (Raby 2009, 3). With reference to Raby's comprehensive definition of community college models, I would outline the necessary conditions for a college to be categorized as a community college as follows:

- Its mission is to provide affordable higher education and other types of education and training programs for all. If publicly funded, the college charges very low tuition such as instate tuition in US community colleges; if privately funded, the college runs on low-cost strategies, and there is a public financial support system for all those who are willing to pursue higher education.
- It does not exclude any adult who wants to learn based on his/her previous educational preparation.
- It serves local education and training needs.
- It is run with the participation of local academics, employers, and students.

With this definition of community college, a for-profit college can function as a community college as long as the tuition is low enough, or there is a public financial aid system for students who need it.

Utilizing this functional definition, we can broaden the concept of a community college to include virtual organizations that perform the same mission. A virtual organization is a set of independent organizations (legally and financially) that work together organically with agreed rules for a common mission with shared resources. The common mission does not exclude each organization's own mission or interests but is built into the operating agreement and is realized by the design of the virtual organization. In the case of the community college structure we propose, one organization oversees the operations of the education facilities and campus and a number of groups provide all sorts of education programs on the campus; jointly all groups work together to provide their community with the type of educational services that would be provided by a community college.

One example may make this clearer. If a local market sells only products that it grows, it is a market that serves the local needs for foods. The market eventually changes its way of doing business, and it does not make food anymore. Instead it only sells products produced by others. It is still a local market that serves the local needs for foods even better with competition among the suppliers. Thus, by our definition, a traditional community college changes into a community post-secondary education market in that you cannot find a single organization calling itself the community college, but you can find the community education infrastructure administration, various independent education providers, government financial aid agents, and/or a public or community education administration agent that set the rules for these organizations to do business together. In this way, the community college is just an integration of independent organizations that functions as what we see today's community colleges are doing.

A community education infrastructure administrator would manage the physical learning centers, the main campus, all education facilities, any college transportation system or dormitories if available, and all other physical resources on campus. It may also establish and manage some cultural fixtures. This administration gets into contracts with independent education providers to provide education facilities for delivering their programs, to manage the daily use of the campus, and to collect rent for using the campus. The administration may provide other services such as representing independent education providers to recruit students, checking and making records of student participation in classes and other activities, and collecting tuition and fees.

Optimization of Education Infrastructures and Avoiding Monopolies

If our goal is to address higher education needs of disadvantaged populations, then the geographic distribution of these populations suggests the need for a new model of tertiary institutions, with a separation of education infrastructure and program providers. Such populations include migrant workers, people living in rural areas, small towns, remote areas, and/or slums, who lack a means of transportation to access education, as well as a social support system for enhancing learning where they live. If an education infrastructure (campus and equipment) provider is also the education program provider, this provider will have a monopoly power over the education supply locally in the place where the disadvantaged population lives, generally resulting in higher fees and fewer options. Our model posits one learning center to provide the local education infrastructure for each basic learning grid or small community with a concentration of disadvantaged learners, who could then access a variety of offerings from many providers through that infrastructure.

Our experience suggests that a key metric for placement of learning centers is that most of the local learners can reach the center in less than 20 minutes by walking or biking from their workplaces or living areas. There are many types of small communities that can be considered fitting for a basic learning grid. They can be one apartment complex with 5,000–15,000 migrant workers in manufacturing areas; a big village or a group of small villages in rural areas; a small town; a remote residential mining, forest, or high mountain area; a small slum or a small section of a big slum; a temporary tent camp; or a section of a large tent camp established due to an earthquake, war, or other reasons.

A learning center can be as simple and as small a location with two or three computers to serve a village or can be quite sophisticated and big. Based on our experience, a learning center ideally includes one or more computer rooms depending on the size of the population served: one multimedia minitheater room to deliver attractive educational programs with entertainment features; one or more classrooms for teaching, individual and group learning, or study circle meetings; and a minilibrary. Such a library does not have to be a physical one and can be a "floating library" where people use a central online facility to rotate the books they have. The online library can be shared with other learning centers, since there are economies of scale in digitizing articles and books that can be accessed by the Internet. Such an infrastructure is a base on which any serious educational program can be run. A learning center can also be very big if it is located in a very densely populated area such as in a manufacturing area with 30,000 or more workers.

A learning center must also create a local social environment for fostering learning. The academically less prepared learners especially need some structure in the management of their learning processes for out-of-class learning activities. Based on research conducted in China, the research team observed that migrant workers had not developed the study skills for self-learning, and they need the teachers to help structure management of their time allocation in favor of learning. They need peer support and teamwork to support their learning and avoid the isolation and loneliness of self-learning. Working together with peers keeps learning interesting and allows students to motivate each other. A learning center will therefore not just provide the learning facilities but will also serve to create a small local social environment that will support learning.

There can also be a hierarchy in the structure of learning centers. In addition to local learning centers, there may be a more sophisticated facility to serve some needs that are not met by the learning centers in the neighborhood communities. The integration of such a central campus and its satellite learning centers form a community education infrastructure to serve a relatively larger area with a population from a quarter to a half million people in manufacturing, rural, remote, slum, and tent camp areas. In today's world, more than half of the world population lives in these areas. In the United States and Canada, especially in rural, mining, and remote areas, many universities do have established satellite campuses or learning centers to serve the local needs for higher education. Such experiences are actually what inspired us to formulate our model. However, our model differs in that these satellite facilities are currently established by, and part of, a single college or university. In our model, the campus or the learning center is just a physical condition for providing education, and the infrastructure should be a public facility that is open for any qualified individual or organization to come to deliver their education programs.

Central campuses and satellite learning centers in the neighborhood can be linked by transportation services depending on the local geographical, social, and income situation. In a manufacturing park a shuttle bus may be the most convenient means to transport learners around the learning centers and to the central campus for different educational services. In many of China's rural areas, most villagers have motorcycles and abundant bicycles, and in some more developed rural areas there are bus systems that link villages and towns. These various means of transportation support a relatively large area in which the villagers can move around conveniently, creating the potential for an ecosystem where clusters of satellite learning centers and college campuses plus local transportation systems form a local community education infrastructure that builds a physical gateway to access post-secondary education in the local communities.

Because of its very convenience and high accessibility, however, a local learning center in a highly concentrated residential area may pose a natural monopoly in the local educational market. In fact, once a community education infrastructure is established, the only postcompulsory education local people can access is most likely the education programs running on this community education infrastructure. If a single education provider establishes the education infrastructure and provides all education programs, it is going to create a local monopoly education market. While I believe that such a monopoly is better than what is available today in most of the areas where disadvantaged learner populations live, there can be a better way to deliver education, and a local education monopoly is not unavoidable.

This problem is fairly easy to understand if we look into the utility markets. In each residential area, we do have just one physical telephone system, yet, this telephone line system allows different telephone companies to provide different telephone services. Similarly, there is also just one power system in a residential area, yet different power service companies can compete along the same physical power system. It could have a devastating effect if a single company ran all rail transport to any location just because it owned the railway. In that case, other companies that would like to compete for train services would have to build their own railways, which is obviously very inefficient. I propose to run an open educational system in that no one would have exclusive rights to the community education infrastructure to the exclusion of all the other education providers. The owner of an education infrastructure may run its own courses and programs, yet it must open its networked campuses (the learning centers) and all the other facilities to other education organizations.

Who then, has the incentive to provide the infrastructure for this supermarket? There is no one single model of starting up community education infrastructures in diverse areas, regions, and countries. It is possible that local governments, businesses, communities, existing schools, and individuals can initiate the building of one or more local learning centers, or even a complete physical community education infrastructure. They may adopt different models to administer the education services operating on the infrastructure. If there is no public intervention, there is a tendency for the investor in the education infrastructure, be it a private or public, a local entity or a remote one, to monopolize or to control the education services provided in its own interest. This phenomenon is recognized in economics as a natural monopoly, which means that if economically there can be just one supplier in a certain market, the supplier will have a natural monopoly power that will lead to the advantage of the owner of the supplier. The market is so small that both the new and old suppliers cannot get sufficient business to compensate for the cost occurred to enter the market. Unless one education infrastructure is completely controlled by the people of the community, the control of an education infrastructure will have a tendency to lead to monopoly of education offerings in the community.

This suggests that in the future a legal framework that guarantees an open education market on the community education infrastructure might be needed. At this time we strongly suggest that local and international funding agencies, governments, and nongovernmental organizations (NGOs) require community education infrastructure be open to all qualified providers during the funding process. Ideally, as long as an organization or even an individual can solicit enough students via the open information system available as a part of the education infrastructure and agrees to pay all the standard costs and fair rent for using the education facilities, it should be allowed to offer and run courses and programs on the networked learning centers. In this way no one can monopolize the campus, and the campus serves as a mini-education market or "education supermarket."

Within the proposed open education systems built on the local education infrastructures around the world, we would eventually expect to see some major education providers emerge to deliver programs across multiple markets. As such the open education infrastructure becomes a battlefield for competition among education providers, which will potentially bring the best education offerings to disadvantaged populations in localities previously served by limited, likely monopoly organizations with programs of varying quality. Because the education market is often monitored and controlled by national governments, we don't expect to see it open immediately to international education providers without restriction but maintain the goal of sustaining a national open education market for disadvantaged learners.

Social Recognition of Learning Achievement: Education Credentials and Accreditation

What would this open education market look like? In his book *The World Is Open*, Curt Bonk (2009) has built a learning model coined "WE ALL LEARN" based on the availability and the development of ICT and Web 2.0. Bonk asserts that open education sources, sharing, participation and cooperation, social networking, and globalization are increasingly driving learning to become more personalized. He has made some thought-provoking predictions: the standard 12-year education obligation will double; the number of teachers will increase significantly; teachers will be subdivided mainly into education advisors and teachers who are more like facilitators and mentors; there will be some free degrees; and learners may design their own learning and degree programs with the help of advisors. Colleges can outsource everything except degree granting (Bonk 2009).

Today many of us would in principle agree with the WE ALL LEARN model and believe we are approaching a world in which anyone can learn any time, any place, and from anybody. With the Internet we can access all the open courseware, free software, Wikimedia, learning portals on virtually any topic, and worldwide human resources for collaboration and sharing. We are entering a phase of lifelong learning, sharing, and teaching. With this model not just we all learn, but also we all teach, or we all help others to learn. This vision dovetails with the virtual educational organization to support an infrastructure on which anyone can teach in any time, place, and with any methods of his/her choice. However, it raises two fundamental questions: Who is qualified to teach, and how can qualified teachers become organized on their own to provide education programs? The design of a virtual organization frees scholars from having to make an expensive physical investment to provide education, which is a big step toward the emancipation of qualified scholars, but how can a scholar secure recognition for his qualifications? Even in a WE ALL LEARN society and particularly in our community college model, there is still a need for the recognition of qualifications of scholars and accreditation mechanisms for the social recognition of the quality of independent scholars and education organizations.

If people were learning just for the intrinsic value of learning, the satisfaction of gaining the knowledge to meet personal interests and skills, there would be no need for social recognition of learning achievements. The reality is that we are learning for both consumption and as an investment in developing our own human capital. Education credentials serve as a path to most attractive jobs. Due to information asymmetry between applicants and employers regarding the content and value of various programs of study, employers use education credentials as an indication of the level, quality, and category of education a job applicant has. An education credential is a concise indication of a few important real education processes: (1) the level of education, (2) the subject of education, (3) the way of learning, such as online or traditional, and (4) the institution that provides the education. Educational credentials are particularly important to disadvantaged learners investing in education as a means to move up the social and economic ladder. As we envision the open education system move toward a WE ALL LEARN model, it will be crucial that learners have access to the education credentials that allow them to achieve social recognition of what they have learned as well as obtain the social support for making the investment. If so, then who will accredit the program of self-directed learners? How will qualified educators and programs outside the current system become accredited?

Currently there are various models of accreditation around the world. In the United States, colleges have united to form associations of their own to provide accreditation services, so that the NGO model solves education market failures such as the creation of "diploma mills" (Harcleroad 1980; Petersen 1999; Bloland 2001; Alstete 2006). In most European countries, Japan, and many more countries, the governments assume the authority of education accreditation through national accreditation systems established by laws and administered independently from government agents, colleges, business, and student organizations (Brown 2004; Yonezawa 2005; CNE

2008; GAC 2008). In many developing countries, including China, the education accreditation system is a subsystem of the government education administration, and degree credentials are under the control of the government. In fact, in China, not only accreditation but also quotas for degree granting are set by the government education administration. In a short period of time, there is little chance that a new degree credential and accreditation system would come to accommodate the WE ALL LEARN society, but it is worthwhile to explore how a new system may evolve to support this model.

Outside the education markets, we have seen that accreditation markets provide solutions to deal with market failures due to information asymmetry. In the organic food market, the organic accreditation market helps to identify and eliminate fake organic food producers. In physical capital markets, an accreditation market is the major solution to information asymmetry problems with Lloyd's Register in the ship building industry serving as one example. Even in the financial market, we have rating agencies such as Moody's and Standard & Poors. ISO 9000 has been applied to manufactures and services to signal the quality of specific products or services. A market-based approach to education credentials may also be able to provide the flexible, yet credible education accreditation system needed for a WE ALL LEARN society. An NGO education accreditation organization is limited in its interests by its constituency and is unlikely to be interested in international accreditation markets. Similarly, an education accreditation organization in the public sector has its jurisdiction within its national boundary. Although there are international education accreditation organizations based on interstate government treaties and cooperation, the international education accreditation market is largely an area to be explored. Here I will just present one education accreditation market solution that will allow a smooth operation of the minieducation-market community colleges.

We envision an education accreditation market existing alongside all the networks of community education infrastructures. Different types of accreditation organizations would include NGOs, government administered, and privately owned organizations working on both domestic and international levels. Any individual or organization, as long as it is accredited, should be allowed to deliver programs on the community education infrastructure. Education programs and providers, whether public, private, or governmental in nature, are accredited by different agencies to signify differences in standards and styles. These accredited education organizations may issue diplomas and certificates of degree or provide nondegree programs to their students once they have met education program requirements. Alternatively, those who are not granted the independent rights to confirm education credentials by accreditation agents need to issue diplomas and certificates along backed by the accreditation agency.

Academically qualified individuals should also be free to deliver education programs including degree programs if accredited as an individual education program provider. Let's call this individual a Degree Program Advisor (DPA). A DPA is accredited to advise learners on self-designed degree programs in specific subject areas. Although an admitted advisee may design a degree program, the customized program must completely conform to the accreditation agency's degree standards and be approved by the DPA. By the time of the completion of the customized program, the DPA can recommend the student be granted a degree by the accreditation agency. Here an accreditation revolution takes place. An accreditation agent will not only accredit education providers but also finally sign a degree document on the recommendation of a DPA who the accreditation agent recognizes as a qualified DPA. Such an accreditation agency has some functions that a university has today.

The support of an accreditation market with diversified education accreditation agents will allow any academically qualified organization to deliver the type of education programs it deems fitting to the market formed by a network of community education infrastructures. This ease of entrance and exit helps create a more flexible and diversified market with competition that fosters educational innovation and opens doors to all types of students who have a wish to learn. This means for example, that a student with a DPA would have the flexibility to take courses that fulfill the degree requirements of a customized learning program from any accredited individual or institution in the world without sacrificing the systematic learning process and credit control that help create value in a degree. If we can make this type of customized degree programs widely available, then we will have a WE ALL LEARN society, and all of us will have freedom to learn and to teach that will only be limited by our qualifications. This is the kind of education that will make the teaching and learning activities on the networks of community education infrastructures flourish.

Building Networks of ICT-Based Community Education Infrastructures and Open Education Systems around the World

The proposed model would have immediate benefit to a variety of populations around the world.

Disaster-Hit Areas Such as Haiti

After the devastating earthquake of 2010, almost all the local university facilities were damaged, many faculty members lost, and university organizations no longer functioned. A version of our open education model offered on a community-based infrastructure adapted to Haiti could provide the basis for sustainable social and economic development as one solution to building local human resource capacity across society. If international agencies work with the local people to develop a network of community education infrastructure based on telelearning centers for running open education programs, a variety of needs could be met. For example, college students could obtain access to programs from both domestic and international universities and still complete their studies locally. In addition, once the community education infrastructure is established, international education organizations as well as local ones can deliver a variety of programs that might include everything from public health information sessions to professional training.

Manufacturing Areas, Rural and Remote Areas, and Small Towns

As discussed, this education model has been developed to solve the education access problems in China's manufacturing areas. This model can be expanded to China's rural and remote areas and small towns. Half of China's population—roughly 650 million people—lives in these areas, but China's higher education is concentrated in large and midsized cities. Our learning center–based community college model has competitive advantages in addressing the future needs of higher education in the vast rural areas of developing countries. A community college built on a cluster of learning centers could be an engine of local, social, and economic development by boosting human development and creating information hubs to facilitate community functions such as e-government, e-business, agriculture exchanges, and technology development. Agricultural education programs are particularly ripe for boosting local and national economic development. For at least half a century, economists and educators have found that the returns to education are the highest to farmers (e.g., see Jamison and Lau 1982). Because farmers have more discretion in their work, the potential to apply "allocative ability" to take advantage of, for example, new ways of production and marketing is high, education can help farmers gain more returns (Schultz 1967). So in the years to come a new green revolution will heavily depend on more education to the farmers and better information and e-business access to the farmers in China, India, African countries, and many other countries where farming population is still a large proportion of the population. This model can help to reach the UN Millennium Development Goals.

Rural to Urban Migrants and Slum Dwellers around the Developing World

According to the United Nations Population Fund (UNFPA) report "State of World Population 2007," between 2000 and 2030, Asia's urban population will increase from 1.36 billion to 2.64 billion, Africa's from 294 million to 742 million, Latin America and the Caribbean from 394 million to 609 million (UNFPA 2007). Roughly 40 percent is due to a combination of migration and reclassification, in other words based on rural to urban migration caused by social and economic changes. The human development of these new urban dwellers will be a big challenge that could in part be met through education based on our model. Another problem related to rapid urban growth in developing countries is the densely populated slums with very little infrastructure for their residents. The slum population includes one out of every three city dwellers or a billion people that is equal to a sixth of the world's population, and over 90 percent of them are in developing countries (UNFPA 2007). Learning centers of various sizes can be setup in these densely populated areas with facilities that can accommodate the local infrastructure and linked to sustain an open community education. Such a local and accessible education system would allow residents to develop their human capitol within their neighborhoods.

According to Bonk (2009), only about 1 billion of the 6.7 billion people in the world have Internet access. This proposal to build networks of community education infrastructures all over the world for disadvantaged populations would make a significant contribution to addressing access issues, and billions of people will be free from restrictions to education due to social and natural causes. I believe that technology can play an important role combined with our telelearning center–based community education model in facilitating the freedom to access effective and relevant education as well as to provide such education services in a broad variety of social and economic settings.

Acknowledgement

This chapter is part of our work on a currently running project titled "Social Choices and Their Efficiencies of Higher Education Accreditation Institutions Among Nations" sponsored by China's National Natural Science Foundation

(Project No. 70973036); also based on our earlier work sponsored by the Ford Foundation from 2005–2008 on migrant worker education.

REFERENCES

Alstete, Jeffrey. 2006. *College Accreditation: Managing Internal Revitalization and Public Respect.* New York: Palgrave Macmillan.

Bloland, Harland G. 2001. *Creating the Council of Higher Education Accreditation* (CHEA). Phoenix, AZ: The Oryx Press.

Bonk, Curt J. 2009. *The World Is Open: How Web Technology Is Revolutionizing Education.* San Francisco: Jossey-Bass.

Brown, Roger. 2004. *Quality Assurance in Higher Education: The UK Experience Since 1992.* New York: RoutledgeFalmer.

Coase, Ronald H. 1993. "The Nature of the Firm (1937)." In *The Nature of the Firm. Origins, Evolution, and Development,* ed. Oliver E. Williamson and Sidney G. Winter, 18–33. New York: Oxford University Press.

CNE (Comité National d'Évaluation). 2008. *Introducing the CNE–Main Characteristic of the Evaluation.* Paris: CNE. Available online at: http://www.cne-evaluation.fr.

GAC (German Accreditation Council). 2008. *Report on the Evaluation of the Foundation for the Accreditation of Study Programmes in Germany (German Accreditation Council).* Bonn, Germany: GAC. Available online at: http://www.enqa.eu .

Harcleroad, Fred F. 1980. *Accreditation: History, Process, and Problems.* Washington, DC: American Association for Higher Education.

Jamison, Dean, and Lawrence Lau. 1982. *Farmer Education and Farm Efficiency.* Baltimore, MD: Johns Hopkins University Press.

Petersen, John C. 1999. *International Quality Assurance in Higher Education Occasional Paper, July 1999.* Washington, DC: CHEA.

Raby, Rosalind Latiner. 2009. "Defining the Community College Model." In *Community College Models–Globalization and Higher Education Reform,* ed. Rosalind Latiner Raby and Edward J. Valeau, 21–38. Dordrecht, The Netherlands: Springer.

Raby, Rosalind Latiner, and Edward J. Valeau, eds. 2009. *Community College Models–Globalization and Higher Education Reform.* Dordrecht, The Netherlands: Springer.

Rashdall, Hastings. 1936. *The Universities of Europe in the Middle Ages.* 3 vols. (revised in 1987 by F. M. Powicke, and A. B. Emden). Oxford: Clarendon Press.

Schultz, Theodore. W. 1967. "The Rate of Return in Allocating Investment Resources to Education." *The Journal of Human Resources* 3: 293–309.

UNFPA. 2007. *State of World Population 2007. Unleashing the Potential of Urban Growth.* New York: UNFPA. Available online at: http://www.unfpa.org.

Wingfield, Brian Monday. 2010. *America's Most Expensive Colleges and Universities.* New York: Forbes.com. Available online at: http://www.forbes.com.

Yonezawa, Akiyoshi. 2005. "The Reintroduction of Accreditation in Japan: A Government Initiative." *International Higher Education* 40 (Summer): 20–22.

Part II

Capacity Building

Chapter 4

Innovative Learning Support for Teaching Large Classes

Charl C. Wolhuter, Hennie J. Steyn, Elsa Mentz, and Ferdinand J. Potgieter

Introduction

There are two forces currently impacting on higher education in South Africa. The first is a steep rise in student numbers and the pressure (socially, politically, demographically, as well as economically) to increase enrollments even more drastically. The second force is the effect of the global economic revolution on higher education, namely demands for an enhancement in productivity, for example, an increase (quantitatively and qualitatively) in the successful throughput of graduates with less input costs. Teaching of large classes is a reality throughout the world, especially because higher education institutions have been forced to increase class size in recent years if they wanted to remain profitable. It is therefore not surprising that the teaching of large class sizes has become a challenge to many lecturers. Despite the accepted dictum that the quality of teaching and assessment is more important than class size, the reality seems to be that large classes are here to stay (Muller 2010). Although most students and lecturers declare a preference for reduced class sizes and believe in their superior efficacy over large classes, the economy in the consumption of resources (both human and financial) accomplished in large classes will ensure their continued employment in the future (Muller 2010). Moreover, for many higher education institutions the increasing importance of guaranteed graduate throughput has seemed to accentuate the belief that there is a substantial trade-off between class size and student learning (Muller 2010; Van der Walt et al. 2011).

Higher education tends to use technology in teaching and learning to increase productivity (Dreyer 2005), and an efficient way to include education technology is to use it in tandem with other teaching methods by means of the so-called multimodus (or blended) approach in teaching. Multimode teaching refers to the thoughtful, logical integration of different teaching methods in order to support successful learning of students. This means that the different modi support each other in their strong and weak points (Osguthorpe and Graham 2003; Garrison and Kanuka 2004).

From literature on teaching large classes it is clear that lecturers are facing a number of challenges administering and lecturing large classes. One way around these problems would be to develop a strategy for managing large classes in higher education without increasing the human resources budget and without aggravating the problem of internal inefficiency. We propose an innovative multimodus teaching strategy (MTS) for teaching and learning in large classes that utilizes digital modes to provide content and facilitate administration of the classes in a flexible and accessible manner allowing lecture time center on reenforcing knowledge with assessments and group work. We claim that this strategy increases productivity in higher education by supporting students in their understanding and applied knowledge acquisition to become more self-directed learners while decreasing the unit cost of higher education. In addition to the increase in productivity the strategy has also had some unintended results, namely the fact that learners with different mother tongues can be effectively accommodated in one class and that the teaching experience and quality of work life of the assigned lecturer increases discernibly. The MTS for teaching large groups includes the following teaching modi, namely the study guide and learning material, the teaching team, the digital book disk (DBD), the structuring of the class meeting in a particular format, eFundi as web-based learning management system (LMS), and the different assessment procedures.

Trends in Access and Productivity in Education

The above-mentioned strategy was decided upon within the context of rapidly increasing enrollments, burgeoning class sizes, and limited resources. Similar to the rest of the world, developing countries are faced with the challenge to improve the quality of higher education while decreasing the ever-rising cost of higher education.

Table 4.1 Gross Enrollment Ratios in Various World Regions

Region	Gross Secondary Education Enrollment Ratio	Gross Tertiary Enrollment Ratio
World		27
Central and Eastern Europe		65
North America and Western Europe		72
Developing Countries Regions		
Arab countries	67	22
Central Asia	97	24
Latin America and the Caribbean	90	37
South and West Asia	56	13
Sub-Saharan Africa	36	6

Source: UNESCO (2011).

Developing countries face a number of problems related to access to and participation in higher education. Participation rates in higher education are low compared to the developed countries (see Table 4.1). A bottleneck exists between secondary education and higher education. Inside higher education internal inefficiency is an enormous cost. In South Africa only 22 percent of students complete their studies in the prescribed time (James 2010). A big obstacle in expanding access to higher education is a shortage of faculty. It is difficult to acquire in countries scarce in highly trained human resources due to the "brain drain" of educated and skilled people to more developed countries and the high cost of offering competitive salaries to those available; human resources are the most expensive item on the running budgets of higher education institutions.

One way around this problem would be to develop a strategy for handling large classes in higher education without increasing the human resources budget and without aggravating the problem of internal inefficiency. The authors believe they have developed such a strategy in South Africa and have put it through a successful trial run.

Enrollment Explosion

Since the mid-twentieth century, and especially since the 1990s, higher education worldwide has been characterized by a continuous sharp growth in enrollments. The recent past (since 1990) has been driven by the economic boom and by the demands of the nascent knowledge society (i.e., a society that has progressed from an economy based exclusively on agriculture), then by industrial production and service delivery, to a stage where the production of knowledge is the principal axis of the economic machine. Between 1999 and 2006 tertiary education enrollments worldwide increased by roughly 50 percent from 94.7 million to 142.1 million (UNESCO 2011).

South Africa has been no exception to international trends. On the contrary, political pressures (e.g., the drive for equity in higher education enrollments, the historical weight of the slogan "the doors of learning shall be opened to all," and the role assigned to higher education as instrument for the societal transformation of South Africa) bolster pressures for enrollment expansion at higher educational institutions even more. Higher education enrollments in South Africa increased from 495,355 in 1994 to 632,911 in 1999 and again to 741,380 in 2006 (UNESCO 2011), while the responsible minister has set the target of a further 100,000 students in the near future (Rademeyer 2007). Furthermore, in 2009 the minister of higher education declared that the current system, whereby a mere 18 percent of matriculants gain university admission, should be revised as it denies too many matriculants university education (SAPA 2009).

The Imperative to Raise Productivity

Currently a worldwide process of economic liberalization and privatization is taking place. By the 1980s it was clear that the Western welfare state was overextending itself (Davidson and Rees-Mogg 1992). Consequently conservative governments in Western Europe and Northern America lodged a neoclassical free-market revolution in economic theory and practice (Redwood 1993; Watson 1996). This trend, of moving away from state intervention, monopoly, and regulation also spread to Eastern Europe as part of the post-1990 total societal reconstruction, while most developing countries were forced on the same road by means of Structural Adjustment Program agreements they had to sign with the World Bank in order to obtain financial aid. As a result of the neoliberal economic revolution, business principles (profit motive, efficiency, productivity) are carried into many areas where they had been thus far nonexistent. One such area is the university. The imperative for raising productivity (i.e., increasing output at minimum cost) is underlined by the levelingoff of governmental financing of higher education worldwide (cf. Wolhuter et al. 2010). This trend too has not bypassed South Africa. One indicator of the extent of government support for higher education is public expenditure per tertiary student as percentage of per capita gross domestic product. In South Africa this figure decreased from 65.2 percent in 1999 to 47.1 percent in 2004 (World Bank 2006)–steeper than the decline in the world mean (cf. Wolhuter et al. 2010). State appropriations per weighted full-time equivalent university student in South Africa decreased from 25,125 R,[1] in 1986 to 16,119 R in 2003–a decrease of 36 percent (De Villiers and Steyn 2009).

What must further be factored into this equation of the demand "to do more with less" is the high attrition rate at South African universities. Only 22 percent of students complete their courses in the prescribed study time (Anonymous 2008). Of the 120,000 students who entered higher education for the first time in 2000, 30 percent dropped out during their first year of study. A further 20 percent dropped out during their second and third years (Anonymous 2008). For many fields of study the figures are even higher. To worsen matters, the dropout rates for Black students are substantially higher (see Table 4.2), thus to a large extent wiping out any gains made on the equity count at the point of access.

There are many indications that the quality of students entering university each year is deteriorating. In 2009 a spate of newspaper reports appeared, reporting on the poor quality of the first-year intake, ill-prepared for university study and of much poorer quality than previous years (Dibetle 2009; Rademeyer 2009), later to be confirmed by Higher Education South Africa's National Benchmarking Test Project (Blaire 2009).

The basic strategy used by many South African universities to meet the challenge of increased numbers and decreased funding is still the traditional strategy of contact education that is illustrated in Figure 4.1.

Table 4.2 Percentage of Students Who Graduate in the Prescribed Period (Based on the 2000 Intake)

Field	Black Students	White Students
Business Management	11	43
Life and Physical Sciences	11	35
Mathematical Sciences	13	33
Social Sciences	14	43
Languages	13	52

Source: Gower (2008).

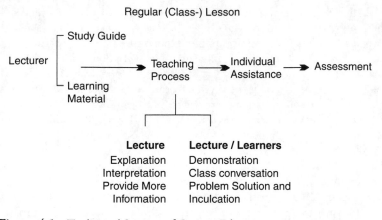

Figure 4.1   Traditional Strategy of Contact Education.

In the traditional strategy of contact education, the lecture by a lecturer is still a central feature. Presently it is recognized that the method of lecturing is by all measures not geared for this task to increase productivity in education. It should be borne in mind that the lecture method was developed in the Middle Ages, before the invention of printing, when the only way to disseminate knowledge was for the professor to read (the word "lecture" is derived from the Latin word "lektio" that means "I read") the text and for students to copy word by word. It was rendered obsolete by the invention of printing in 1453 and has become even more of an anachronism in an age of free access to knowledge (information and communication technology), shift from an emphasis on "teaching" to "learning" at all levels of education, rise of constructivism in teaching and learning, progress from memorization and reproduction of knowledge to higher-order educational competences, and shift from content-based education to outcomes-based or competency-based education. That the age of the lecture has passed is not only well-substantiated in a series of publications in the last 50 years, such as the well-known writings of B. F. Skinner (1954) and Donald Bligh (1972), but also from students voting with their feet in their diminishing attendance of lectures worldwide. Some researchers state that 25 percent or more of students are likely to be absent from lectures on any given day (Friedman et al. 1999). In recently published research on this topic, Yolanda Jordaan (2009) found student absentee rates of 23.74 percent and 15.83 percent respectively for male and female students at a South African university.

Conceptual and Theoretical Framework

Our innovative multimodus teaching system was developed based on particular teaching and learning theories, specifically within the context of teaching large groups. When thinking about improving teaching and learning in large classes, most researchers take cognizance of emerging perspectives on learning, teaching, and technology. These include, for example, learning and cognitive theories such as information processing, Piaget's constructivism, Les Semenov Vygotsky's constructivism, Bloom's taxonomy, situated cognition, social constructivism, and connectivism (see, for example, Verhagen 2006; Hill and Kop 2008; Orey 2008). Depending on the nature and scope of the intellectual conundrum that they are trying to solve with regard to teaching and learning in large classes, they may also be expected to read up on *learner-centered theories* that would, typically, include emergent theories on motivation, multiple intelligences and learning styles, teaching and learning in the affective domain, creativity, adult learning, and so on (cf. Jaschik 2010; Moloi et al. 2010; Mompo and Redoli 2010). How these learner-centered theories may inform *practical inquiry strategies*, such as constructionism, learning by design, project-based learning, problem-based instruction, i-search, and case-based learning, will also have to be taken into account (see also Read 2010). The same would probably apply to emergent inquiry strategies interested in *effecting change in students' minds*, such as conceptual change and transformative learning (Orey 2008).

These theories and strategies are, however, mostly useless in and of themselves, unless their conceptual and theoretical principles can be innovatively and justifiably captured in instrumentation that will encourage and facilitate change in students' *learning behavior*. In this regard, *tools for teaching and learning* such as cognitive apprenticeship, scaffolding, articulation, critical reflection, resource-based learning, and experiential learning have already demonstrated their scientific worth over the past number of years (Orey 2008).

As we explain below, cooperative learning is an important modus in our own multimodus approach toward teaching and learning in large classes (cf. De Leng et al. 2010). Cooperative learning practice, per se, is based on Lev Vygotsky's zone of proximal development (1978), which is located within the social constructivist paradigm. For this reason, we justify the epistemological bedrock of our research within social constructivism. One of the assumptions of social constructivism is that individuals gain knowledge and insight through interaction with each other and their environment (Kim 2008). Alison King (2002) also found that the inter-action of learners with each other creates the opportunity for them to model their thought processes on each other. This results in the creation of new knowledge and comprehension. New knowledge could thus be con-structed via social interaction and the application of previous knowledge (Alexandrov and Ramirez-Velarde 2006).

The social constructivist view stresses the fact that the most optimal learning environment is one in which there exists a dynamic interaction between the teachers, the learner, and the task to create, develop, and discover own knowledge through interaction (Derry 1999). Cooperative learning is the instructional use of small groups through which students actively work together to maximize their own and each other's learning through the accomplishment of a shared or common goal (Zakaria and Iksan 2007; Johnson and Johnson 2009). Linked with social constructiv-ism, the aim of cooperative learning is to transform students from passive recipients of subject matter into active constructors of their own and other peoples' knowledge (Schunk 2000; Slavin 2000; Smith 2000).The goal is reached through interdependence among all group members with both personal and team accountability for conceptual understanding. All mod-els of cooperative learning utilize the basic elements of positive interdepen-dence, individual accountability, face-to-face interaction, social skills, and group processing. The lecturer's role in cooperative learning changes from being in front of the students ("sage on the stage"), doing most of the talk-ing, to becoming a facilitator ("a guide on the side") who guides students' learning. In this way students can take more responsibility for their own learning and as a result become self-directed learners. Research shows that appropriately planned group work promotes deeper and boarder-learning outcomes for more students, improves critical thinking and problem solv-ing skills, and contributes to better social and life skills (Cheng and Warren 2000; Johnson et al. 2000; Terwel 2003).

Five years ago, Margo O'Sullivan (2006) concluded that class size has a negative impact on teaching and learning–both for the students and for the lecturer. This conclusion might be viable for deductive teaching strate-gies such as the traditional lecture, but according to Richard Felder and Rebecca Brent (1999) the larger the class, the more essential it is to focus on teaching strategies that promote active learning. They argue that in a traditional lecture class with 15 students, it is not too difficult to get almost everyone actively involved in asking and answering questions and participating in discussions of course material. In a class with 40 students it is extremely difficult to do so, and in a class of 75 or more it is virtu-ally impossible. The challenge is that lecturers who have never used active learning in a large class usually envision two problems. They worry that some students will refuse to participate under any circumstances and that the noise level during the activity will make it difficult to regain control of the class (Felder and Brent 1999).

The responsibility of and duties with regard to teaching large classes can be pedagogically consuming and the lecturer is often dwarfed by the sheer enormity and extent of the task at hand (Muller 2010). Not only is it problematical for lecturers to establish effective rapport with their students in large classes, but they also often feel isolated and deserted. On top of this, they also have to put up with many and varied behavior-related problems (Anonymous 2010) from the side of their students—often without the luxury of having access to ready-made, on-the-spot solutions to and remedies for such problems. These behavior-related problems are exacerbated by the (often deliberately chosen) anonymity (Bruff 2009) and passivity of their students and the ensuing frustration that the teachers often experience as a direct result of having to attend such a large class (Muller 2010).

From results of the Australian Universities Teaching Committee (AUTC) research project (2001) on teaching large classes in Australia, it seems that small group discussions were the most effective and popular method currently being used to teach and assess large classes (Herbert and Hannan 2002). The lecture method was indicated as one of the least successful strategies for teaching large classes. Felder (1997) avers that the lecture, as didactic modality, has little educational value in large classes. Virginia Slaughter (1998) makes a similar claim and this is echoed five years later in the work of Peter Cantillon (2003) who avers that the *lecture* is not an effective way of teaching skills, changing attitudes, or encouraging higher-order thinking in large classes. Effective group work in large classes can help students clarify ideas through discussion and debate and develop interpersonal and communication skills. Student-to-student feedback may be as useful to learning as feedback provided by lecturers, with the added bonus of lessening the burden on teaching staff.

Students' perceptions of teaching-learning in large classes furthermore suggest that large class sizes can create obstacles to learning. Students admit to being afraid to ask or answer questions in large classes, and they complain that there is little to no chance of receiving proper, one-on-one feedback in large classes (Slaughter 1998). In large classes instructors tend to use predominantly lectures as a teaching method with activities (in the form of homework) mainly focusing on memorizing, comprehension, and application of subject matter (Van der Horst and McDonald 1997; Malan 2000). In most instances lectures compel students to take responsibility for the mastering of their own higher-order thinking skills (such as analysis, evaluation, and synthesis) with limited or no support from the lecturer (Shaughnessy 2005).

The fact that research on teaching large classes suggested that the traditional lecture should be replaced by other teaching strategies does not imply that the kind of information that is usually transferred via the lecture method no longer needs to be available to students. This kind of information is necessary but could be provided in a more productive manner, namely through modern communication technologies. The communication technologies can be utilized to present to students the valuable information, explanations, and demonstrations usually provided during the lecture. Modern communication and digital technologies can be used to deliver, support, and enrich teaching and assessment (Derek Stockley 2003). Through these technologies nontraditional "classrooms" are provided where the educator is educationally and didactically present (Willocks 1996). It was also found that teaching and learning in the virtual classroom are as effective as in the traditional classroom, but most probably more productive (Russell 1999).

In the virtual classroom use is being made of virtual reality and virtual interactivity. The DBD is an e-book based on DVD-technology developed to provide the kind of information usually delivered via lecture to learners to be assessed in their own place and at their own time and speed. Through the use of the DBD, the implementation of different learning theories, such as the constructivist learning theory, the cognitive learning theory, and the behavioristic learning theory, is consciously aimed at (Feden 1994; Marton and Booth 1997; Schunk 2000; Mowrer 2001). These theories provided the following guiding principles for our strategy. The use of digital technology should be teaching based–it should be used to increase the quality of education and decrease the cost of education. The point of departure should not be: "See what technology can do," but "What is required from technology to deliver quality education support?" The impressive nature of technology should not cause loss of the education message. The use of technology should also not be to package traditional teaching in a new format, namely, to use technology to continue with "chalk and talk." The use of technology requires a new teaching paradigm, namely to accept that the learners are not lecturer dependent regarding their learning activities. The learners should be able to study at their own pace and time and according to their own situation. The technology should also not be unknown to the learners, but should preferably be inherently part of their day-to-day life (Steyn 2010).

Teaching large classes via the implementation of cooperative learning still needs good support from teaching assistants and lecturers to be successful. Not only do they need to provide learning support but also teaching support, which is equally important. Lynn Burnett (2009) found in her research on good practices in teaching large classes that it is important to let students know where they can go to find assistance. Clear communication channels need to be available and study objectives should be clearly stated. Another major challenge associated with teaching in large classes is the administrative and logistical inconveniences that are intrinsically associated with it.

Recent research indicates that solutions for dealing with these administrative and logistical challenges in large groups are–almost by definition–significantly different from those for dealing with the administrative and logistical challenges of teaching small classes (Muller 2010). Lloyd Rieber (2004) emphasizes the important supporting role that professional teaching assistants can play in the teaching of large classes. These assistants can provide an inexpensive and educationally beneficial means for teaching, assessing, evaluating, and grading writing in large group classes. Provided that they attend all the large class meetings that their lecturer-in-chief is scheduled to lead and provided that they meet regularly to plan for and discuss the students' work (Rieber 2004), they can help to reduce the overall assessment (and evaluation) load of lecturers significantly. They can also help to save costs, and because the students who have to attend the large classes now have additional (and more easily available) individual support and access to better and quicker feedback, they (the students themselves) are–once again–empowered and capacitated. One possible disadvantage of using professional teaching assistants is that lecturers run the risk of alienating themselves from the academic and professional development of their students because their teaching assistants seem to become more familiar with their students than they do (Rieber 2004).

The Innovative Multimodus Teaching Strategy

Background

In our case, the initial development of an alternative to the traditional *lecture* method was brought about by the departure of the lecturer who was responsible for the module "Introduction to the Philosophy of Science," and our subsequent, unsuccessful attempts to assign a suitable replacement at short notice. "Introduction to the Philosophy of Science" is a compulsory core module for all second-year BEd-students, introducing them to the philosophy of science and education theory. The challenges were threefold: (a) to provide teaching support to a large class, (b) to cater for both Afrikaans- and English-speaking students in the same class-groups, and (c) to break down the habitual skepticism of the students regarding Philosophy as compulsory module in their curriculum. Eventually we decided to take-up these challenges by introducing a strategy for the teaching of large classes or the MTS.

The MTS Strategy: Components

The above-mentioned strategy of teaching large groups was implemented by using a purposeful combination and integration of the following teaching modi, namely the study guide, learning material, teaching team, the DBD, class meetings characterized by cooperative group work, eFundi as electronic LMS, and particularly planned assessment procedures.

The Study Guide

The study guide acted as a basic road map to support the learners in the management of their own learning. The study guide provided, for example, the basic learning outcomes to be achieved, the identification of the contents to be used, the topics to be covered per week, and the dates and nature of assessments activities.

The Learning Material

The learning material used was similar to those used in traditional teaching and learning. However, information provided in the DBD also served as "learning material," and many students reported that they used the DBD to study, most probably because it serves the needs of auditory learners.

The DBD

Compared to available computer-based learning and teaching support materials, the DBD has proved to be more readily accessible to the majority of our students living in a developing community. Although the majority of them still do not have access to computer-based technologies, they do have access to DVD technologies, such as a TV and DVD player. The DBD furthermore allowed the authors as instructional designers to contract the best available expertise in the field to present and/or copresent (audiovisually) the various content specializations in the module.

At the start of the module, each student received a complete DBD-set in either Afrikaans or English, according to the student's preference. On each DBD the lecturer accepted responsibility for those elements of the class meeting that have traditionally been regarded as the duty of the lecturer, namely the explanation and interpretation of the learning content, as well as the supply of additional information and the explication of difficult concepts, using relevant examples. Besides the possibility that visual materials may also be included, the DBD has the added advantage of individualization–the student can watch the presentation at a time when and as often as he/she wants to at his/her own pace (especially using the pause/rewind functions).

Each DBD is manufactured using about 40 different specifically developed techniques and rules to ensure the acceptance thereof by the students and to make sure that the DBD supports the different aspects from the different learning theories and guidelines to ensure the contribution of the DBD to achieve effective learning.

The Teaching Team

The teaching team consisted of the assigned lecturer as teaching manager and assistant lecturers (who were all full-time BEd [Hons] students [one per 250 students]). The teaching team as a unit took joint and full responsibility for the effective teaching support rendered to all the students in the module.

Scheduled Class Meetings

Scheduled class meetings broadly followed the following sequence (and included the following five learning opportunities) that are provided simultaneously in Afrikaans and English:

- Ten multiple-choice test questions projected onto a screen by a computer data projector have to be answered by all students on a computerized answer sheet (learning opportunity 1) before the start of the cooperative group work session. These marks are used to calculate the students' participation marks. This "forces" students to acquire ("prepare") the knowledge required during the rest of the class meeting. A cooperative group work assignment (activity) is then announced and explained as introduction by the lecturer (learning opportunity 2).
- The groups (consisting of pairs of students) complete the group work assignments in class (learning opportunity 3).
- The groups then exchange their completed assignments for peer-group assessment. The lecturer provides guidelines for grading purposes. The students' own peers then allocate marks to a particular pair's written assignment, also offering reasons for the marks that they are allocating (learning opportunity 4).
- Assessed group assignments are then handed back to the original authors for their perusal and reflection, allowing for their comments and questions of clarification regarding the assessment and mark allocation, if necessary (learning opportunity 5).
- Assessed assignments are then submitted for moderation by the assistant lecturers and for official recording of the marks on the official student record database.

The exercise of and training in identified academic and professional competencies that education students are obliged to acquire, including problem-solving skills (features of the traditional *lecture*), formed the focal point of scheduled class meetings. In these meetings, the mastery of specific learning outcomes through the communal practice of selected learning activities, based on group work as cooperative learning strategy, became the focus. The five essential principles of cooperative learning as defined by David Johnson and Roger Johnson (2009)—namely positive interdependence, individual accountability, group processing, face-to-face promotive interaction, and social skills—were applied in all group work activities. Each of these five principles are adhered to in the planning, implementation, and assessment of assigned group activities to ensure that all the students were continually, actively, and equally involved.

eFundi as LMS

Due to rapid technological development, an ever-changing higher education landscape, as well as evolutionary changes in users' needs and demands, the North-West University (NWU) decided in 2007 to investigate a web-based LMS that caters for these needs. An LMS is a web-based software application for the administration, documentation, tracking, and reporting of training programs, classroom and online events, e-learning programs, and training content.

The NWU adopted SAKAI's version as a web-based LMS in January 2009 and labelled it *eFundi*. It is used at the NWU to enhance students' learning experiences in an e-learning environment. It has proven to be a powerful communication instrument as far as assisting students in large class-groups is concerned—especially when these students need to timely receive correct course-related information.

Assessment

The following modes of assessment were used in a planned and integrative manner:

Formative Assessment.

- Class test: Every week a class test, consisting of ten multiple-choice questions took place. These tests were scored electronically (by means of optical mark–reader software), subsequent to which the marks were electronically uploaded on eFundi, were students could have instant and easy access to them.
- Group work assignments: Although group work (mainly done in pairs) was primarily employed as a collaborative, active learning technique,

the assignments were also assessed and scored by the students' peers and subsequently moderated by the assistant lecturers to foster positive interdependence. During every scheduled class, meeting students were given a written assignment that was to be completed in pairs.

• Individual assignments: Students were also required to complete an individual written assignment, which was subsequently assessed and scored by the assistant lecturers to foster individual accountability within the cooperative learning environment.

• Semester test: The formative semester test (as formal *assessment* opportunity) covered the work up till a given date, and it was subsequently assessed and scored by the assistant lecturers.

Summative Assessment. The summative assessment opportunities were aimed at providing the opportunity of determining the level to which the students were able to integrate and apply the required competencies. In this case the summative assessment primarily was the semester examination that, as formal *evaluation* opportunity, covered all the study units in the module.

An important feature of the strategy is that students using different languages of teaching and learning, namely Afrikaans and English, were easily catered for in the same class-group and in the same class-meetings. This was effected by providing all the modi of the strategy in both languages. The study guide was provided in both languages, and learning material was provided according to the requirements in both languages. The DBDs were also provided in both languages, as were the class meetings. It was possible to manage the class meetings in both languages because the setup of the class meetings provided the opportunity to use both languages simultaneously, for example, the class test is set in both languages, and because the introduction of the group work topic is short, it can be explained in both languages afterward to the two language member groups, provision could be made for full participation and peer assessment in the language of choice. The other assessment activities and the LMS are also provided in both languages. The precondition is that at least one member of the teaching team should be fully conversant in one of the languages.

Investigating the Effectiveness of the MTS

Population

The module had 579 registered students to be served in three on-campus class groups of about 190 students each.

Measuring Instruments

To interrogate the efficacy of our strategy, we used the following methods: two structured questionnaires that were completed by students (a premodule and a postmodule questionnaire), as well as a calculation of the costs and benefits (measured by final results of students) compared to the costs and benefits of the conventional *lecture* method.

Findings

Premodule Questionnaire

The premodule questionnaire and the responses to the closed questions appear in Appendix 1. At the outset of the course there were some students who were in one way or another negatively prejudiced toward the module: 45 percent stated that they were not interested in the module, 13 percent regarded it as a waste of time, 20 percent were of the view that it could make no contribution to them becoming better teachers, while 30 percent believed that it had nothing to do with the learning area that they intended teaching at school. In the open section, some of the recurrent answers to the question "What do you know about the module Philosophy of Science?" included: "All students on campus study the module," "I have no knowledge about the module," and "other students find the module to be a waste of time." Where answers touched on the content of the module, it was clear that the majority of the students conceptualized this particular module as one that addresses obscure issues of (what they perceived to be) "philosophy," as well as dealing with scientific research methods and related issues such as values and ethics. A significant number of the participating students failed to relate the relevance of the module to the teaching profession and/or to their own future teaching praxis. Some of the answers (presumably from the more positively inclined students) to the question, "What do you expect to learn in the module Philosophy of Science?" however, reflected cautious expectations that it might, in some way, assist in preparing and equipping them for the teaching profession.

A small percentage of students expressed negative feelings toward group work. The majority (58 percent) liked to work in groups and 53 percent were of the opinion that they learn more in class when they work in groups than when they work alone. These responses may possibly be understood in light of the fact that 52 percent of the students were of the opinion that not all group members necessarily pull their weight during the cooperative group work exercises in class. Nevertheless, only 32 percent actually did not prefer working in groups during scheduled class meetings. Finally, 62 percent of the students were of the opinion that the advantages of group work outweighed the disadvantages.

It should, however, be noted that 42 percent of students indicated that they did not prefer to manage their own learning, and 36 percent indicated that it is the lecturers' task to manage their learning.

The participants were more positive as far as the use of technology in teaching and learning was concerned: 82 percent agreed that the use of eFundi as LMS assisted them in improving their own academic achievement. 85 percent of the students expressed the opinion that the more advanced the technology is, the better the support for learning would be. They (91 percent) reported having a good understanding of how eFundi works, and how it ought to be applied and managed.

Postmodule Questionnaire

The postmodule questionnaire and the responses of the students appear in Appendix 2. Regarding the use of the DBD, 74 percent of the students reported that they found the DBD useful in helping them to understand the subject content, and 71 percent recognized the positive support value of the DBD in helping them to prepare for tests.

The participants' experience of the cooperative group work exercises and frequent short class tests were also positive: 76 percent of them responded that the group work exercises were designed to help them gain an improved understanding of the subject content matter. In addition, 70 percent of them agreed with the statement that the group work exercises support them in preparing for the semester test. Similarly, 86 percent of the participants agreed that the regular class tests were also designed to help them gain an improved understanding of the subject content matter.

The participants' overall experience of the strategy was convincingly positive: 81 percent of them preferred it to the traditional, conventional lecture method. From a series of follow-up informal individual interviews and observations, we suggest that the remaining 19 percent of the students did not support our strategy for the teaching *of* and facilitation of learning *in* large classes, mainly because they are used to and do, in fact, prefer "spoon-feeding". Based on our interviews and observations, we also suggest that these students, many of whom indicated that they also wish to achieve good academic grades, appear to be much lecturer-dependent. They also appear to have a relatively low level of self-confidence in their own abilities and competence to construct their own knowledge bases. They have also indicated that they prefer a teaching-learning scenario where the lecturer actually teaches each class, so that they may only have to make notes of which subject content is more important and, subsequently, have a relatively informed idea of what exactly to study for their final summative exam.

Discussion

As Felder (1997) points out, the teaching of large classes can be rewarding, provided that all students accept coresponsibility for their own learning and development. Teaching should, after all, never be concerned with coverage of the material. The real issue should always be the depth of coverage (Meltzer 2002) and, as such, this requires students to reciprocate as best they can.

We wish to point out that our research into the teaching *of* and facilitating of learning *in* large classes is not about e-learning per se. Instead, what we have done is, if anything, typical of the multimodus teaching approach (De Leng et al. 2010). Having made eclectical use of the work of, amongst others, Karl Smith (2000); David Meltzer (2002); Cantillon (2003); Rieber (2004); Johnson and Johnson (2009); Bas De Leng, Diana H. J. M. Dolmans, H. L. M. Donkers, Arno M. M. Muijtens, and Cees P. M. Van Der Vleuten (2010); Martin Muller (2010); and Rafael Mompo and Judith Redoli (2010), we would venture to define multimodus learning, in our own case, as the integrated use of a specifically selected range of teaching support and assistance to provide a more rounded teaching support service to students (De Leng et al. 2010). In the case of our own work, interfaces that were researched and that we report on below include the class meeting (focusing on cooperative learning in small groups), the use of DBD's, the use of paper-based teaching and learning support materials, as well as the use of our own, locally developed eFundi. Although maybe not entirely original or inventive in the true sense of the word, what we have done nevertheless constitutes, in our opinion, a blended and pedagogically innovative step forward.

The aim behind the implementation of our strategy for the teaching *of* and facilitation of learning *in* large classes in this particular module was to test its effect on education productivity at the tertiary level. An increase in productivity is determined by an increase in quality—in this case an increase in academic achievement by the students, as well as a decrease in the costs calculated in terms of lecturer-in-front-of-class time teaching a particular group of students.

We now present a summary of our findings with regard to education productivity, emanating from this pilot study in the teaching of the module "Introduction to the Philosophy of Science" to large classes:

- In the final summative examination, an average of 66 percent[2] was achieved by the students, with 23 percent of them obtaining a distinction. Only 9 percent of the students either did not obtain permission to sit for the exam or failed the exam. These results indicate a significant improvement on the results of the previous year. In addition to the improvement of their academic achievement, the attitudes of students toward philosophy have also improved noticeably.
- We calculated that if the teaching of these students had been done according the traditional *lecture* method, it would have required 750 working hours of the lecturer alone. Using our strategy for the teaching *of* and facilitation of learning *in* large classes, it required only 290 working hours from the lecturer, consequently saving 460 working hours of the lecturer. The extra cost of implementing the strategy was 31,000 BRL. This can be understood to mean that in the case of teaching these 500+ students, 440 working hours of a lecturer was effectively "bought" at the cost of 31,000 BRL or 70.45 BRL/hour. This suggests that the cost of lecturing these 500+ students was lowered, because the average cost of keeping a lecturer in front of a class for 440 hours, calculated at 150 BRL/hour, would have been at least 66,000 BRL.
- One of the by-products of our strategy for the teaching *of* and facilitation of learning *in* large classes is that it seems to have contributed to finding a more amiable solution to the existing problem of medium of instruction at tertiary level. By using this strategy, the teaching was to all intents and purposes delivered completely bilingual in each of the class-groups, neglecting neither Afrikaans nor English, and without any attempts at subdividing the language groups into two separate, parallel groups.
- Another by-product is that extra lecturer hours become available; the teaching experience of the lecturers was increased positively. Most lecturers find teaching to large class-groups particularly stressful. The stress levels of the responsible lecturers appear to have been reduced as a result of our strategy for the teaching *of* and facilitation of learning *in* large classes.

Our study indicates that the strategy as outlined above seems to contribute positively toward an increase in students' academic achievement and a reduction in overall input costs. It also decreases the total number of the lecturer's lecturing hours that may otherwise have been required to teach a large class-group of 500 students.

Conclusion

Indications are that our strategy for the teaching *of* and facilitation of learning *in* large classes was largely successful. The productivity of both teaching and learning related activities was raised. In particular, the levels of students' academic achievement were better than expected for a module such as "Introduction to the Philosophy of Science," and the overall input costs were substantially reduced.

An unexpected outcome of the project was the way in which the strategy seemed to endorse, encourage, and support the promotion of multilingualism, at least as far as the use of English and Afrikaans as media of instruction are concerned. In this regard, it should be noted that positive feedback was received from students who preferred English as medium of instruction—especially as regards the English version of the DBD, the use of English in group discussions, and the equal and equitable facilitation of all scheduled class meetings in English and Afrikaans.

The initial success of our strategy for the teaching and facilitation of learning in large classes led to an executive decision by the dean and the management committee of the faculty to extend this strategy to the teaching and learning of other generic and compulsory undergraduate modules. Other lecturers in the faculty as well as in two other faculties at NWU requested assistance in implementing this strategy during the second semester of 2010. As this strategy is introduced to other generic subjects at different levels of undergraduate study in our own faculty as well as in other faculties, it will be possible for researchers to track and plot its success.

Finally, we are of the opinion that it may also be worth experimenting with this strategy in an attempt to realize the seemingly illusive ideal of developing and empowering the other official languages (apart from Afrikaans and English) of South Africa (i.e., the indigenous African languages of learning and teaching at tertiary educational institutions in South Africa).

NOTES

1. Exchange rate, on 15 January 2012: US$1 = 8,17 R (BusinessDay.com.za 2012).
2. At South African education institutions, grading is given in percentages.

REFERENCES

Alexandrov, Nia, and Paul V. Ramirez-Velarde. 2006. "Educational Meta-Model and Collaborative Learning." Paper presented at the ICBL2007 Conference held in Florianopolis, Brazil, 7–9 May 2009. Available online at: http://cs/. mty.itesm.mx.

Anonymous. 2008. "Red Onderwys" ["Save education"]. "Rapport" ["Rapport"] 7 September 2008: 18.

Anonymous. 2010. "Teaching Large Groups in Mathematics." In *Teaching Large Groups*, ed. Hennie J. Steyn. Potchefstroom: Academic Support Services, North-West University (Potchefstroom campus).

Blaire, Sheila. 2009. "New Maths Curriculum Does Not Add Up." *Business Day*. Available online at: http://www.businessday.co.za.

Bligh, Donald A. 1972. *What's the Use of Lectures?* Harmondsworth: Penguin

Bruff, Derek. 2009. *Teaching with Classroom Response Systems: Creating Active Learning Environments*. 4th ed. San Francisco: Jossey-Bass.

Burnett, Lynn. 2009. "An Institution-Wide Approach to Retaining and Supporting First Year Students." *ALTC First Year Experience FYE Curriculum Design Symposium* 2009. Brisbane: Queensland University of Technology. Available online at: http://www.fyecd2009.qut.edu.au.

Cantillon, Peter. 2003. *ABC of Learning and Teaching in Medicine: Teaching Large Groups*. London: BMJ Group. Available online at: http://www.bmj.com.

Cheng, Winnie, and Martin Warren. 2000. "Making a Difference: Using Peers to Access Individual Students' Contributions to a Group Project." *Journal of Teaching in Higher Education* 5 (2): 243–255.

Davidson, James D., and William Rees-Mogg. 1992. *The Great Reckoning–How the World will Change in the Depression of the 1990s*. London: Sidgwick & Jackson.

De Leng, Bas A., Diana H. J. M. Dolmans, H. L. M. Donkers, Arno M. M. Muijtens, and Cees P. M. Van Der Vleuten. 2010. "Instruments to Explore Blended Learning: Modifying a Method to Analyse Online Communication for the Analysis of Face-to-Face Communication." *Computers in Education* 55 (2): 551–644.

De Villiers, Pierre, and Gert Steyn. 2009. "Effects of Changes in State Funding of Higher Education on the Output in South Africa." *South African Journal of Higher Education* 23 (1): 43–68.

Derek Stockley. 2003. *Definition of E-Learning*. Melbourne: Derek Stockley Pty. Ltd. Available online at: http://derekstockley.com.au.

Derry, Sharon J. 1999. "A Fish Called Peer Learning: Searching for Common Themes." In *Cognitive Perspectives on Peer Learning*, ed. Angela O'Donnel and Alison King, 197–211. Mahwah, NJ: Lawrence Erlbaum.

Dibetle, Monako. 2009. "First-year Jumble." *Mail & Guardian Higher Learning*, May 2009: 1.

Dreyer, Chris. 2005. "Attacking the Digital Divide–Designing Electronic-Mobile Learning Environments for Improved Teacher Training in Developing

Countries." Paper presented at the International Congress for School Effectiveness and Improvement, Barcelona, Spain 2–5 January 2005.

Feden, Preston D. 1994. "About Instruction: Powerful New Strategies Worth Knowing." *Educational Horizons* 73 (1): 18–24.

Felder, Richard M. 1997. "Beating the Numbers Game: Effective Teaching in Large Classes." Paper presented at the ASEE Annual Conference, Milwaukee, WI, June 1997. Available online at: http://www4.ncsu.edu.

Felder, Richard M., and Rebecca Brent. 1999. "FAQs-2: (a) Active Learning vs. Covering the Syllabus; (b) Dealing with Large Classes." *Chemical Engineering Education* 33 (4): 276–277. Available online at: http://www4.ncsu.edu.

Friedman, Paul J., Fred Rodriguez, and Joel McMomb. 1999. "Why Students Do and Do Not Attend Classes." *The Scholarship of Teaching*, February 1999: 1–27.

Garrison, D. Randy, and Heather Kanuka. 2004. "Blended Learning–Uncovering Its Transformative Potential in Higher Education." *The Internet and Higher Education* 7 (2): 95–105.

Gower, Primarashni. 2008. "A Four-Year Undergrad Degree?" *Mail & Guardian*, October 10: 13. Available online at: http://mg.co.za.

Herbert, D., and R. Hannan. 2002. *AUTC Project 2001. Teaching Large Classes: A Survey of Large Class Teaching Around Australia.* Brisbane: Teaching and Educational Development Institute, University of Queensland.

Hill, Adrian, and Rita Kop. 2008. "Connectivism: Learning Theory of the Future or Vestige of the Past?" *The International Review of Research in Open and Distance Learning* 9 (3). Available online at: http://www.irrodl.org.

James, William. 2010. "Righting Ancient Education Wrongs is About Quality Teachers, Not Numbers." *Cape Argus,* December 28: 9.

Jaschik, Scott. 2010. *The Lost Arts of Teaching.* Washington, DC: Inside Higher Ed. Available online at: http://www.insidehighered.com.

Johnson, David W., and Roger T. Johnson. 2009. "An Educational Psychology Success Story: Social Interdependence Theory and Cooperative Learning." *Educational Researcher* 38 (5): 365–379.

Johnson, David W., Roger T. Johnson, and Mary Beth Stanne. 2000. *Cooperative Learning Methods: A Meta-analysis.* Malverne, NY: Table Learning Systems, Inc. Available online at: http://www.tablelearning.com.

Jordaan, Yolanda. 2009. "Influencing Factors on Lecture Attendance at a Tertiary Institution." *South African Journal of Higher Education* 23 (1): 98–112.

Kim, Beaumie. 2008. "Social Constructivism." In *Emerging Perspectives on Learning, Teaching, and Technology*, ed. Orey, Michael. Bloomington, IN: Association for Educational Communications and Technology.

King, Alison. 2002. "Structuring Peer Interaction to Promote High-Level Cognitive Processing." *Theory into Practice* 41 (1): 33–39.

Malan, S. P. Trichard. 2000. "The 'New Paradigm' of Outcomes-Based Education in Perspective." *Journal of Family Ecology and Consumer Sciences* 28: 22–28. Available online at: http://www.up.ac.za/saafecs.

Marton, Ference, and Shirley Booth. 1997. Learning and Awareness. Mahwah, NJ: Lawrence Erlbaum Associates.

Meltzer, David A. 2002. "Transforming the Lecture-Hall Environment: The Fully Interactive Physics Lecture." *American Journal of Physics* 70 (6): 639–654.

Moloi, Konnie C., K. Peter Dzvimbo, Ferdinand J. Potgieter, Charl C. Wolhuter, and Johannes L. van der Walt. 2010. "Learners' Perceptions as to What Contributes to their School Success: A Case Study." *South African Journal of Education* 30 (3): 475–490.

Mompo, Rafael, and Judith Redolli. 2010. "Some Internet-Based Strategies that Help Solve the Problem of Teaching Large Groups of Engineering Students." *Innovations in Education and Teaching International* 47 (1): 95–102.

Mowrer, Robert R. 2001. *Handbook of Contemporary Learning Theories*. Mahwah, NJ: Lawrence Erlbaum Associates.

Muller, Martin L. 2010. *Nature of the Effect of Class Size on University Learning and Teaching Experiences: A Research Report*. Stellenbosch, South Africa: University of Stellenbosch.

O'Sullivan, Margo C. 2006. "Teaching Large Classes: The International Evidence and a Discussion of Some Good Practice in Ugandan Primary Schools." *International Journal of Educational Development* 26 (1): 24–36.

Orey, Michael. 2008. *Emerging Perspectives on Learning, Teaching, and Technology*. Bloomington, IN: Association for Educational Communications and Technology.

Osguthorpe, Russell T., and Charles R. Graham. 2003. "Blended Learning Environments–Definitions and Directions." *The Quarterly Review of Distance Education* 4 (3): 227–233.

Rademeyer, Alet. 2007. "Pandor sê nog universiteite is dalk nodig: Staat mik na 100 000 ekstra studente" ["Pandor Says More Universities are Perhaps Necessary: Government Aims at 100,000 Extra Students"]. *Beeld [Image]*, November 28: 6.

Rademeyer, Alet. 2009. "Net 17% van eerstejaars slaag Chemie" ["Only 17% of First Year Students Pass Chemistry"]. *Beeld [Image]*, April 9: 3.

Read, Charles. 2010. "Grootgroeponderrig in Natuurwetenskappe" ["Large group teaching in the Natural Sciences"]. Paper presented at the Workshop on Teaching Large Groups, Potchefstroom, South Africa, 21 August 2010.

Redwood, John. 1993. *The Global Marketplace–Capitalism and Its Future*. London: Harper Collins.

Rieber, Lloyd J. 2004. "Using Professional Teaching Assistants to Support Large Group Business Communication Classes." *Journal of Education for Business* 79 (3): 176–178.

Russell, Thomas L. 1999. *No Significant Difference Phenomenon (NSDP)*. Raleigh, NC: North Carolina State University.

SAPA (South African Press Association). 2009. "Matriek in Minister Nzimande se Visier" ["Matric in Minister Nzimande's Visor"]. *Die Burger [The Citizen]*, July 1: 1.

Schunk, Dale H. 2000. *Learning Theories: An Educational Perspective*. 3rd ed. Upper Saddle River, NJ: Merrill.

Shaughnessy, Michael F. 2005. "An Interview with Trevor Tebbs: Talking about Higher Order Thinking and Teaching About It!" *Education News*, September 15. Available online at: http://www.educationnews.org.

Skinner, Burrhus F. 1954. "The Science of Learning and the Art of Teaching." *Harvard Educational Review* 24 (2): 86–97.

Slaughter, Virginia. 1998. *Teaching Psychology in Large Classes: An International Survey of Solutions.* Brisbane: University of Queensland.

Slavin, Robert E. 2000. *Educational Psychology: Theory and Practice.* 6th ed. Boston, MA: Pearson/Allyn & Bacon.

Smith, Karl A. 2000. "Going Deeper: Formal Small-Group Learning in Large Classes." *New Directions for Teaching and Learning* 81 (Spring): 25–46.

Steyn, Hennie J. 2010. "DBD in Education: Improve Quality in Education Provision." Paper presented at Faculty of Education, Unisa, Pretoria. 11 April 2010.

Terwel, Jan. 2003. "Co-Operative Learning in Secondary Education: A Curriculum Perspective." In *Co-Operative Learning: The Social and Intellectual Outcomes of Learning in Groups,* ed. Robyn Gilles and Adrian Ashman, 54–68. London: Falmer.

UNESCO. 2011. "Enrolment in Tertiary Public and Private Institutions." 2011. Montreal, Canada: UNESCO Institute for Statistics. Available online at: http://www.uis.unesco.org

Van der Horst, Helen, and Ria McDonald. 1997. *Outcomes-Based Education: A Teacher's Manual.* Pretoria: Kagiso.

Van der Walt, Johannes L., Charl C. Wolhuter, Ferdinand J. Potgieter, Philip Higgs, Leonie Higgs, and Isaac M. Ntshoe. 2011. "The Academic Profession in the Third World: A Comparative Study." *Journal of Third World Studies* 28 (2): 1–31.

Verhagen, Plon. 2006. *Connectivism: A New Learning Theory?* Available online at: http://www.surfspace.nl.

Vygotsky, Lev S. 1978. *Mind in Society: The Development of Higher Psychological Processes.* Cambridge: Harvard University Press.

Watson, K. 1996. "Education Provision for the 21st Century–Who or What is Shaping the Agenda and Influencing Developments?" In *Education and National Development in Southern Africa,* ed. Priscilla T. M. Marope and Shelden G. Weeks, 1–21. Gaborone: Botswana Educational Research Association.

Willocks, Stephanie D. 1996. "Our Classrooms and Chaucer's Canterbury Tales: How to Make Them Work Together." *English Journal* 85 (7): 122–124.

Wolhuter, Charl C., Philip Higgs, Leonie Higgs, and Isaac M. Ntshoe. 2010. "How Affluent is the South African Higher Education Sector and How Strong is the South African Academic Profession in the Changing International Academic Landscape?" *South African Journal of Higher Education* 24 (1): 196–214.

World Bank. 2006. *World Development Indicators.* Washington, DC: The World Bank.

Zakaria, Effandi, and Zanaton Iksan. 2007. "Promoting Cooperative Learning in Science and Mathematics Education: A Malaysian Perspective." *Eurasia Journal of Mathematics, Science & Technology Education* 3 (1): 35–39.

Appendix 1

Precourse Questionnaire and Responses

1 What do you know about Philosophy of Science?
2 What do you expect to learn in the module Philosophy of Science?

Closed Questions:

		Percentage Distribution of Responses		
Question	Disagree Entirely 1	Agree to Some Extent 2	Agree to a Large Extent 3	Agree Totally 4
1. I am interested in the module Philosophy of Science	5	40	43	12
2. The module Philosophy of Science is a waste of time	30	57	11	2
3. The module Philosophy of Science can make no contribution to make me a better teacher	46	34	17	3
4. The model Philosophy of Science has nothing to do with the subject that I intend to teach at school	27	43	16	14
5. I like to work in class in groups	17	25	34	24

(Continued)

Closed Questions:

	Percentage Distribution of Responses			
Question	Disagree Entirely 1	Agree to Some Extent 2	Agree to a Large Extent 3	Agree Totally 4
6. I learn more in class when I work in groups than I do when working alone	20	27	32	21
7. When doing an assignment in class, I prefer to work alone	32	27	19	22
8. When doing group work in class all group members pull their weight	17	35	33	15
9. According to my judgment the advantages of group work are more than the disadvantages	8	30	46	16
10. In the module I would prefer to work during class time in groups	9	23	43	25
11. I think e-learning is used in order to reduce the lecturer's work	19	50	24	7
12. I prefer to manage my own learning	14	28	40	18
13. The more advanced the technology, the better the support for learning	2	13	46	39
14. A lecturer's task is to manage my learning	23	41	25	11
15. Technological support for student is expensive	8	28	46	18
16. I have used eFundi at some stage	3	5	14	78
17. I visit eFundi on a weekly basis	2	5	26	67
18. Lecturers encourage me to use eFundi	2	16	32	50
19. When I visit eFundi, it is only to read announcement	28	43	20	9
20. I know exactly how to use eFundi and how to obtain information	1	8	31	60
21. The information that I get on eFundi helps me to improve my marks	2	16	35	47

Appendix 2

Post-course Questionnaire and Responses

	Percentage Distribution of Responses			
Question	Fully Agree	Agree	Disagree	Fully Disagree
1. I used the DBD at least once a week	14	27	31	28
2. The DBD supported me to better understand the subject contents	35	39	11	15
3. The DBD supported me in my preparation for the semester test	36	35	16	13
4. The group work supported me to better understand the subject content	32	44	16	8
5. The group work supported me in preparing for the semester test	22	48	19	11
6. The class tests supported me in understanding the subject content	33	53	11	3
7. I prefer the strategy used in the Introduction to Philosophy of Science (WTOL 221 module) to the traditional lecture method	34	47	11	8

Chapter 5

Success Factors in the Implementation of e-Learning in a UK Higher Education Institution

The Case of One Faculty

Tricia Coverdale-Jones

This chapter considers the implementation of strategies, policies, and actions to improve the use of e-learning within a United Kingdom (UK) university. This university is an example of a wider class, in that it is a post-1992 university, one of the 36 former "polytechnics" that were changed to public universities on a national level under the Further and Higher Education Act (1992). Other new public universities have been created since then. The university is located in Southern England with over 20,000 students, 84 percent of whom are undergraduates. The university describes itself as "a top modern university for student satisfaction." Many of the degree programs available include some vocational aspects, and over half of the courses are accredited or validated by professional organizations. The author was variously faculty of Humanities and Social Sciences e-learning coordinator and Learning and Teaching coordinator from 2005 to 2011.

In the UK, the adoption of e-learning is rather generally accepted as necessary by universities, especially but not exclusively in the more undergraduate-teaching-focused newer universities. The Open University has, of course been a pioneer in the field of e-learning, starting in the 1980s when the technology only allowed MS-DOS text-based interaction (Hardwick and Cooper 2009). There are also numerous Anglophone publications on the use of e-learning with over 550 references in the university library, including e-books and e-journals; many of these were published in the period 2000–2005, when the ideas were taking root on a more widespread basis. The majority of university managers and academics are convinced of the validity of the e-learning approach based on the social construction of learning mooted by Lev Vygotsky (1978), and there are leading proponents of e-learning (Salmon 2004a; Littlejohn and Pegler 2007). Opposing views include those of Robin Goodfellow and Mary Lea (2008, 1) who offer an alternative, "a language- and literacies-based approach to teaching and learning," to the adoption in higher education of the Vygotskian principle. Goodfellow and Lea (2008, 50–51) also refer to the "taken for granted discourses of e-learning in the university." However, they are in the minority in their view of e-learning. This university followed the more accepted model. The idea has also been put forward that e-learning is an essential requirement for a global university: "But investment in online learning will allow universities to benefit from economies of scale and meet increasing demand from developing countries. A growing number of higher education institutions are taking this forward" (Katsomitros 2011, 1).

The perception is that students, especially the majority of younger students, are "digital natives" (Prensky 2001), or users of computer-mediated communication since early childhood who do not need to learn new rules to use technology for social, professional, or educational purposes. This assumption has been questioned on the basis of experience that shows differences in competence between learners, the "digital divide" (Leier 2011; JISC 2012b). According to their website, the UK government-funded JISC (Joint Information Services Committee), founded in 1993, "aims to provide vision and leadership to universities, and bring about technology developments for the benefit of all universities and colleges." JISC also manages the UK's network infrastructure for universities through the Joint Network Team Association (JANET). This year JISC also funds its first research and development project to stimulate innovation and to share knowledge and benefits across higher education, while shouldering the risk for individual universities (JISC 2012b). This report, based on two phases of a large-scale research project in 2005–2009, generally upholds the view of learners as "digital natives," but with exceptions. It identified the students' needs and expectations of technology as an essential part of their lives for most students (JISC 2012b). Among the key points were that technologies were integral to the "Google generation" learners' lives; they extract information online and from image and video; they use informal collaboration; they value quality academic content; and they have high expectations of the technology but feel that technology should be balanced with face-to-face and paper-based learning. It was noted that "some learners, including many disabled learners, are agile adopters and explorers of technology." On the negative side there was still a "narrower but deeper digital divide" and also conservatism in the adoption of new software or technology (JISC 2012b).

These findings confirm a general impression in discussions in British society, political fora, and the media as well as within universities that learners have changed and that education needs to cater for this. The need for digital skills is also generally accepted (Lane Fox 2011). In the context of student expectations, almost all UK universities have followed the trend of developing online learning resources and the use of a virtual learning environment (VLE), some more quickly and profoundly than others. The situation in the UK is one where competition between universities for students is quite fierce, and no university would wish to "lag behind" the others. The need to cater to student expectations and not to fall behind competitors is expressed in the self-description "a top modern university for student satisfaction" referred to above.

Bobby Elliott (2009) believes that we still have to fully develop an "eLearning Pedagogy." This view is also confirmed by Isobel Falconer and Alison Littlejohn (2007). However, this has not deterred attempts to develop e-learning in higher education through trialing different uses of technologies and government and other organizations' investment in supporting this process (JISC, EUROCALL, HEA Subject Centres).

As in the JISC report referred to above, the wish is to enable learning in the context where younger students are already operating (i.e., online). Even though some reports in the past have shown that students prefer to keep some areas of their online use for personal and social uses (Sutton-Brady et al. 2009; Leier 2011), the distinctions are blurring (Tian et al. 2011), so universities have developed YouTube, Facebook, and Second Life applications and course materials. A VLE provides a separate development of this—a virtual space for learning.

When the university was implementing its new e-learning policy in 2007, this was very much a "live" topic, with government-funded initiatives also through the well-established organization JISC and the more recent HEA Subject Centres as providers of training, online advice, funding for symposia, meetings, and projects (HEA 2012).

Context within the University and Initial Actions

Within the wider UK context, the university implemented a policy to boost the use of e-learning in 2007 to improve the learning experience for all students. A combination of "push" and "pull" strategies was used, with the "push" strategies being based on "university-wide commitment to the further development of e-learning and a central steer from the Directorate of the university; faculty-buy-in and faculty and departmental leadership to drive the project forward" (Starie 2011, 1).

The faculties and schools also drew up their own policies and priorities to build up the support of academics at all levels across the university. At that time the VLE software available on the university network was Internet course tools (WebCT), and the use of this facility depended on the interest of the lecturer, with the result that there were relatively few enthusiasts. There was a tradition of putting materials (mostly Microsoft Word files) on an internally accessible drive on the university network for students to read or download, though a few academics created web pages to publish documents as well; hence, the model for the use of the network was as a repository for the transmission of information from the lecturer to the student. Under the new policy, funding for technical and pedagogical support was boosted both centrally and within the five faculties. Building on the existing use of WebCT, the aim was to make the application of e-learning more universal, and to change the Teaching and Learning culture, renamed as Learning and Teaching to refocus on student-centered learning. As part of the "push" strategy within the university, university-wide minimum standard was set at a VLE presence with at least the unit handbook for all new units by September 2007 and all Level 1 (first year) and master's level units by 2010; in fact this was achieved across almost all current units a year earlier. The e-learning position of this university in comparison to others was in the middle range, where some UK universities were more advanced in e-learning, others less so.

The university policy aimed at facilitating and enhancing e-learning use. Littlejohn and Pegler (2007, 10) in their initial definitions of blended learning, especially the use of the VLE, include points that can be observed on different types of degree programs in the the Portsmouth context as a newer post-92 teaching-focussed university:

- Access to a wide choice of resources on your personal computer drawn from international as well as institutional digital repositories, accessed via a single log in that personalizes the "blend" of learning that you are offered.
- Personalized content delivered through a customized interface with RSS (Really Simple Syndication) alerts to flag new content relevant to individual interests.
- Using a VLE to access course materials and ask questions whether on or off campus.

- Assembling and publishing an e-portfolio of your work from courses studied across several institutions.
- Successful and rewarding student-teacher relationships initiated and maintained through online communication without ever meeting face-to-face.

The e-learning policy publication and implementation emphasized the use of the VLE and coincided with the transfer from WebCT to Blackboard. As noted, a relatively small number of unit coordinators were already making use of WebCT as an online platform. Blackboard was branded as "Victory" at the University of Portsmouth, named after Nelson's famous battleship that can still be seen in the Historic Dockyard in Portsmouth (University of Portsmouth 2012). There was frequent discussion among the team of developers described in the next section on how to arrange the material.

Unit coordinators have "ownership" of their units (named modules in some universities) that are the components of a degree program. UK degrees usually follow a fixed program for each named degree award. A degree program consists of a number of core, or compulsory, units, with a limited number of option choices at each level. The unit coordinator has responsibility for the course content, which is also subject to the normal validation and review procedures as part of the quality assurance processes.

Perhaps as a result of using web pages for degree programs, or even sending the materials out on paper or on a CD-ROM for distance learners, a small number of course coordinators or subject leaders wanted to have a set of materials and activities for a whole degree program or year group on the VLE, rather than for each subject or unit module within that program. Others were happy to follow the recommended organization within separate units. Gradually most coordinators who requested the whole program approach have come round to the unit organization pattern, with a few programs still using web pages in addition to modules on the VLE and others using "hubs" for resources shared across programs and levels (e.g., research management, subjects such as fraud, terrorism, cybercrime, and others).

There were also different priorities with some schools in the faculty that were more active in distance-learning degrees for mature employed learners (e.g., Criminal Justice, Education, Translation and Applied Linguistics in the School of Languages) than others. There were differences between schools in the balance between undergraduate and postgraduate student numbers; as referred to above, the university as a whole has 84 percent undergraduates (University of Portsmouth 2011a), most of whom are UK-based "home" students who enter at age 18 and study on campus. In the implementation of the e-learning policy, the needs of other student groups, such as older learners, part-time and distance learners, students with disabilities, and international students had to be kept in mind.

The e-Learning Coordinators' and Online Course Developers' Roles in the Faculty

The faculty of Humanities and Social Studies, along with other faculties, appointed an e-learning coordinator who was answerable to the associate dean (students) who is concerned with the quality of the student learning experience, among other things. This post was paid for for two years out of an initial central budget, then a further two years were funded by the faculty. The coordinator was responsible for consultations, dissemination of good practice, information sharing, and facilitation of staff development. These actions were also delivered, in part, centrally by the university's academic development department, the Department for Curriculum and Quality Enhancement. The emphasis was on the improvement of learning. All this was part of the "pull" strategy to bring e-learning into the mainstream activities of academic staff.

The five faculties decided to use their autonomy to organize this in different ways; all had a faculty e-learning coordinator, but in some cases (Technology) it was felt that the academic and other staff already had expertise in setting up websites and software, so it would not be necessary to appoint additional developers. One large faculty appointed only one developer, now two; another (Creative Arts) gradually extended the use of the online medium. The faculty of Humanities and Social Sciences, however, initially funded the appointment of five online course developers (OCDs) in 2008. The creation of these specific posts was also to drive the project forward. The job description for these developers shows the emphasis on the responsibility of academic staff to improve the learning experience:

- To work with members of academic staff to prepare online materials,
- To work with academic members of staff to convert existing learning materials for online delivery using established templates and processes as well as assisting in the development of new templates and processes, and
- To assist in the development of these materials into interactive, problem-based exercise.

The support work of these developers is not exclusive to the University of Portsmouth, but is a feature of practice that has enabled progress most strongly—one of the success factors was "the creation of specific posts such as the Faculty E-Learning Coordinator and online course developers to drive the project forward" as noted by the associate dean (Starie 2011). With reference to the roles of academic moderators and technical support, Gilly Salmon (2004b) offers a five-stage model for "Running E-tivity plenaries." In this model she identifies the five steps and the level of activity to be undertaken by the moderator or teacher and the technical support required. Salmon (2004b) explains these stages in the following terms:

> Each stage requires participants to master certain technical skills (shown in the bottom left of each step). Each stage calls for different e-moderating skills (shown on the right top of each step). The "interactivity bar" running along the right of the flight of steps suggests the intensity of interactivity that you can expect between the participants at each stage. At first, at stage one, they interact only with one or two others. After stage two, the numbers of others with whom they interact, and the frequency, gradually increases, although stage five often results in a return to more individual pursuits.

The five stages are (1) access and motivation, (2) online socialization, (3) information exchange, (4) knowledge construction, and (5) development. Each stage describes the role of technical support and e-moderating staff (Salmon 2004b).

What is interesting here is that participants are seen as all persons involved, including learners and facilitators (faculty members, learning support staff, or technical support staff). The increasing levels of interaction are part of the whole process, and the OCDs as well as students at Portsmouth are involved to different degrees up to Level 5, which includes *supporting and responding* on the part of the e-moderator and *providing links outside closed conferences* on the part of the technical support. This is far from the more traditional model of the "transmission" of knowledge and embraces the Vygotskian (1978) model of the social creation of knowledge referred to above as a largely accepted norm in UK higher education.

The technical support offered by the OCDs fits this model to a large extent, although, despite not fulfilling a purely technical role, they do not take part in conferencing with students (Level 4 in Salmon's model); their interactions are mainly with the academic unit coordinators. The roles vary according to the needs of the school, so searching for links and checking copyright, as in the job descriptions (Level 5 in Salmon's model), was used more but not just for distance-learning courses. In some cases the distant students can and do e-mail or telephone the developers for advice on accessing the VLE.

As can be seen in the job description, these developers were appointed as *support* for lecturers in the four schools to transform their existing files,

CDs, or in some cases paper-based learning materials into online materials suitable for the VLE and to create new e-learning materials, offering advice to unit coordinators on exercise and online activity types. In other words, the OCDs had a defined role that involved more than just technical help. It was agreed within the faculty that the OCDs would initially spend time in helping staff rather than uploading files for them; the pedagogic responsibility would still be with the lecturer, but the OCDs could suggest ways of implementing ideas.

The technical migration of units from WebCT to Victory/Blackboard was the first priority. However, when the OCDs were first appointed, as a log of lecturer inquiries in the first few weeks shows, they were dealing largely with technical issues such as how to add files to Victory units. This was still in the phase where many academics saw the VLE as a place to lodge materials rather than for activities. The OCDs worked in the buildings for their assigned schools, but twice a week they came together to work in the Learning and Teaching room, together with the e-learning coordinator; this facilitated the exchange of development ideas across the schools and enabled the enhancement of Victory presentation and design, sharing templates. This also allowed the coordinator to check progress across the faculty; additionally there were "Show and Tell" meetings where new developments could be seen in more detail. The experience of work with the developers was so positive that in 2009 there were additional appointments of assistant OCDs, so there is now a team of nine.

Disseminating Good Practice: The Faculty Webpages and Conferences

The e-learning coordinator arranged that the faculty would have a separate webpage for disseminating news, ideas, sharing practice, and links to external sites. In the early days guidelines written by the team and placed on the Learning and Teaching web pages were fairly basic ("Getting started with Victory"). The current version of the website is more advanced, containing for example copyright guidelines and links, accessibility guidelines, and a set of "Best Practice in using the VLE" guidelines.

As an example of the information made accessible for university academic and technical staff, and also outsiders, the following subheadings are provided under the main heading "eLearning and Victory":

- Victory
- Wimba "voice tools"–tool built in to Victory for recording podcasts and running "live online classrooms"

- online discussions and chat rooms
- quizzes and online assessment, for example, using Questionmark Perception
- e-portfolios
- ASK–includes many online study skills resources
- online resources available through the library (e.g., e-books, journals, databases)
- digitizing reading list service
- distance learners library pages
- multimedia and images–the library has access to many copyright cleared databases or your online course developer has access to further databases
- video and audio studio facilities in the faculty
- copyright
- Web 2.0 and social networking–includes many things like Facebook, Twitter, Flickr, You Tube, blogging, JISC Web 2.0 project
- Google apps and e-mail–all students have university Google accounts
- Turnitin–plagiarism detection and online submission tool
- there will be a number of changes happening over the next few years, including the introduction of a new VLE.

There were also staff development events, (e.g., a podcasting workshop open to academics from other universities), sometimes at the request of course teams or schools, drop-in "surgery" times, varied programs of development work for each school, and annual school action plans with reference to the university e-learning action plan as well as ongoing consultations with heads of department and course teams. Visits were supported to staff development events at other universities, often nationally funded (HEA) and to those set up centrally within the university (Department for Curriculum and Quality Enhancement). These included training events and sharing practice discussions in which staff were able to enroll themselves.

One of the main ways of sharing practice was through the preestablished annual Faculty Learning and Teaching Conferences in June and the University Learning and Teaching Conferences (University of Portsmouth 2011b, 2011d) in December every year. The aim of all these actions was to gradually increase awareness of the possibilities for e-learning, to show that colleagues were able to develop their successes in teaching through e-learning, which is a culture change overall. In one sense, this was "word-of-mouth" dissemination of ideas and thus much more effective than remote examples. As well as staff development, a small fund was made available for academics to bid for small-scale projects in developing e-learning materials and processes, again aiming at improvements at grassroots level.

Was This a Success?

The improved use of e-learning within the faculty can be seen as a result of audits of the units in two of the schools. The results show movement from only partial presence in the early days to almost 100 percent presence at the minimum or higher standard(with gaps arising only in units that are not currently running). Audits of the units in two schools, Languages and Area Studies, and Social, Historical, and Literary Studies in 2010–2011 (Faculty of Humanities and Social Studies, Learning and Teaching 2012) have clearly shown increased take-up of the following features:

- weblinks, links to journal articles (including RSS feeds to academic journals)
- use of online reading lists and a link to the library subject pages
- video
- quizzes
- discussion board use
- links to study skills resources
- assignment submission
- use of Turnitin (plagiarism-monitoring software is used by most UK universities)
- e-portfolios

Clearly the relevance of all these features will vary according to the subject. The use of academic journals is more practicable in some subject areas than in others. Turnitin cannot check foreign language essays or dissertations but can be useful for checking essays in related units. Discussion board use is more relevant to distance learning courses, one example being a course set up for an external contract for foundation degrees in government aimed at civil servants or a master's degree aimed at those in the police force.

There were many other examples of good practice initiated in this period, for example:

- Journalism students make an online newspaper in a limited time (assessed work) (University of Portsmouth 2011c; also on Facebook).
- Students watch a video of themselves in a business meeting, and the reflection they write about this forms a part (15 percent) of the assessment (unit in business communication).
- Distance-learning students in the Institute of Criminal Justice Studies (ICJS) do activities online with instant feedback (e.g., matching) or videos, and thinking points are embedded in the online text. Discussion activities are also assessed.

- ICJS also use film of interviewing a suspect with related evaluative activities and links to journal articles.
- The Terrorism Hub contains many examples of discussion between students and RSS feeds to the Chatham House (2012).
- History students in a group produce a webpage on a given topic. This replaces the poster on paper that they used to use and can more easily be seen and commented on by other students.
- Education students keep an e-journal in their e-portfolio of their teaching experience, available to the tutor and small student group only (also dentistry students in another faculty).
- Streamed links to recordings from TV programs, for which copyright permission from the BBC was obtained. The streaming server allows students to view, but not to download the video recordings. As the VLE is password-protected, the copyright of the BBC or the lecturer is protected.
- Language students are asked to make voice recordings using the software in Victory or other audio software and to "post" these in the Victory unit for other students or the tutor to listen to. Or the students make short films using photos they have taken during their year abroad and adding a commentary in the foreign language.
- Lecturers make "podcasts" recordings of introductions to each week's theme, or add audio to a PowerPoint presentation, which students can then use to revise the previous lectures. These can be released only after the lecture has taken place, if the lecturer wishes. It is also possible to make "podcasts" for feedback on assessed work.

These activities are not unique to this university, of course, but their take-up is nonetheless an indication of success. The success criteria were agreed as the increased use of e-learning and improved acceptance by academic staff of the usefulness of this, with the aim of improving student learning. This clearly involved a culture change, which can be observed amongst the academic staff, though not directly measured. There is improved acceptance of the use of Blackboard as the norm and hardly any discussion of "Why should I do this?" or "What is the benefit of changing my tried and tested teaching methods?" or "I think we should discuss the philosophy of eLearning before we do anything." We have certainly made progress since 2007, with the emphasis on improving the learning experience for students. The associate dean has noted some key success factors, among others:

- the successful dissemination and communication of the project aims in order to overcome the concerns of some staff about the project and to facilitate the buy-in of academic and support staff,

- an emphasis on the pedagogical merits of the project and the integration of pedagogy with the latest technological developments (rather than a concentration on technology),
- training programs and staff development to facilitate the pedagogical and technological challenges of the project, and
- an understanding that the primary purpose of the project was to improve the student learning experience and to engage with and meet student expectations. (personal communication from Pete Starie, December 2011)

As a result of these priorities and their focus on human and organizational support, which can be "as important to the successful introduction of new ways of working as the technical aspects" (JISC 2012a), staff attitudes have moved on from a decision on *whether* to put materials in Victory to a focus more on *how* to enhance the use of the VLE and other platforms for student learning. There are still "early adopters" of newer technological developments, but a wider use of e-learning has led to less reliance on these few colleagues for the implementation of e-learning projects. The reaction from students has been typically to assume that VLE is normal, a right and not a privilege. Student feedback in the first two years after 2007 did mention improvements in the use of online learning as positive factors, but since then feedback has involved comparisons between units and suggestions for improvements in some cases, that is, the use of the VLE is taken as the norm. It is clear that student expectations of the use of technology have an impact on their perceptions of ways of learning, so most may be considered as "digital natives" (Prensky 2001). The impact of raised tuition fees is likely to change the student expectations even more—this is an unknown quantity!

What Does the Future Hold?

We have moved on from the period where e-learning change implementation was the priority. Other examples of the way in which consultation has been used to give a strong foundation for change, such as consultations on electronic submission in line with administrative systems and assessment regulations, and discussion of the move to Google applications for students in the period described above are ongoing, however. Future developments under consideration include adaptations to handheld devices, the subject of a future EUROCALL publication (Webb 2010; Thorne et al. forthcoming). The university and the faculty have confidence in the achieved embedding of e-learning as a core activity of academic staff. A newer focus, influenced also by the British government agenda, is on employability, so the faculty e-learning coordinator has been replaced by a faculty employ-ability coordinator. Additionally all these developments are influenced by a university-wide revised academic structure, which is to come into effect in the autumn of 2012; all units have been rewritten, course struc-tures have been streamlined, and the academic year structure has changed from a semester base to an annual base. Soon after this the transfer from Blackboard to Moodle will take place. So the impact on e-learning will be widespread but firmly based on the rooted experience and culture change of the last four and more years.

Lessons Learned

As in other spheres any change in the academic world requires support at all levels if it is to be successful. At the same time there is an awareness of the competitive climate in UK higher education, which motivates stake-holders to consider change. Prior consultations with departments across the university before the drawing up of the institution-wide e-learning policy gave a solid foundation to the development of e-learning. Important factors in the culture change and successful development of e-learning as a normal activity for academics were

- an institution-wide philosophical commitment to the improvement of learning experiences at university, faculty, and department level,
- a "push" strategy with a minimum standard for all units by a deadline,
- a "pull" strategy, which involved the celebration and sharing of good practice by word-of-mouth communication,
- human and organizational factors were not ignored,
- faculty financial commitment and support in the appointment of team members, with selection of pedagogically aware as well as tech-nically competent personnel,
- allocation of OCDs to schools, so that specific subject needs could be met,
- OCDs meeting as a team for the whole faculty to enable the sharing of practice across schools,
- a strategy of assisting faculty members in the creation of new and revised and redesigned learning materials for the VLE, with "owner-ship" and content decisions remaining firmly with the academic staff,

- additional support from and open communication with a central department (Technology Enhanced Learning) in collaboration with the e-learning coordinator and the OCDs, and
- enabling enthusiasts to develop ideas into practice through support for bids for project funding.

These developments are of course part of a continuing process where future changes such as the new VLE, the use of mobile devices, and the new course structures are currently being discussed, planned, and implemented.

References

Chatham House. 2012. *Homepage*. London: Royal Institute of International Affairs Chatham House. Available online at: http://www.chathamhouse.org.

Elliott, Bobby. 2009. *e-Pedagogy: Does e-Learning Require a New Approach to Teaching and Learning? Presented at e-Learning Symposium.* Southampton, UK: University of Southampton, Centre for Languages, Linguistics and Area Studies (LLAS). Available online at: http://www.llas.ac.uk.

Faculty of Humanities and Social Studies, Learning and Teaching. 2012. "Staff Essentials: Humanities and Social Sciences Learning and Teaching." Portsmouth, UK: University of Portsmouth. http://www.port.ac.uk.

Falconer, Isobel, and Alison Littlejohn. 2007. "Designing for Blended Learning, Sharing and Reuse." *Journal of Further and Higher Education* 31(1): 41–52.

Goodfellow, Robin, and Mary R. Lea. 2008. *Challenging e-Learning in the University: A Literacies Perspective.* Buckingham: Open University Press.

Hardwick, Kath, and Richard Cooper. 2009. "Obituary, Robin Mason Advocate of e-Learning in Higher Education." *The Guardian*, July 6. Available online at: http://www.guardian.co.uk

HEA (Higher Education Academy). 2012. "Subject Support." Heslington, York, UK: Higher Education Academy. Available online at: http://www.heacademy.ac.uk/subjectcentres.

JISC (Joint Information Services Committee). 2012a. *Be Prepared for Change: Enable Your Staff to Work More Effectively with Digital Technologies.* Bristol, UK: JISC, University of Bristol. Available online at: http://www.jisc.ac.uk.

JISC. 2012b. *Learner Experiences of e-Learning: Phase 2.* Bristol, UK: JISC. Available online at: http://www.jisc.ac.uk.

Katsomitros, Alex. 2011. "Why Global Universities Should Adopt e-Learning." Redhill, Surrey, UK: Observatory on Borderless Higher Education. Available online at: http://www.obhe.ac.uk.

Lane Fox, Martha. 2011. "Teachers Must Think Internet-First." *The Guardian*, June 20. Available online at: http://www.guardian.co.uk.

Leier, Vera. 2011. "A Podcast Project in the German Programme of the University of Canterbury, New Zealand." *The EUROCALL Review* 19, pp18–29, September 2011.

Littlejohn, Alison, and Chris Pegler. 2007. *Preparing for Blended Learning.* Abingdon, UK: Routledge.

Prensky, Mark. 2001. "Digital Natives, Digital Immigrants." *On the Horizon* 9 (5), pp 1–6, October 2001. Bradford, West Yorkshire, UK: MCB University Press.

Salmon, Gilly. 2004a. *E-Moderating: The Key to Teaching and Learning Online.* Abingdon: Routledge.

Salmon, Gilly. 2004b. "5-Stage Model of e-Learning." *All Things in Moderation Website.* London, UK: ATIMOD Company. Available online at: http://www.atimod.com.

Starie, Pete. 2011. "Important Factors in Enabling the Progress of e-learning in the University and the Faculty" (personal e-mail communication to Tricia Coverdale-Jones, 9 December 2011).

Sutton-Brady, Catherine, Karen M. Scott, Lucy Taylor, Giuseppe Carabetta, and Steve Clark. 2009. "The Value Of Using Short-Format Podcasts To Enhance Learning And Teaching." *ALT-J, Research in Learning Technology* 17 (3): 219–232.

Thorne, Steven L., Frederik Cornillie, and Piet Desmet.(forthcoming). "ReCALL Journal Special Issue: "Call for Papers: Digital Games for Language Learning: Challenges and Opportunities" (e-mail message to EUROCALL e-mail list from June Thompson, 13 May 2011). Available online at: http://www.eurocall-languages.org.

Tian, Stella Wen, Angela Yan Yu, Doug Vogel, and Ron Chi-Wai Kwok. 2011. "The Impact Of Online Social Networking On Learning: A Social Integration Perspective." *International Journal of Networking and Virtual Organisations* 8 (3/4): 264–280.

University of Portsmouth. 2011a. *Facts and Figures 2011.* Portsmouth, UK: University of Portsmouth. Available online at: http://www.port.ac.uk.

University of Portsmouth. 2011b. *Changes in Learning and Teaching in Our Faculty.* Portsmouth, UK: Faculty of Humanities and Social Sciences, University of Portsmouth. Available online at: http://www.port.ac.uk.

University of Portsmouth. 2011c. *Milldam Mail Homepage.* Portsmouth, UK: Milldam Mail, University of Portsmouth. Available online at: http://sshls-dev.port.ac.uk/milldam-mail-demo.

University of Portsmouth. 2011d. *Re-Thinking Learning, Teaching and Assessment.* Portsmouth, UK: Faculty of Humanities and Social Sciences, University of Portsmouth. Available online at: http://www.port.ac.uk.

University of Portsmouth. 2012. *Victory.* Portsmouth, UK: University of Portsmouth. Available online at: https://victory.port.ac.uk/webct (password-protected access).

Vygotsky, Lev S. 1978. *Mind in Society: The Development of Higher Psychological Processes.* Cambridge, MA: Harvard University Press.

Webb, Stephen. 2010. "A Survey of Student Handheld Devices at the University of Portsmouth." Unpublished internal document. Portsmouth, UK: Department for Curriculum and Quality Enhancement, University of Portsmouth.

Chapter 6

ICT-Enabled Scalable Workshops for Engineering College Teachers in India

Kalpana Kannan and Krishnan Narayanan

Education has evolved over the years from basic reading and writing to the present-day globalized view. As we move from the era of low technology to highly sophisticated technology, there is a growing need for a skilled workforce at all levels of the society. There is a greater demand for continuing professional development and providing equal opportunities for all. However, to reach out to a maximum number of people in the society, it is necessary to break the social, economical, geographical, time, and space barriers in education.

The education system faces many challenges now. Some of the challenges, such as expanding the reach of education, imparting quality education at affordable costs, and shortage of qualified and experienced faculty, cannot be solved by the traditional system of education. We need a new approach to address these challenges. Implementation and integration of information and communication technology (ICT) into the education system can address some of these challenges.

ICTs have become a major factor in shaping the new global economy and thereby producing the rapid process of changes in the society. In recent years, there has been a growing interest in how best we can make use of ICT to improve the efficiency and effectiveness of education at all levels. Literature shows that many developed and developing countries are using ICT-enabled education in a big way at all levels. Research shows that ICT-enabled education has a positive impact on teachers and learners (Looi and Hung 2004; Williams 2005). Some developing countries have adopted ICT tools to improve the gross enrollment ratio (GER) in higher education (Sridhar 2005), teacher training (UNESCO 2001), and distance education through television and radio (Dixit 2009). The application of ICT has also revolutionized and enriched education and skill development in rural areas (Ramos et al. 2007). People with disabilities (Wild 2004; Taylor 2005) and women who could not earlier participate in the learning process due to sociocultural barriers now can (Sridhar 2005). Thus, ICTs are powerful tools for extending educational opportunities outside the boundaries of traditional classrooms. ICT can help reach out to a larger population–rural population, women, minority groups, persons with disabilities, the elderly, and/or those who because of cost or lack of time were previously unable to participate in scheduled learning activities.

Improving the quality of education and training is a critical issue, particularly in developing countries. It is important to improve higher education in developing countries, as higher education trains people to take up different economic roles in society and spurs the technological innovation that drives economic growth. An analysis of enrollment in higher education across nations suggests that there is broadly a positive correlation between the GER in higher education and the per capita gross domestic product (GDP) of nations (Agarwal 2006, 155). This is understandable as higher education has an important role in imparting useful skills that are particularly crucial in the knowledge-based modern economy. However, the GER in higher education is very low in most developing countries. According to the UNESCO Institute for Statistics (2009) the GER in higher education for India is 16 percent, China 24 percent, and Brazil 36 percent, whereas most developed countries have a GER of more than 50 percent. For example, the GER for the United States is 89 percent, Japan 59 percent, Australia 76 percent, and the United Kingdom 59 percent. In India, the Ministry of Human Resources Development plans to increase the GER in higher education from the present 16 percent to 30 percent by the year 2020 (Sibal 2010). To achieve this target, skilled manpower is needed in a short time span.

Teachers play an important role in building human capital. As they must satisfy the growing demand for better skills and employability of their students, present-day teachers need more opportunities than ever before for lifelong learning. According to many international reports the attention given to teachers' education and their continuing professional development has in many cases lagged behind that given to other areas of the education system (UNESCO 1998, 2000; OECD 2001). In fact, according to a UNESCO report on higher education, in some countries teachers can expect one week's in-service professional development only once in five-ten years (UNESCO 2001). Therefore, it is important to significantly scale-up the training activity for teachers in most developing countries. One of the ways to scale-up the professional development activity is through ICT.

This chapter presents the details of how ICT was used to promote the professional development of college-level engineering teachers using a model for large-scale synchronous distance mode workshops, via satellite and the

Internet. These workshops have the potential to scale-up the professional development of college teachers. Apart from learning subject content and new teaching methodology using ICT, these workshops also encourage teachers to make collaborative contributions of teaching-learning material that gets published in open source through the workshop portal. This chapter discusses the need for ICT-enabled training for engineering college teachers and the model used for synchronous distance mode workshops. It also discusses the challenges encountered in conducting the synchronous distance mode workshop. The chapter concludes that although workshops of this kind are extremely beneficial, particularly to those in rural areas, utilizing familiar technologies and training the implementing staff to prepare for potential technical support issues are critical factors for success.

Background on ICT for Teacher Training

Literature shows that many countries are using ICT for schoolteacher training, whereas, very few countries are using ICT for professional development of college teachers. For example, in South Korea, the Cyber Teacher Training Centre (CTTC) provides teacher professional development opportunities to in-service teachers through the Internet (Tinio 2010). CTTC is mainly training a large number of primary and secondary school teachers. Similarly in China, China Central Radio and TV University conduct large-scale radio and television based teacher education (Tinio 2010). In India, the National Council for Educational Research and Training (NCERT), in collaboration with the Indira Gandhi National Open University (IGNOU 2011), conducted a teacher-training program in the year 1996. A satellite-based one-way video and two-way audio-conferencing was used and was supplemented by print materials and recorded video. Eight hundred and fifty primary teachers were simultaneously provided training in 20 centers in the state of Karnataka, and fourteen hundred primary teachers were provided training in 45 centers in the state of Madhya Pradesh. The teachers interacted with remote lecturers by telephone and fax (Arora and Pandey 1998).

Though ICT-enabled education is seen as a way to improve the quality of education, its implementation is complex. Many factors must be taken into consideration, such as the availability of technology, time, training and support, coordination and management, individual attitudes, beliefs and motivations, characteristics, and ethos of the organization (Tearle 2004). It also costs a lot of money to build and maintain the ICT infrastructure. Technology obsolescence is another challenge. ICT-enabled education requires pedagogy that is different from the traditional way of teaching and learning. Teachers who are used to the traditional way of teaching might find it difficult to reorient themselves in the new ICT framework. For example, it is not easy to convert a good teacher into a good online teacher. Although many problems of the developing world, such as poverty, illiteracy, and inequality can be addressed with the help of an ICT-enabled education, it is found that most developing countries do not have the necessary ICT infrastructure for implementation. Furthermore, many developing countries cannot afford the high cost to build and maintain the ICT infrastructure. As a result, very few people in developing countries have access to ICT, and therefore cannot reap the benefits.

Despite the challenges, many developing countries have adopted national polices to stimulate ICT-enabled education. ICT-enabled education has the potential to impact quality education for all, at a very low cost over the long term. As ICT awareness in society is growing, more and more people can adopt, use, and participate in ICT-enabled education. Thus, it also has the potential to be inclusive.

There are several initiatives undertaken by the Indian government, both at the center and the state level, to facilitate skill upgradation of college teachers in technical institutions. This chapter provides the case of ICT-enabled large-scale teacher-training for engineering college teachers, undertaken by the Indian Institute of Technology (IIT) Bombay, under the National Mission on Education through ICT, sponsored by the Ministry of Human Resource Development, Government of India (NME-ICT 2011).

This study analyses the data drawn from the participants of a workshop, conducted in the synchronous distance mode in June 2011, for mechanical engineering faculty members. Specifically, the subject matter covered the field of thermodynamics. We conducted a survey toward the end of the workshop to address the following research questions. What were the most important motivating factors for the participants to join the ICT-enabled workshop? How does the motivation for joining the workshop differ based on gender, age, qualification, and location of colleges in urban/rural areas? Are there any differences in the levels of satisfaction of the participants based on the location of colleges in urban/rural areas? What were the participants' overall perceptions of the ICT-enabled workshop?

Need for ICT-Enabled Training for Engineering College Teachers

In India, there has been a rapid expansion of institutions of higher education since independence in 1947. From 20 universities and approximately 500 colleges in the year 1947, there are about 400 universities and 20,000 colleges in the country today (UGC 2011). Every year about 500,000 undergraduate students graduate from various engineering disciplines (AICTE 2009). There are about 3,000 engineering colleges and 150,000 teachers teach in these colleges (AICTE 2009). In spite of the large numbers, the quality of undergraduates is low, and many students do not find appropriate jobs. The quality of engineering education has suffered due to a variety of reasons, such as, a shortage of qualified and experienced teachers following the sudden expansion of colleges, low salaries in the teaching profession, unmotivated students, and lack of infrastructre. Today, the biggest resource crunch in higher technical education is the nonavailability of experienced and qualified teachers (Kannan and Narayanan 2010). Raising the quality of engineering education in the country is a national-level problem, for which there is no one solution. Given the large number of engineering colleges and teachers in the country, the existing mechanism of training teachers through India's Quality Improvement Program (QIP), where about 40–50 teachers are trained at a time, is not scalable (Kannan and Narayanan 2011). A possible solution is to train a large number of teachers in core engineering subjects using ICT.

It has been observed that many engineering colleges in the country have very few faculty members with doctoral and even master's degrees. In many colleges, fresh undergraduates join as faculty members with no teaching experience. These young teachers are not motivated to build a long-term academic career due to low salaries and the poor academic environment in colleges. Hence, the quality of education in most engineering colleges is badly affected. It is therefore very important to scale-up the training activities for engineering college teachers in the country.

Model Used for Synchronous Distance Mode Workshop

IIT Bombay is involved in a number of initiatives that use ICT to improve the quality of technical education in the country. Since 2002, IIT Bombay has been involved in both synchronous and asynchronous distance engineering education programs (Moudgalya et al. 2008).

Under the National Mission on Education Through ICT (NME-ICT 2011), sponsored by the Ministry of Human Resource Development of the Government of India, a project team led by D. B. Phatak at IIT Bombay (henceforth referred to as the IIT Bombay team) has been conducting workshops for engineering college teachers in core engineering subjects through a synchronous distance mode. The objectives of the workshop have been to significantly scale-up the professional development activity in the country and to reach out to a large number of college teachers located in urban, rural, and remote areas of the country. The IIT Bombay team started with an objective of conducting ten workshops in core engineering subjects over a period of three years, training 1,000 college teachers per workshop. The idea was that by training the teachers, the impact would be high, as one teacher can influence hundreds of students. Through this model, one can train a large number of teachers in a short time. Thus, it was expected that the quality of teaching in the engineering colleges would significantly improve.

Since 2009, a team of faculty members from IIT Bombay has conducted five large-scale teacher-training workshops in the synchronous distance mode. These workshops are a first of their kind where a large number of teachers are engaged simultaneously through the satellite network and the Internet.

The model that is being used for conducting large-scale synchronous distance mode workshop is briefly explained now. IIT Bombay acts as the hub. The workshop is conducted in two parts: coordinators' workshop and the main workshop. Two months prior to the main workshop, the IIT Bombay team invites teachers from various engineering colleges for a one-week coordinators' workshop. During this workshop the coordinators are given an orientation on various teaching-learning technologies, the laboratory facility required, software, and hardware required for the conduct of the main workshop. To ensure that the teaching-learning material is useful to majority of colleges in the country, a common syllabus of the subject to be covered in the main workshop is finalized. These coordinators help conduct the main workshop in the respective remote centers.

The publicity for the workshop is done through brochures, websites, and e-mails. A web-based centralized online registration is set up for the workshop registration (eOutreach 2011). Teachers who have taught the subject in various engineering colleges are invited to register online at the remote center nearest to their colleges. Figure 6.1 shows the model used for synchronous distance mode workshops for college teachers.

There are typically about 30–35 remote centers in each workshop. Every remote center has about 30–60 college teachers attending the workshop. The remote centers are connected through Educational Satellite (EDUSAT), launched by the Indian Space Research Organization (ISRO) (EDUSAT 2011) and an Internet-based software A-VIEW (2011) that allows two-way audio-video connectivity between the hub and the remote centers. EDUSAT became nonfunctional in September 2010; due to this technical problem, now only A-VIEW is being used for transmission.

The A-VIEW screen has three windows: A, B, and C. Window-A shows the video of the course instructor. In window-B, the participants' video is displayed. Window-B has two other modes: the chat window and users' window, which can be selected at any time. Whenever participants have

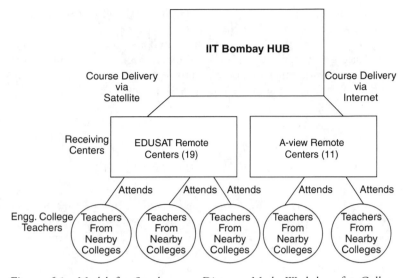

Figure 6.1 Model for Synchronous Distance Mode Workshop for College Teachers.
Source: Created by the authors.

a query they can electronically raise their hand through users' window. A question mark indicates that the center has raised a query. The instructor at the IIT Bombay hub can select the remote center with a raised hand and then answer the query. Window-C is used for displaying the presentation slides or as a whiteboard. The sizes of all the windows are adjustable and can be increased or decreased depending on the requirement.

During the main workshop, the lectures are transmitted live from IIT Bombay, and the laboratory sessions and group assignments/tutorials are managed locally at the remote centers. The open source learning management system (LMS), Moodle (2011), is used extensively for uploading assignments. Queries are handled through live interaction, e-mail, and chat. For answering quizzes during the workshop, Moodle and a classroom response system, "Clickers" are used. Clickers, is any system used in a face-to-face setting to gather immediate feedback in response to questions posed by instructors (Deal 2007); its usage is explained later.

After the main workshop, the teachers are given assignments to be completed in their respective colleges for another two weeks. Participating teachers submit the assignments, in the form of question bank and student projects, on the Moodle site. After postproduction editing, all the contents of the workshop—lecture slides, audio-video recording of the lectures, and the assignments submitted by the participants—are released in open source through the subject portal. Given that there are about 1,000 teachers participating in this exercise, the learning material collected is expected to be enormous. For example, after the workshop on computer programming, the participating teachers had submitted a total of 3,870 questions and projects that would be useful for the teaching-learning community. Thus, it is expected that the teaching-learning community would widely use the teaching-learning material generated in these workshops.

Workshop on Thermodynamics for Mechanical Engineering Faculty

In June 2011, a workshop for a course on thermodynamics for mechanical engineering college teachers was conducted. There were about 960 registrations for the workshop. In the end, 779 faculty members attended the workshop in the distance mode. These teachers were from 248 engineering colleges located in 208 cities and towns spread across the country. As the number of engineering colleges is higher in the states of Maharashtra and Tamil Nadu, the maximum participants were from these two states, 37 percent and 28.6 percent respectively.

Methodology

The primary objective of this research was to explore engineering college teachers' perceptions of the workshop delivered through a synchronous distance mode. Survey methodology was used to address the research questions. An online questionnaire toward the end of the workshop was posted on Moodle and the participants were given two days' time for submission.

Sample

Teachers who had taught the first level thermodynamics course in mechanical engineering in any engineering college were invited to join the workshop; 779 teachers attended. Out of 779 participants, 684 responded to the survey. Of these, 84 (12 percent) were female and 600 (88 percent) were male; 313 (46 percent) were in the age group 23–30 years, 263 (38 percent) were in the age group 31–40 years, and 108 (16 percent) were above 41 years; 197 (29 percent) were undergraduates, 416 (61 percent) were postgraduates, and 71 (10 percent) were doctorates; and 306 (55 percent) came from colleges located in urban areas and 378 (45 percent) from rural areas.

Instrument

The questionnaire contained a total of 42 questions. It had five sections: General Information with 12 questions, Participants' Background with 6, Infrastructure Related with 1, Workshop Related with 19, and Overall Experience with 4. A five-point Likert scale was used for most of the questions. However, the last section also included open-ended questions for comments, feedback, and suggestions. The questionnaire was first tested in the pilot workshop conducted through the distance mode and then some questions were modified to improve the reliability of the instrument. The Cronbach's alpha for each of the factors was computed as follows: (a) motivation 0.64, (b) organization support and infrastructure 0.84, (c) course structure 0.77, (d) distance mode interaction 0.69, (e) usefulness and adoption of course material 0.81, and (f) overall satisfaction 0.60.

Survey Results

The survey was analyzed based on gender, age, qualifications, and location of colleges in urban/rural areas. The scores in each of the categories were calculated for comparison.

Research Question No. 1

What were the most important motivating factors for the participants to join the ICT-enabled workshop?

The participants were asked to rank the three most important motivating factors for joining the workshop from a list of ten factors. The survey results show the following:

a. *To learn new teaching methodology* was ranked as the number one motivating factor by about 50 percent of the respondents.
b. *To learn from IIT teachers* was ranked as the number two motivating factor by about 33 percent of the respondents.
c. *To experience distance mode teaching* was ranked as the number three motivating factor by about 25 percent of the respondents.

Research Question No. 2

How does the motivation for joining the workshop differ based on gender, age, qualification, and location of colleges in urban/rural areas?

The average scores for each of the motivating factors were analyzed based on gender, age, qualification, and location of colleges in urban/rural areas. Table 6.1 gives the results of the analysis. Only the factors that were statistically significant are reported in the table. Some of the factors, such as "for certification," "to reduce preparation time for the lectures," "to get IIT brand name," "because the course is fully sponsored" and the "management of the institute asked to attend," did not vary much with age, gender, qualification, and location of colleges in urban/rural area. They were thus not included.

The results indicate that teachers with undergraduate (UG) and postgraduate (PG) degrees had joined the workshop to learn new teaching methodology, as compared to teachers who had doctorate degrees. Similarly, both UG and PG teachers wanted to learn from IIT teachers as compared to teachers with doctorate degrees. The results indicate that teachers who were above 40 years had joined the workshop to experience distance mode teaching. Interaction with other college teachers was an

Table 6.1   Analysis of Motivating Factors for Joining the Workshop

Motivating factor	Variable	Sample size (N = 684)	N	Mean	SD	F/t-Ratio
To learn new teaching methodology	Qualification	UG	197	4.53	0.71	4.13**
		PG	416	4.56	0.60	
		PhD	71	4.32	0.80	
To learn from IIT teachers	Qualification	UG	197	4.58	0.60	5.88**
		PG	416	4.56	0.64	
		PhD	71	4.29	0.70	
To experience distance mode teaching	Age group	23–30 yrs	313	3.8	0.83	3.49**
		31–40 yrs	263	4.0	0.81	
		Above 40 yrs	108	4.1	0.67	
To interact with other college teachers	Gender	Female	84	3.6	0.88	3.87**
		Male	600	3.8	0.78	
It will help in promotion	Age group	23–30 yrs	313	2.8	1.16	7.36***
		31–40 yrs	263	3.2	1.11	
		Above 40 yrs	108	2.9	1.11	
	Qualification	UG	197	2.8	1.14	5.04**
		PG	416	3.0	1.16	
		PhD	71	3.3	1.08	

Note: UG = Undergraduate degree in engineering, PG = Postgraduate degree in engineering, PhD = Doctorate degree in engineering.
** Indicates 5 percent level of significance, *** indicates 1 percent level of significance.

important factor for male respondents as compared to their female counterpart. Career growth in terms of promotion was a very significant motivating factor for teachers in the age group 31–40 years and for the teachers with PhD degrees.

Research Question No. 3

Are there any differences in the levels of satisfaction of the participants based on the location of colleges in urban/rural areas?

Our survey shows that about 45 percent of the teachers came from engineering colleges located in rural areas. The analysis of data based on the total level of satisfaction shows that rural college teachers (N = 306, Mean = 11.80, and SD = 1.62) were more satisfied (t = 4.82**, significant at 5 percent level) with the workshop than urban college teachers (N = 378, Mean = 11.78, and SD = 1.88).

Research Question No. 4

What were the participants' overall perception of the ICT-enabled workshop?

From the survey, we found that overall workshop experience of the participants were either good or excellent. About 47 percent of the participants had rated their overall workshop experience as excellent, about 44 percent as good, 8 percent as satisfactory, and 0.30 percent as poor. Although about 91 percent of the respondents had rated the overall experience of the workshop as good or excellent, there were a few centers that had experienced technical and audio-video problems during the workshop.

Some of the feedbacks received from the participants are given below:

a. "I liked this innovative method of teaching which reduces the time needed to impart knowledge to a number of students at the same time."

b. "Only this kind of workshop will help lecturers like me to get such input, which otherwise may not be possible. IITs should reach out to faculty members of all Engineering institutions through this kind of workshops to build a strong knowledge base, so that we can build a stronger India. I hope we will get more support from the Government. The teaching methodology was another learning aspect which I have picked up which will surely help me teach better and benefit my students too."

c. "Although it is distance mode still interaction level between instructor and participants is good. Direct interaction among same field teachers in a country at the same time."

d. "It is a very good opportunity to learn the basics of Thermodynamics from a senior and highly resourced professor. Professor's delivery is excellent. I wonder how he writes legibly the entire lecture and so it is easy for us to follow the subject and this is going to be my future resource material. I appreciate his confident and clear discussion."

e. "These type of workshops are very useful to rural engineering colleges. I personally enhanced my confidence to teach my students."

f. "Attending the workshop in my own city has saved me a lot of trouble like travel, accommodation etc."

Some of the suggestions and comments received from the participants are given below:

a. "There was time lag between the audio, video and the whiteboard. If technology can be improved it will be of great help."

b. "Due to its distance mode, there was some lack of interest in participants. During Q & A sessions most remote centers were having less number of participants."

c. "Whenever participants responded from their remote centers, we were not able to hear the responses properly due to noise interference."

d. "Sometimes the audio/video quality was poor. It is not as effective as in regular classroom teaching. However, a large number of people were benefited by the distant education."

e. "Sometimes there was problem with Internet connectivity and because of that I lost some part of the content."

f. "The only thing which I found difficult is we could not ask doubts as and when they get into our mind. We had to wait till the time for interaction is allowed."

g. "Exposure for asking the doubts in an audio format is poor. Many a time, we wished to ask subsequent question but because of lack of time and other college participants, we were left with doubts in our mind."

Discussion

Our study suggests that most participants had joined the workshop to learn new teaching methodology, to learn from IIT teachers, and to experience distance mode teaching. The limitation of our study was that the participants were asked to answer from the ten motivating factors given in the questionnaire, therefore, we do not know if participants had some other motivation for joining. Some of the disadvantages of a distance mode frequently cited in the literature are lack of interaction and a high dropout rate (Fox 2002). In this model, these disadvantages were less, as the participants could interact with the faculty through live-interaction, chat, e-mail, and discussion forum. They also had face-to-face interaction with fellow participants and the coordinators of the remote center; therefore, the feeling of isolation was not there. As the workshop duration was only for two weeks, most of the participants regularly attended the workshop.

The center coordinators were asked to maintain a record of the participants attending the workshop. From the coordinators' feedback we came to know that in most centers about 80 percent of the participants were regular and actively participated in the program. Thus, interaction and regularity was imminent in this distance mode workshop.

In the conventional model, imparting uniform training to a large number of people spread across geographical locations is costly and difficult to achieve, whereas, in the synchronous model, it is possible to impart uniform training to a large number of teachers spread across the country. In the thermodynamics workshop, 779 teachers from 248 colleges spread across 208 cities and towns received training in a short period of two weeks. We found from our survey that a large number of college teachers from rural colleges participated in the workshop. Thus, uniformity, outreach, and inclusion of different sections of the society are highly reflected in this model.

The survey suggests that even though the lectures were transmitted in the distance mode, the participants' satisfaction across various categories was high. We found that a large number of participating teachers (about 91 percent) found the overall experience of the workshop to be good or excellent and were likely to adopt the contents in their teaching. It was found that the level of satisfaction was significantly higher among the rural college teachers than urban college teachers. One of the reasons could be that the rural college teachers have fewer opportunities than the urban college teachers to attend workshops. From the survey, we also found that about 46 percent of the respondents were in the age group 23–30 years and were interested to learn new teaching methodology and subject content from IIT faculty. If a large number of young teachers join the workshop, the benefits would be significant, as they would be highly motivated to impart the new knowledge and new teaching methodology to their students.

The workshop model used for teacher training in the synchronous mode has taken into consideration some of the advantages of both–the distance mode and the conventional mode. The advantages of the distance mode such as, cost-effectiveness, scalability, accessibility, and selection of place as per the convenience of the participants makes it very attractive for both the organizers and the participants. As there are fewer subject experts in the country and most of them are hard pressed for time, the distance mode workshop gives them an opportunity to share their knowledge and experience with the larger audience in a short period of time.

Measuring Learning Outcomes Using ICT

Measuring learning outcomes in ICT-enabled workshops where the participants are geographically spread out is a challenging task. In the first three workshops, the classroom response system, clickers were used. In the subsequent workshops, the learning management system Moodle was used to conduct online quizzes. In this section, the experience of conducting quizzes is briefly explained.

Clickers

In any distance mode teaching, instructors and participants have limited visual cues as they are physically separated. They also miss out on the body language. As a result, it becomes very difficult for the instructor to gauge and comprehend if the participants have understood the learning material. A possible way of addressing this problem is to use pedagogical tools used in face-to-face classrooms, such as the classroom response system, clickers. Use of such systems improves teaching effectiveness as the instructor gets immediate feedback from the participants and accordingly s/he can clarify or review the teaching material (Tiwari et al. 2010).

The classroom response system consists of hardware and software. The hardware consists of handsets with keypads that function as clickers and receivers that are connected to a computer. Both clickers and receivers communicate using infrared or radio frequencies based wireless technologies. The responses from every remote center first gets collected locally and then gets transferred to the hub through file transfer protocol (FTP). The software allows the instructor to collect and store the responses in the database and display the responses in the form of graphs and charts.

During the workshop, while clickers worked well in some remote centers, they failed in others. Five problems for the failure were identified. First, the remote center coordinators were not able to setup the software and hardware. Second, the participants were afraid to use the clickers as most of them were first time users and were not familiar. Third, the responses collected had about 40–50 percent timeouts, (i.e., participants could not enter their responses in the time in which the responses were collected by the system). Fourth, some centers were not able to send their responses through file transfer protocol (FTP). And finally, the lack of trained technical manpower at some remote centers was one of the reasons that contributed to the inability to understand instructions and manuals provided with the clicker system (Tiwari et al. 2010).

Even though the clickers did not work as well in the distributed classroom setting as they work in the regular classrooms, their use in the workshop excited most of the participants, and some expressed their desire to use clickers in their own classrooms (Tiwari et al. 2010).

Online Quiz through Moodle

In thermodynamics and basic electronics workshops, the learning management system Moodle was used to measure the learning outcomes. Two quizzes were conducted in each workshop. The first quiz was conducted on the second/third day of the workshop and the second quiz was conducted toward the end of the workshop. Each quiz was 40 minutes in duration and contained about 20 multiple-choice questions. The time window given to take the online quiz was 90 minutes. Each participant could start the quiz at any time within the time window. Some of the precautions taken to avoid malpractices during the online quiz were (a) the questions were selected randomly from the question bank, (b) the sequence of questions in the quiz and the answer options were randomized, and (c) the participants were automatically logged out of the quiz, if they remained idle for five minutes or more.

About 750 participants took the final online quiz in thermodynamics and about 1,150 participants took the quiz in basic electronics. Some of the problems faced during the online quiz were as follows: (a) in the first quiz, many participants got zero marks, as they did not save their answers and were logged out due to timeout; (b) some participants by mistake pressed the wrong button, "Submit All and Finish" instead of the "Save and Continue" button, therefore, they were logged out; and (c) one center had a power failure during the quiz and all the participants in that center were logged out during the quiz.

Some common mistakes made by the participants in answering the first quiz helped the instructors to modify the instructions. In the subsequent quizzes, only two questions per page were presented, and the participants were asked to save the answers after every page before continuing to the next page. Correct answers were displayed on Moodle after the quiz time. The analysis of quiz results helped the instructors to find out the topics where many participants went wrong, and accordingly they clarified the concepts in that topic. After the quiz, the participants used the Moodle discussion forum extensively to discuss quiz related questions.

Challenges

Technology issues

There is high dependence on technology in the synchronous mode. Initially, the satellite based technology EDUSAT was used for transmission. As there were fewer remote centers with EDUSAT setup, the feasibility of using an alternate Internet-based technology A-VIEW was explored in the "Computer Programming" workshop conducted in July 2010. Eleven receiving centers were connected through A-VIEW and 19 centers were connected through EDUSAT (see Figure 6.1.) There were five centers that had used both EDUSAT and A-VIEW to receive the lectures. Feedback received on the quality of audio-video from these five centers was compared. Most centers gave positive feedback on the quality of audio-video through A-VIEW. However, in September 2010, the ISRO announced that EDUSAT was nonfunctional and would not be available for transmission for few months. Thus, in December 2010, all the remote centers were connected through A-VIEW, as EDUSAT was not available. The shift from EDUSAT to A-VIEW was relatively easy as some centers had used A-VIEW earlier and were satisfied with the quality of reception. As A-VIEW is a new technology, there were some teething problems. The quality of reception in some centers was low, as the available bandwidth was less. Based on the user feedback, the A-VIEW team made improvements in the software. The current software is user friendly, and the quality of transmission has improved.

During the coordinators' workshop the coordinators were made familiar with the use of new software related to live-transmission, query handling, and other guidelines required for handling distance mode workshops. In spite of the training, some coordinators did not know how to handle queries in the distance mode, and how to solve technical issues related to live-transmission. The support team at IIT Bombay provided online support and troubleshooting guidelines to help solve some of the problems. Live testing sessions between the hub and remote centers were conducted one week before the main workshop to check the connectivity and audio-video quality. Many technical problems at the remote centers were resolved during the testing sessions.

As most of the participants were for the first time introduced to new teaching aids and software such as clickers and Moodle, the guidelines on the use and installation of clicker software were posted on the workshop website. Initially, most participants were not very comfortable in using clickers. Toward the end of the workshop, however, participants were more comfortable with this technology tool. Similarly, participants took some time in taking online quizzes through Moodle.

Management and Coordination

Managing a distance mode workshop needs a lot of planning and coordination. Lack of coordination and planning can become an obstacle to the program. As the remote centers are located in 30–35 different cities and towns, the center coordinators play a very important role in local management and coordination at each center. Therefore, a one-week coordinators' workshop at the hub was very important, as this gave them an orientation on how to manage and coordinate the workshop in the distance mode. During the initial workshops, the IIT Bombay team had to provide a lot of online support and troubleshooting guidelines to help solve some of the problems. In the subsequent workshops, as the coordinators became familiar with the use of technology, they were able to manage better. Thus, familiarity and experience in handling distance mode workshop are very important for the success.

Future Work

Further research is required to assess the impact of such large-scale training programs on the teaching-learning community in the country. Some of the questions that could be answered through further research are as follows:

- Is the training program able to contribute to student learning?
- What is the frequency of adoption of teaching material given in the training by the teachers?
- Is there any significant difference in students' learning, after the adoption of new teaching methods and material?
- What is the change in teachers' conceptual understanding of the learning material?

Summary and Conclusion

In this chapter, we discussed the synchronous distance mode workshop model used for training a large number of engineering college teachers spread across India. In the conventional face-to-face model, imparting uniform training to a large number of people is costly and difficult to achieve, whereas, in the synchronous model, it is possible to impart uniform training to a large number spread across the country in a short time. Although the concept of teacher training in the distance mode is new, the survey results show that the participants' satisfaction is high, and the workshop is found to be effective by a majority of the participants. The survey also shows that some of the objectives of the workshop such as outreach and inclusion of different sections of the society, for example women and teachers from rural colleges, are partially achieved.

Further, ICT-enabled training provides greater exposure and better knowledge to teachers in engineering colleges located in less developed regions of India. In the future, such training activity could be significantly scaled up, and this would help in human capital formation. Such workshops could improve the quality of higher education and could facilitate appropriate use of demographic dividend that India possesses.

Acknowledgements

We would like to thank Professor U. N. Gaitonde for conducting the teacher-training workshop on thermodynamics and for allowing us to carry out the survey and Professor D. B. Phatak and his team for organizing and coordinating synchronous distance mode workshop. The financial support for conducting the teacher-training workshop was made available by a grant from the National Mission on Education through ICT (NME-ICT), Ministry of Human Resource Development, Government of India. The Indian Space Research Organization gave the EDUSAT support. The Amrita Vishwa Vidyapeetham provided the e-learning software A-VIEW, also supported by NME-ICT.

References

A-VIEW. 2011. *Amrita Virtual Interactive E-learning World (A-VIEW) Software.* Kolam, India: A-VIEW. Available online at: http://aview.amrita.ac.in.

Agarwal, Pawan. 2006. *Higher Education in India: The Need for Change.* ICRIER Working Paper No. 180. New Delhi: ICRIER.

AICTE (All India Council for Technical Education). 2009. *Annual Report, 2008–2009.* Janpath, New Delhi: AICTE. Available online at: http://www.aicte-india.org.

Arora, G. L., and Saroj Pandey. 1998. "Teachers' Continuing Education: Shifting Focus on Distance Mode." *Indian Journal of Open Learning* 7 (3): 255–265.

Deal, Ashley. 2007. *Technical Report: A Teaching with Technology White Paper, Classroom Response Systems.* Pittsburgh, PA: Carnegie Mellon University. Available online at: http://www.cmu.edu.

Dixit, Usha. 2009. "The Use of ICT in Teacher Training: Nepal's Experience." Paper presented at the 13th UNESCO-APEID International Conference on Education, Hangzhou, China, 15–17 November 2009.

eOutreach. 2011. *Website for Workshop Registration.* Mumbai: Affordable Solutions Lab, Indian Institute of Technology Bombay. Available online at: http://ekalavya.it.iitb.ac.in.

EDUSAT. 2011. *Educational Satellite Launched by Indian Space Research Organization.* Bangalore: EDUSAT. Available online at: http://www.isro.org.

Fox, Seamus. 2002. "Arguments For and Against the Use of Technology and Learning Technologies in Higher Education: What Do They Tell Us?" OSCAIL Technical Report. Dublin: National Distance Education Centre.

IGNOU (Indira Gandhi National Open University). 2011. *Indira Gandhi National Open University.* New Delhi: IGNOU. Available online at: http://www.ignou.ac.in.

Kannan, Kalpana, and Krishnan Narayanan. 2010. "ICT Enabled Teacher Training for Human Capital Formation: A Study of IIT Bombay Initiative." Paper presented at the International conference on Science, Technology and Economy: Human Capital Development, Mumbai, India, 11–12 November 2010.

Kannan, Kalpana, and Krishnan Narayanan. 2011. "Model and Learner Feedback for a Large Scale Technology Enabled Teacher Training Program." Paper presented at the IEEE International Conference on Technology for Education, Chennai, India, 14–16 July 2011.

Looi, Chee Kit, and David Hung. 2004. "Singapore's Learning Sciences Lab: Seeking Transformation in ICT Enabled Pedagogy." *Education, Technology R&D* 52 (4): 91–115.

Moodle. 2011. *Open Source Software for Learning Management System.* Perth, Australia: Moodle. Available online at: http://moodle.org/.

Moudgalya, Kannan M., Deepak B. Phatak, and R. K. Shevgaonkar. 2008. "Engineering Education for Everyone: A Distance Education Experiment at IIT Bombay." Paper presented at Frontiers in Education, Sarotoga springs, New York, 22–25 October 2008.

NME-ICT (National Mission on Education through ICT). 2011. *NME-ICT Homepage.* New Delhi: Ministry of Human Resource Development. Available online at: http://www.sakshat.ac.in.

OECD (Organisation for Educational Co-Operation and Development). 2001. "Education Policy Analysis." Paris: Center for Education Research and Innovation, OECD.

Ramos, Angelo J., Genevieve Nangit, Andelina I. Range, and Jerome Trinona. 2007. "ICT Enabled Distance Education in Community Development in the Philippines." *Distance Education* 28 (2): 213–229.

Sibal, Kapil. 2010. *Opening Remarks of Honorable Human Resources Minister Kapil Sibal at the 57th Meeting of the Central Advisory Board of Education held on 19th June 2010.* New Delhi: Ministry of Human Resource Development. Available online at: http://education.nic.in.

Sridhar, Sangeetha. 2005. "E-Government–A Proactive Participant for E-Learning for Higher Education." *Journal of American Academy of Business* 7 (1): 258–268.

Taylor, Margaret. 2005. "Access and Support in the Development of a Visual Language: Arts Education and Disabled Students." *International Journal of Art and Design Education* 24 (3): 325–333.

Tearle, Penni. 2004. "A Theoretical and Instrumental Framework for Implementing Change in ICT in Education." *Cambridge Journal of Education* 34 (3): 331–351.

Tinio, Victoria L. 2010. *Technical Report: ICT in Education.* New York: UNDP. Available online at: http://www.apdip.net.

Tiwari, Divya, Richa Sehgal, Jayant Bansal, and Sahana Murthy. 2010. "Clicking Away the Distance from Education." Paper presented at the IEEE International Conference on Technology for Education (T4E), Mumbai, India, 1–3 July 2010.

UGC (University Grant Commission). 2011. *Technical Report: Higher Education in India, Strategies and Schemes during Eleventh Plan Period (2007–2012) for Universities and Colleges.* New Delhi: UGC.

UNESCO. 1998. *Technical Report: World Education Report: Teachers and Teaching in a Changing World.* Paris: UNESCO.

UNESCO. 2000. *Technical Report: The Dakar Framework for Action: Education for All: Meeting our Collective Commitments.* Paris: UNESCO.

UNESCO. 2001. *Technical Report: Teacher Education through Distance Learning: Technology, Curriculum, Cost, Evaluation.* Paris: UNESCO.

UNESCO Institute for Statistics. 2009. *Gross enrolment ratio (%) and gender parity index of GER.* Montreal, Canada: UNESCO Institute for Statistics. Available online at: http://www.uis.unesco.org/Education/Pages/tertiary-education.aspx

Wild, Mary. 2004. "Screen or Page: Will the Use of Computer Aided Education Improve Phonological Skills in Year 1 Classes?" Paper presented to British Educational Research Association Annual Conference, University of Manchester, UK, 16–18 September 2004.

Williams, Peter. 2005. "Lessons from the Future: ICT Scenarios and the Education of Teachers." *Journal of Education for Teaching* 31 (4): 319–339.

Chapter 7

Taking Teacher Certification in Specialized Subjects Online

Lessons Learned from Preparing Special Education Teachers to Become Highly Qualified in Math

Ellen Clay and Michel Miller

Introduction

Online programs can provide valuable access to continuing education or certification opportunities for teachers and other professionals. However, to be successful, this type of program, whether in developed or developing countries, must overcome the time constraints of both the learners and the course facilitators, as well as the other challenges involved in moving from a face-to-face to an online environment. This chapter outlines our experience in creating, evaluating, and adjusting a specific course in mathematical concepts for special education teachers. We found that a program, which capitalizes on frequent and quality contact among classmates around support structures that have been built into the course design, can produce a sustainable model for online professional development of teachers and which does not overtax the time of course facilitators, can be created. Once created, and shared, these models can be adapted for fields as diverse as teacher education and health sciences that are crucial for both developing and developed countries alike.

In the United States, the No Child Left Behind Act (NCLB) and the Individuals with Disabilities Improvement Act (IDEA) have set forth a priority that educators are highly qualified. "Highly qualified" is defined as full certification, a Bachelor's degree, and demonstrated content knowledge in all core subjects taught. The guidelines specify that all teachers were to reach highly qualified status by the 2005–2006 school year. One especially high-needs area in the United States is mathematics. However, despite this timetable, there are still numerous teachers currently teaching who are not highly qualified in all core subjects taught. According to research by Bonnie Billingsley, Anna Marie Fall, and Thomas Williams (2006), less than 3 percent of early career special education teachers hold secondary teacher certification in mathematics. Due to this current situation, funding has become available to support teachers in gaining the mathematical knowledge needed to remedy the problem.

Higher education institutions (HEIs) have an obligation to provide these teachers the content knowledge they need to become highly qualified as well as the pedagogical content knowledge to support student learning within the content domain; they must provide this instruction to practicing classroom teachers even as they are teaching. In addition, many of the teachers required to demonstrate content knowledge in these areas may also be insecure about their own abilities. It is therefore critical to provide the support teachers need to sustain learning and development in the in-service programs.

Online professional learning opportunities may be one means to support teachers in building their content knowledge for teaching. Traditional advantages of an online environment include a flexible schedule to accommodate a teacher's already busy day–travel time is not required–and access to people from many different geographic areas (Wooten and Hancock 2009). This type of opportunity may be especially useful to groups of teachers who find themselves beholden to these new policies, such as special education teachers, who are now required to hold secondary mathematics certification, or elementary teachers, who need middle-level mathematics certification–both of whom need these additional certifications to teach the upper grades of their original certifications. These teachers often work in isolation from the rest of the mathematics education community, thus their access to valuable mathematics education is especially limited. With this in mind, The Math Forum at Drexel University, in conjunction with the School of Education at Drexel's Goodwin College, created the Moving to Mathematics (M2M) program to provide access to valuable and sustainable professional learning opportunities in mathematics for practicing general and special education teachers.

We use the word access to imply both spatial access, described above, and access to mathematical content knowledge for teaching. This implies enabling teachers to interact with the rigorous mathematics provided in a mathematics department, but facilitated with pedagogically appropriate methods an education program might offer, focusing on the mathematical concepts rather than just the procedures (Ball and Bass 2000).

At Drexel University, we have created an online master's level program in the Learning and Teaching of mathematics. The first year of coursework involves learning the mathematical concepts underlying the middle and secondary level mathematics curriculum used nationwide and allows teachers to use this learning in their classrooms. Our work in this program has allowed us to develop online strategies that support deep mathematical and pedagogical learning for a very diverse group of teachers.

The Pennsylvania Department of Education has funded this project including the design of all courses in the sequence and implementation of two full cycles of the sequence, of which we are reporting on the first cycle. This funding has also allowed for ongoing analysis of the program as we proceeded through the first cycle of implementation as well as reflective analysis following the first full implementation. This type of funding, from state, federal, or international government, nongovernmental organizations, and/or foundations will be crucial for HEIs to design, test, and modify models for quality online programs. Once created, the individual programs can be offered as professional development opportunities to support practitioners, in this case teachers, who find themselves in need of expanded educational opportunities due to policy changes or changing demands for services. These courses, once developed, can be offered as a four-course sequence in cost-effective ways with approximately 30 teachers in each course. Running over four semesters, the cost to a school district would be approximately US$500 per teacher per year. In the United States, this is equivalent to approximately one credit of a university course per year. In addition, these courses are of the quality and the content necessary for university credit and in fact are the basis for the middle level teacher education program we are in the process of creating for the new certification requirements of our state. Thus despite the claim that massification (Altbach et al. 2010) and online education are diminishing the quality of education today, we believe that the need to balance both access and quality is improving our traditional programs in ways that face-to-face instruction in the traditional university setting did not provide.

In addition to the need for valuable professional development, defined by the conceptual nature of the mathematics that can be transferred to the classroom, our work provides research into providing this access in a sustainable form for both the participants and the agencies providing the opportunities. This chapter discusses the potential for online professional development for all teachers who provide content instruction through a focus on the M2M program.

Background

Educational research highlights the need for mathematics teachers to possess an understanding of the subject that goes beyond rote memorization and procedural manipulations to be able to teach it. These teachers also require the abilities to use multiple representations to express mathematical concepts in different ways, provide explanations for rules and procedures, and analyze students' solutions and explanations. Educational research also suggests that general education teachers and special education teachers often lack content knowledge in the mathematics they teach (Ma 1999; Ball et al. 2005; Greer and Meyen 2009). This is despite the Council for Exceptional Children's (CEC) Policy on Academic Subject Matter Content of General Curriculum and Special Educators, which emphasizes the following in regards to the importance of content knowledge for special education teachers:

> When a special education teacher assumes sole responsibility for teaching an academic subject matter class at the secondary level, the special educator should have a solid subject matter content knowledge base sufficient to assure the students can meet state curriculum standards. (CEC, n.d. 1)

The teachers in the M2M program are participating in a series of online professional development courses that are designed to help teachers to prepare for the Pennsylvania mandated Mathematics Praxis II, which will lead to certification in mathematics. The program implementation was funded by the Pennsylvania State Department of Education as an attempt to also increase the content knowledge of general and special educators. In offering the program, the funders placed a priority on partnering with high-needs school districts in Pennsylvania. High-needs schools are generally defined as those that have a high percentage of students from low social economic brackets and who are below grade level academically as well as have teachers who lack appropriate licensing. We believe that the definition of high-needs should also include the lack of access to professional development. Granting agencies often partner institutes of higher education with local high-needs school districts to provide face-to-face professional development. To provide access to high-quality professional development in historically defined high-needs school districts *and* rural areas often lacking access to professional development, we offered the program online to ensure wide participation of teachers from all types of districts.

Embedded in the M2M program is a research agenda regarding how to create a space, facilitated by the Math Forum, in which the participants in our program engage with each other in meaningful ways around mathematical content. This does not mean facilitators do not take part in the course. It means the facilitator's participation is reserved for higher-level conversations such as offering powerful representations and making connections among topics, thus making it sustainable for the professional development model. The research agenda also seeks answers on how to support participants in the program to ensure they complete the series of professional development courses in the M2M program. There is a real need among our participants for knowledge to support their certification efforts. In other words, if we do not retain our teachers in this program then it is hard to claim that we provided access to content knowledge that was valuable to them. Specifically our research questions are as follows:

1. What structural supports were taken advantage of by the participants within our program?
2. What differences were found in the participatory interactions of those teachers who remained in the program versus those who left the program before completion?
3. How can one facilitate an online program that is high-touch and sustainable?

To promote understanding of our research, we first provide the reader a detailed description of our program, including the types of learning supports available to teachers. Then using a subset of our population, we analyzed within course data to determine differences in the ways the teachers were able, or not able, to take advantage of these supports within the time frame of the courses. Finally, we spent some time focusing on the facilitation of the course, as the facilitation must be sustainable to continue to provide access to the courses.

The Moving to Mathematics Program

In creating the Moving to Mathematics program, we set out to provide access to valuable and sustainable mathematics teacher education to as many teachers as possible. We also were interested in studying the process of providing quality professional development to teachers who may not otherwise have such access. By quality we mean sustainable support for the teachers in need of time and energy and deep conceptual mathematical instruction. Teachers are extremely busy. This is especially true for special education teachers who have individualized plans for each student in their care. It is thus important that the teachers maximize their learning while minimizing the time spent in the program. The current US school structure does not generally provide regular scheduled time in the workplace for continuing education; therefore we must ensure that our program is sustainable for practicing teachers. Quality mathematics is often defined by Mathematics Departments and taught in ways that teachers are unable to bring to their own classrooms. In our program, implemented by a mathematician, a special educator, and two mathematics educators, we offer courses that are centered around fundamental mathematical concepts but are studied through the examples commonly found in the middle level and secondary curricula in our country, so that as the teachers learned the mathematics they could see that it was immediately relevant to their classrooms.

Program Participants

We chose to offer the program online to reach as many people in the state as possible. We contacted human resources in our two partner districts and sent letters to all special education supervisors across the state to recruit teachers for the M2M program. The teachers who were interested in participating in the program had to submit an online application. In fact, in the first year of the program we received applications from many more teachers than our funding supported. We had initial funding for 50 participants in year one but had well over 100 applications for the program. We were able to secure additional funding from the Pennsylvania Department of Education to add more participants. Thus, we began immediately to consider the issues of sustainability for the facilitators. When year one began we had 89 participants involved. This reflects on applicants who followed through by enrolling in the first course. A majority of the teachers participating in year one of the program were female and Caucasian. Also, over 85 percent of the teachers had a certification in special education. Participants were randomly assigned to one of the sections of the first course in the program. Each section had 16–20 participants. To better understand the experiences of those who began the program, we then randomly selected one section of the course to use in our research. The section we selected had 18 teachers, 3 of whom discontinued the program due to a change in status at their school during the introductory course in which they were required to attain other coursework (for example, reading specialist rather than mathematics specialist). We did not analyze the data from these three participants, thus we analyzed the work of 15 teachers (n=15). Our cluster sample of 15 participants matched our overall participant demographics primarily being female, Caucasian, and certified in special education.

When we show discussion threads from our participants, we use only the first letter of their name to maintain confidentiality. When there were two or more individuals with the same first letter, we added in the second letter in their first name to differentiate participants.

Program Courses

Much of our work to date has been balancing the needs of the teachers to learn high-quality mathematics that could be used in their classrooms as well as topics on the mandated Praxis II exams with the level of facilitation necessary for a model that could be used widely for continued professional education of teachers. Even as funding provided the opportunity to implement a program of valuable professional learning activities, it created tensions between providing test preparation and providing mathematics knowledge for teaching, with its full repertoire of multiple representations, explanations, and analysis of mathematical thinking. We hypothesize that if we teach fundamental mathematical concepts that underlie the entire curriculum, we provide teachers with mathematical knowledge that cuts across many of the questions on the test as well as cutting across much of the mathematics they teach in the multiple grades at their schools.

The courses in this program include

- Understanding Data,
- Proportional Reasoning,
- Algebraic Reasoning,
- Functions, and
- Geometric Reasoning.

These topics encompass the big ideas of the middle and secondary mathematics curriculum in the nation. The instruction surrounding the content knowledge includes useful representations and language of mathematics that support student learning as well as methods of teaching elementary mathematics that impact underprepared middle- and secondary-level students. Each course is run through an online model that breaks the subject matter of the course into content modules.

Program Instructional Model

Our program's instructional model was adapted from the Online Asynchronous Collaboration (OAC) model currently used in mathematical instruction throughout the Goodwin College of Professional Studies at Drexel University, both in the School of Education and the Math Forum. The goals of the M2M Program include supporting teachers' development of mathematical understanding that will lead to success in fulfilling their certification requirements while being introduced to verbal, pictorial, graphical, and symbolic representations that will support their students in coming to a deeper, more connected understanding of the mathematics of middle and high school.

In the implementation of our professional development, we felt the tension between current models of highly facilitated online education used in course delivery and the ability to provide professional development through an online educational environment that was valuable and sustainable. In refining the OAC model of Jason Silverman and Ellen Clay (2010) for our continuing education grant, we wrestled with the traditional thinking of content delivery where the facilitator is the "sage on the stage" providing and controlling the learning in current practices of online education. In addition, research by Vincent Tinto (2006–2007, 2) has shown that "frequency and quality of contact with faculty, staff, and students has repeatedly been shown to be an independent predictor of student persistence." To create a valuable online educational environment for professional development that is also sustainable for facilitators, we wanted to move away from a focus on providing frequent and quality contact with faculty to focusing on developing a space where participants have frequent and quality contact with each other during learning.

The OAC model, shown in Figure 7.1, currently includes three phases within each of the content modules, *initial thinking* about mathematics, *discussion of collective thinking,* and *revision of individual thinking.*

These three phases are each introduced by an announcement/e-mail from the facilitator of the class. There are typically seven- to ten-day content modules in a ten-and-a-half-week course.

Phase One: Initial thinking

As each online module opens to the participants, it offers an introduction to a mathematical idea through a short video presentation that introduces

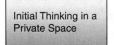

Figure 7.1   OAC Model Flow Chart.
Source: Created by the authors.

the mathematical topic of the module and sets the tone for thinking about mathematics rather than getting the activity set done. Activities related to these mathematical ideas are assigned at this time. The activities vary significantly. Some are written problems that participants are asked to share their thinking around, which they can do with symbols, language, pictures, or dynamic software. Other activities require verbal description for which they use Jing®, a publicly available software package for capturing the screen of your computer and your voice simultaneously. This phase of the module lasts approximately three days during which participating teachers share their thinking, solutions if they are able to, and questions around the mathematical activities in a private workspace. These activities set focus on describing, thinking, and asking questions, rather than doing mathematical procedures, getting frustrated, and trying to figure things out on one's own.

A sample activity excerpt from our Algebraic Reasoning course, the third in our series is as follows:

> In this activity on the blog, you will find a list of algebraic expressions, equations, inequalities, and functions that are typical of algebra problems on standardized tests. As a bunch, they look rather overwhelming. But your job is to read them aloud focusing on the quantities, the operations, and the relationships.
>
> The goal is to get comfortable with the language. So read a few of them. Pick a couple of easier ones and then a couple that challenge you for the activity (Blackboard 2010–11).

By this point in the program, the mathematics is significantly more challenging for the participants than in their first two courses. Several of our teachers are totally overwhelmed with the ideas in this course, yet they will be tested on them to complete the new certification requirements; thus we had to be especially careful in introducing this course in a way that allowed them to both learn and stay engaged. You can also see in this activity the possibility for differentiation by allowing them to choose the relationships they work with.

We use the blog tool of the Blackboard Learning Platform to provide a private space for participants to record their initial thoughts throughout this phase of the work. We feel this stage is essential for us as facilitators to understand where each of the teachers is meeting us with their mathematical thinking. We cannot support a deep, connected understanding of mathematics within our teachers if we do not know where in the web of mathematics each of our teachers is entering. Once the work becomes public, we lose the opportunity to hear our teacher's uninfluenced thoughts about an activity. This initial private stage is just as essential to our teachers as it allows them time to connect with their own knowledge on which they can then build rather than pasting new unconnected ideas on top of old unconnected ideas, leaving them disconnected and thereby practically useless. The participants have approximately three-four days to complete this phase of the module.

Several of our teachers did find the initial thinking stage quite frustrating as they had little time to spare and were often lacking in confidence. Thus we have created two forms of support to assist them during the private phase. In the first, we provide a public discussion board forum in which we encourage the teachers to ask any questions they encounter in their work. In this way, even as we are in the private phase, teachers can begin to discuss the mathematical ideas of the module. The second way we support teachers in this phase is by the facilitators directly responding to entries made by the teachers in the blog space.

Phase Two: Discussion of Thinking

After the teachers have had approximately three days to post their initial thoughts, questions, and solutions to the private blog, we open up the individual postings for public discussion. We then ask the participants to view each other's thinking and comment on at least two of them, the one directly above and directly below their own post.

We provide a specific set of criteria within each module to assist our participants in analyzing each other's thinking and commenting. In this way, rather than trying to figure out if the answers are right or wrong, we focus on issues, such as which representations are used, the presence of the underlying mathematics, or the consistency of the language. This type of discussion builds confidence and allows the facilitators to orchestrate discussion around the fundamental mathematical topics of the course. In the following excerpt, you can see the specific mathematics and the focus on language that we are asking the participants to think about.

When you read/listen to videos, try to determine which language they used, choosing from the ones below, or describing them in some way.

Reading from LEFT to RIGHT
"x squared plus one"
"Negative two x plus six"
"x squared plus 2"

Main focus on OPERATIONS
"The sum of x squared and 2"
"The product of 5 and 4 raised to the x power"

Main focus on QUANTITIES
"Negative 2 times x"
"x times negative 2"
"x is being multiplied by negative 2"

Phase Three: Revision of Initial Thinking

After the teachers have had three-four days to comment on and discuss their common thinking, we allow the final three days for revisions. Again, we have fine-tuned our facilitation to suggesting revisions that focus on a particular mathematical topic. The following excerpt shown in Figure 7.2 provides an example of our narrowing the scope of the revision as well as the focus on mathematical language in this case.

You can see from this excerpt that we have focused on fewer problems so that teachers could have more time to think deeply about a few problems after having originally worked with a more diverse set of examples. In addition, you can see that we are offering language to assist them as we saw much struggling with this issue in their original thinking. Finally, note that we are asking them to think about what their natural inclination is so that their new ideas can be linked to their current understandings, making learning more likely.

You only have to read the following—not the whole list.

a. $x^2 + 2$

b. $5(4^x)$

d. $2(x - 7)^2 + 5$

f. $y = -1/2\, x + 3$

(2) When reading these 4 algebraic strings, please focus on the quantities and the operations acting on the quantities. You may want to start with,

"I have a quantity x, she's being squared . . ." or

"X is the main character of my story. I'm adding 3 to her . . ."

(3) Before you begin your new pod cast, look back at these 4 problems (or at least the ones you did of those 4), and tell us whether you were reading from left to right, focusing on the operations, or focusing on the quantities and the operations happening to them. Decide what you want to improve on, and tell us anything in particular you'd like us to give you feedback on.

Figure 7.2   Example of Revisions.

Data Analysis

In our program, we offer a unique combination of six learning supports: Introductory Materials, Facilitating the Process of Problem Solving, Ongoing Access, Technology for the Course and the K-12 Classroom, Access to Collaboration with Others in the Field, and Expert Facilitation. These supports have emerged from our ongoing formative assessment of the program. In this section of the chapter, we describe the levels of interaction around the six learning supports we provided. We then describe the grouping of the participants by their level of participation in the program. We then compare characteristics of interaction of those who were able to access the knowledge they needed in an environment that was sustainable for the facilitators as well as those who were not. In the final section of this chapter, we will discuss changes to the implementation that we believe will provide access to even more participants in the second cohort as well as for a more diverse group of learners in general.

Supports for Learning[1]

This section will first demonstrate the levels of interaction around and the learning realized from each of our six learning supports. We will then return to the above-mentioned groups to determine how the two are related.

Learning Support 1: Introductory Materials

This learning support is most like mathematical instruction in the United States. We provide materials that can be read and listened to, along with activities with which the participants are asked to interact. The materials and activities are conceptually based rather than procedural, which is less common in the United States, but is becoming more prevalent (Lampert 1990; Simon 2006). The following excerpts from a discussion board demonstrate participants taking advantage of this learning support. The first two excerpts express dissatisfaction with the amount of information in the text.

> Question 1
> Mean is 15.7, Do not quite understand how to get variance or standard deviation. I read the definitions but can't get started. This problem had too much data–perhaps a smaller problem to start would have been better for me. (Teacher S) (Blackboard 2010–11)

> I agree. I had difficulty with the variance and standard deviation myself. I think I need further explanation–there is only limited information in the book. I need more basic instructions and smaller problems to practice on before I get to the larger problems in the book. (Teacher S) (Blackboard 2010–11)

Whereas, the following demonstrate examples in which participants were able to take advantage of the introductory materials as a learning support.

> In all honesty this was the one exercise that gave me the most frustration. At first my outlook on the assignment was more of a connect-the-dots ideal. However, upon reading prior to the activity and immediately following the activity did add some clarity to my thought process. (Teacher V) (Blackboard 2010–11)
>
> I know what you mean about probability at stats. I did learn a lot from the chapter too and now know how to figure those ideas out when I see them. When it is put into fraction form I think it is easier to understand. (Teacher A) (Blackboard 2010–11)

Learning Support 2: Facilitating the Process of Problem Solving

The facilitators construct a space where participants are required to share their thoughts while building trust that the answers will come in time. The following excerpts demonstrate participant's differing levels of willingness or ability to take advantage of this learning support. The first excerpt shows a participant who is not yet able to move her focus from the idea of getting the answers to the learning of mathematics.

> What I worry about is that when I am stuck on figuring out a math problem I look at the answer and work backward. I also am not a good test taker. When I take the sample PRAXIS test I get them wrong when I think I know what I am doing. I feel that I have gain [sic] a lot of knowledge but still am very fearful of the test. (Teacher P) (Blackboard 2010–11)

The second excerpt demonstrates a participant who is trying to make the move from getting the answers to sharing her thinking. She has not yet accepted that she can think about the problems for a while and then share her thinking regardless of where she is in the problem.

> I am also struggling with this and am somewhat confused with average/ standard deviation and variance. I know we aren't supposed to spend a lot of time on each item but I seem to get caught up and lose track of time. Like tonight. I don't have everything done but I think I will just start fresh tomorrow. (Teacher Mu) (Blackboard 2010–11)

The last of these excerpts demonstrates the same participant who is becoming more comfortable with sharing her thinking, despite the fact that she is not at all sure about her work.

> When I use the progress monitor program it automatically puts in a trend line. I use that trend line as a visual for parents to understand their child's data and where the child is in relation to the line. However, in looking at this data I would put a line on a diagonal through the point of 400 on up through the point 600. I have nothing to back this up but the look of my progress monitoring data. I am actually confused about this one. I'd like to hear others thinking on this particular question. (Teacher Mu) (Blackboard 2010–11)

Learning Support 3: Ongoing Access

One of the benefits of online learning in an asynchronous model is that participants can spend time in the course at any time they desire. Thus participants can post thoughts, look for ideas, review introductory materials as often as they want within the week.

The most outstanding issue the data revealed was that only about 9 percent of the entries, both initial and responses, were posted between the hours of 3 p.m. and 5 p.m., what we might think of as the professional development time (after school). Rather, the most hits were between 10 a.m. and noon (34 percent) and between 5 a.m. and 6 a.m. (12 percent). Thus teachers are getting online before they begin their school day and during their lunch/prep periods. In fact, a full 66 percent of the hits in the course came in what we refer to as the school day, between the hours of 8 a.m. and 3 p.m.

Learning Support 4: Technology for the Course and the K-12 Classroom

At the Math Forum technology had always been a large draw. When we offered courses that highlighted technology, we often received many more applications than those on mathematical problem solving for instance. The first and most essential use of technology is the Learning Platform, for which we use Blackboard. The Discussion Board Forums and the Activity Blogs are part of this system. We also incorporated technology that we thought teachers could make use of in their own classrooms with their own students. We believed this to be a real incentive to taking part in our program.

The following excerpts demonstrate participants' different levels of ability to take advantage of this learning support. In the first two excerpts participants are struggling with the technology. In the first, the participant is struggling with the technology we need to facilitate an online course. In the second, the participant is struggling with the technology we provided for them to be able to take to their classrooms.

> Hi all, I have been putting my answers in word and copy/paste into the blog. I just finished the review and was extremely pleased with myself for creating two pie graphs (first time) in excel ... Imagine my disappointment when I wasn't able to copy them into the module 2 blog. Can someone tell me what I might be doing wrong? Also, am I posting the review questions in the right place (module 2 blog)? (Teacher Mu) (Blackboard 2010–11)
>
> Question 3
>   Can't draw a scatter plot on the computer?????
>   I feel like I need more direct instruction on these concepts–it's been a very long time since I studied these in high school/college. I did very well in Math always, but I really do need to revisit these topics from the beginning. I forget some of the basics. The technology piece is slowing me down–I am much more adept at paper and pen calculations then [sic] at using the computer. (Teacher S) (Blackboard 2010–11)

Finally, we share an excerpt from a participant who both struggled with concepts and was able to see the benefits of the technology we provided for use in classrooms.

> I did not find this lesson to be as problematic or overwhelming with details or computations as last week. The activities we did from Module 2 were great practice of the skills we learned but were manageable in their expectations. The new material "probabilties" [sic] allowed us to really be able to show students the efficiency technology can provide. (Teacher C) (Blackboard 2010–11)

Learning Support 5: Access to Collaboration with Others in the Field

Collaboration supported our participants in two distinctively different ways. We know that working on mathematics together and sharing of thoughts around mathematical ideas supports learning (Cobb et al. 2001). In addition, supporting teachers in becoming comfortable with learning together supports learning past the duration of our classes. The second essential benefit of collaboration we discovered in our reflective analysis is that it aids in the facilitation of the course. Individual responses to each participant for each mathematical activity by a facilitator is usually reserved for credit-bearing courses at universities for which the majority of school districts in the United States do not provide funding to their teachers. If participants share their collective knowledge with each other, the facilitator can reserve time for pressing deeper into topics, making connections among topics, debunking misconceptions, and connecting to when and why those misconceptions arise. In other words, s/he can reserve her/his comments for sharing expertise that may not be readily available within the group. We have begun to develop a framework for the levels of participation in which the participants took part. We include here excerpts, which will demonstrate participants' differing reactions and ability to take advantage of the five different levels of collaboration available to them in the program.

Level of Collaboration: Access to the Thinking of Others. The first excerpt expresses the use teachers made of simply having access to others' thinking. It suggests that the participant is a little more comfortable learning from the prepared materials rather than from each other.

> I found these exercises a bit more challenging to understand this week; therefore I will be *needing to reread the information* a few times to figure things out more clearly ... I will *need to reread and look at others post* to help me. It has been awhile for me when refering [sic] to this kind of math and I do better when looking at material. I also need *more time to put into reading the material* and digesting it so I can understand it. (Italics added.) (Teacher T) (Blackboard 2010–11)

These next excerpts demonstrate ways in which participants learned merely from reading the posts of others, not even needing to communicate further with colleagues. They demonstrate participants understanding better, building confidence in their own work and returning to analyze their own work, learning ways to dig deeper into the meaning in both specific ways and in general comments, as well as simply seeing that there are different ways to think about a single problem. Finally, the last quote shares a participant learning about communicating ideas.

> I just finished my trials and I posted them in the activity section for mod 3. I'm looking at everyone else's work now. When I look at other work, it helps me understand better. Thanks! (Teacher T) (Blackboard 2010–11)

> Wow! I guess after looking at your responses to questions 31.2. I must have understood the concept more than I assumed ... I really didn't understand the concept of -1 but after checking my responses against yours I do suppose it made sense. Thank you. (Teacher C) (Blackboard 2010–11)

> I agree your wording was very well organized and It also may [sic] me re-look at my own work. Thanks. (Teacher P) (Blackboard 2010–11)

> K, I liked your interpretation of Figure 1 about most of the kids must live close to school because the majority of them walk to school. I didn't evern [sic] think about that when I looked at the data. (Teacher B) (Blackboard 2010–11)

> Great concept on Fig 1–I didn't think of breaking the information that was represented down further! (Teacher T) (Blackboard 2010–11)

S, I like how you explained the data in Discussion 1a. It [sic] interesting how we all see data in different ways. (Teacher P) (Blackboard 2010–11)

Very well said. I always have a way of drawing out my answers. Thanks for your very direct and clear response! (Teacher B) (Blackboard 2010–11)

Level of Collaboration: Asking Questions of Others. There were questions posed both for learning and supporting the learning of others. In the category of asking questions for one's own learning, teachers took advantage of the collaboration in different ways. We see questions asking for instruction on how to get started and how to do specific tasks.

I am actually confused about this one. I'd like to hear others thinking on this particular question. (Teacher Mu) (Blackboard 2010–11)

R, I am still having trouble with the histogram if you did it with technology could you send me a copy so I can look at it. [provides e-mail address]. If anyone else reads this and has a copy could you send me an example. Thanks. (Teacher P) (Blackboard 2010–11)

The following excerpt demonstrates one of the first to really take full advantage of the collaboration. The participant read several posts and sees that hers is different. She puts her own thinking out there, trusting that someone in the class will support her in her learning.

Females Ave. 2.75 and .793 for SD
Ok I see that mine is different from others.. What am I doing wrong? This is what I did>>.
1. found the mean
2. subtracted the mean from all the grade points
3. found the square roots of all my subtractions
4. add all the square roots together and found the mean
5. found the square root of the mean. (Teacher P) (Blackboard 2010–11)

Finally, as we might have expected with participants who are teachers, they sometimes asked questions that were designed to support the learning of others rather than learning for one's self. This is an example in which a participant supported learning that a facilitator would have found necessary, but in this case did not have to address.

In your coin toss experiment you noted that your definition of success was H/T. Did you actually have no T/H or did you count them as H/T? They should be counted as separate outcomes. H/T is different from T/H I would think it rare that one of them wouldn't show up, almost like standing a coin on edge. (Teacher L) (Blackboard 2010–11)

Level of Collaboration: Answering Questions of Others. There were several times when participants answered the questions of others. These excerpts are typical of traditional mathematical instruction. We share only one example to demonstrate the way in which they supported each other by answering each other's questions noting the usefulness of this practice in sustainability.

> I agree scattered plots are not as interesting until you look at the trend line. I recently finished my action research for my masters and I was amazed at how much scattered plots represent important data when you aren't trying to find dramatic trends. I was always looking for a dramatic upward or downward motion. Yet when my mentor showed me the slight trends a light went on and I saw what the data was actually saying. (Teacher P) (Blackboard 2010–11)

Level of Collaboration: Making One's Own Sense from Revoicing Others. Several of the previous quotes are of teachers telling us what they have already learned. The following excerpts demonstrate participants revoicing what they are reading as they make their own sense of the material. In these excerpts they make their own learning visible for us. We believe these will be beneficial for our own teaching as we can use them as models of how we make our learning visible, not just our initial thinking. The first excerpt shows a consolidation of thinking about tails-heads and heads-tails being "separate" outcomes. The second one demonstrates a shift in thinking about how to read a scatterplot, from looking at small areas to looking at the entire graph, a shift that becomes necessary when we move from one-variable data sets to two-variable data sets. The third shows a connection between order of operations, something the author is obviously familiar with but has not connected to the problems at hand in this module. And the fourth demonstrates the clearest of the revoicing of the thoughts of a classmate of which she has been able to make sense.

> T, Actually I was thinking they were the same so thank you for that clarification. I had it written as seperate [sic] at first but then I second-guessed myself. (Teacher P) (Blackboard 2010–11)
>
> J, I agree with your thoughts on #4 that we should not base our decision on one area we should look at a variety of items before making a decision. (Teacher C) (Blackboard 2010–11)

Yes we are talking about the orders of operations. I just was not thinking. It makes more sense now. Thank you. (Teacher P) (Blackboard 2010–11)

Hi, I agree with your statements about odds, in that I don't think I fully realized before that odds of 7–5 meant 7/12 to 5/12. I was thinking about how sometimes the odds are 2–1, and I thought that meant 50%, but I guess it really means 67%. (Teacher Ma) (Blackboard 2010–11)

Level of Collaboration: Third Party Learning. Finally, we share examples of what we refer to as third-party learning, which occurs when a participant learns by simply taking advantage of a conversation being had by others in the class. The following three posts are excerpts from a single thread. The initial post followed by a second participant shifting her thinking on the definition of odds, and a third, short excerpt, demonstrating that this third party has been able to learn from a conversation between two of her classmates. The indentations imply that the post is a response to the prior post.

Playing the odds- I'm not much of a gambler, but my kids do play sports; so we read the "odds" on how they're [sic] team is suppose to perform in comparison to the opposition. After reading page 638, I now realize that if the odds are 7 to 5, then you add those numbers together, then form the ratio 7/12 or 58%, and 5/12 or 42%. (Teacher R) (Blackboard 2010–11)

Hi, I agree with your statements about odds, in that I don't think I fully realized before that odds of 7–5 meant 7/12 to 5/12. I was thinking about how sometimes the odds are 2–1, and I thought that meant 50%, but I guess it really means 67%. I am into horseracing, and I watch the Triple Crown races, so now I will really understand what those odds mean! (Teacher Ma) (Blackboard 2010–11)

Thanks for you thoughts it help me understand. (Teacher P) (Blackboard 2010–11)

Learning Support 6: Expert Facilitation

Although we attempted to limit the need for expert facilitation, we provided facilitation when we felt the group was not supporting the learning of an individual for reasons such as the responses were not timely or were not raising the level of mathematics. Often these two were intertwined. In other words, participants may have raised the level of mathematics if we had waited longer or encouraged others to participate. Therefore we constantly had to balance supporting teachers in the short term versus supporting effective collaboration in the longer term. We share one excerpt in which the facilitator decided her expertise was necessary and the participants took advantage of it. The excerpt demonstrates persistence in asking questions in the Module 2 discussion. The participant involved asked a challenging question around making connections in Module 1, to which she did not get a response. Thus she is following up in this module. This is an example in which the facilitator decided to respond.

> I agree that the information you are attempting to present or organize drives the type of graph you would use. I asked the question last week as to whether it is mathematically incorrect to use a type of graph you feel more comfortable in creating than one that is better suited for the information. For example, if the information you are presenting is more efficient to show in a bar graph but you choose to use a circle graph is that wrong? Does the question you are attempting to answer determine what you use as well as the information itself? (Teacher C) (Blackboard 2010–11)

Having presented data demonstrating ways in which participants were and were not able to take advantage of the supports we offered, we turn to a discussion of this data and then our choices based on the data.

Use of Supports by Groups

We begin this section with two exchanges from the third and most recent course in our sequence. Although these are not exchanges solely among the participants from the cluster sample, we include them to demonstrate norms of practice of an entire group of participants who take advantage of the supports of our OAC model. Isolating the participants from our sample would not allow us to demonstrate entire exchanges as we continued to randomly assign the participants to sections in each subsequent course. We will return to the participants from our sample to continue our discussion of their participation within this context after demonstrating the types of interactions that developed over a three-course sequence.

> What is the inverse operation of ln? and what is ln? (Teacher W, January 30, 6:17 p.m.) (Blackboard 2010–11)

> Ln is log base e. So its inverse function is e^x. That is, make it the exponent of e. (Teacher H, January 30, 7:55 p.m.) (Blackboard 2010–11)

> The inverse of the exponential function is called the natural logarithm function. Most calculators use ln(x) for the natural logarithm of x and log(x) for the base 10 logarithm of x. (Teacher Sm, January 30, 9:02 p.m.) (Blackboard 2010–11)

> I love your questions. What is the inverse of ln? is the perfect question. If you want to solve an equation with a function in it, you need to know the inverse.

Then you ask, and what is ln? Another great question, which you don't really need to know to get this work done, but how can you not ask what you're taking the inverse of.

Your classmates have answered the individual questions, thanks to them. I'll try to answer in a different way.

Just like you may be familiar with what linear relationships (lines) look like y = 3x + 4 or you might know what quadratic relationships look like y = $3x^2$ + 4, there are two other relationships we'd like you to meet y = ln x and y = e^x. So, when you introduce a new function (relationship) to people, how do you help them to learn more about them.

Why don't you try looking at their graphs?

[instruction on how to on a TI-84 calculator]

One more thing you can do just for fun!

Return to the y = menu and add the function y^3 = x.

Then return to the graph and see if you can imagine that this new line you just graphed is a mirror and the other two functions are mirror images of each other. (Facilitator, January 31, 8:21 a.m.) (Blackboard 2010–11)

Thank you for the explanation, the visual representation of the graphs really does help to see the inverse! (Teacher W, January 31, 3:50 p.m.) (Blackboard 2010–11)

Thank you. Many of my concerns were answered here!!! (Teacher Sp, January 31, 5:14 p.m.) (Blackboard 2010–11)

The first excerpt has several instances of participants taking advantage of the supports offered by the program. A participant who is meeting a new function for the very first time at 6:15 in the evening posts the very first line. She has enough trust to ask questions about the conceptual ideas not just the doing of the problem. She posts, "and what is ln?" and "what is the inverse operation of ln?" Within two hours and twenty minutes, she receives two specific answers to her questions, which would allow her to complete the exercise. These are indented showing that they are responses to the initial post. The next passage, authored by the facilitator, is posted the following morning at 8:21. She is answering in such a way that supports participants learning at a higher level of mathematics, generalizing to the situation of meeting any new function rather than the specifics of the particular activity on which the participant is working. The post immediately following the facilitator's post is a response of gratitude to the facilitator's post at 3:50 the same afternoon, from the initial author, showing that she has returned to take advantage of the information provided. Finally, the last post, approximately two hours later, indented to show that it is a response to the original poster, demonstrates a fifth person in the exchange who has come in approximately 24 hours after the original post and taken advantage of the interaction for his own benefit, another example of "third-party" learning. This excerpt was situated around the learning of mathematics. The commentary on participant's taking advantage of the supports of problem solving, ongoing access, use of technology, access to collaboration, and expert facilitation are all provided by the researchers in this paper, not in the course.

The next post demonstrates that these interactions have become norms of practice (Yackel and Cobb 1996) within the current cohort.

> I think this course really proves that you can learn more if you ask questions and you learn more working with others! I thought some of the equations were challenging and unsure what the answers were. But after some thinking, listening, reading, and asking questions I feel I have a better understanding! Thanks for the help! (Teacher W, February 4, 4:45 p.m.)

> Your words ring very true. I am approaching each assignment as an opportunity to discover something new or solidify my understanding of a concept. It is great to have others to help work through some of the rougher patches along the way. (Teacher Mc, February 4, 7:36 p.m.) (Blackboard 2010–11)

> Very true I am learning so much from everyone. I like that we don't get penalized for being wrong the first time, but allowed to make mistakes and work through them and learn from them. (Teacher D, February 4, 8:10 p.m.) (Blackboard 2010–11)

> Definitely so much better with everyone's help and example. Keep up the good work. (Teacher Y, February 5, 7:10 p.m.) (Blackboard 2010–11)

In this exchange, participants demonstrate through their own thoughts and words that they are taking full advantage of Learning Support 2: Facilitation the Process of Problem Solving and Learning Support 5: Access to Collaboration with Others in the Field.

The initial post describes mathematical activity with words and phrases such as thinking, listening, reading, and asking questions. These are not the usual descriptions of mathematical classrooms for adult learners. The responses she receives all corroborate her thoughts. "The first offers new language, opportunity to discover something new or solidify my understanding of a concept." His comments are again corroborated by a third participant who adds, "I like that we don't get penalized for being wrong the first time, but allowed to make mistakes and work through them and learn from them." Again, descriptions that should be expected in any learning environment, but not very common in higher-level mathematical courses. The participants in this exchange have come to appreciate and take advantage of the problem-solving process and are consciously aware of its advantages.

In addition, they are aware and grateful for the access to collaboration. The first post suggests a participant is taking advantage of the collaboration although she does not state it explicitly because she is thinking, listening, reading, and asking questions of others in the class, and she is thanking her classmates for their help. The second and third posts explicitly mention and express gratitude for the support of others. Finally, the fourth participant in this exchange expresses gratitude along with a little push to keep it up.

This group, engaged in their third course, is taking advantage of the supports the OAC model has to offer in both breadth and depth. We hypothesized that this group, participants still with us after three courses, has learned how to take advantage of the supports we offered. However, when we looked for evidence to support our hypothesis, we found a different story. We thus describe the participatory interaction of the four groups we studied in our cluster sample.

The Story of Group 1: Did Not Complete the First Two Courses

Group 1 consisted of seven participants. In general, the participants in this group were very uncertain about mathematics, a group of teachers we very much intended to support. Six of the seven of them asked many questions about both math and technology, showing that they trusted enough to share their uncertainty. We were not surprised when the one participant who would not share her uncertainty did not continue with our program. Of the other six, we found that although they were willing to share their initial thinking on problems, the majority of them never returned to the boards to comment on their classmates work or read the answers to the questions provided to them by their classmates or the facilitator. We had two exceptions to this pattern. One participant commented on her fear of the Praxis.

> What I worry about is that when I am stuck on figuring out a math problem I look at the answer and work backward. I also am not a good test taker. When I take the sample PRAXIS test I get them wrong when I think I know what I am doing. I feel that I have gain [sic] a lot of knowledge but still am very fearful of the test. (Teacher P) (Blackboard 2010–11)

We are not sure that she trusted that we were supporting her in the Praxis preparation rather than just teaching mathematical concepts. The other participated much more fully yet left the program anyway. This group, which came into the program and did not take advantage of much that the OAC model had to offer, left before completing the first course.

The Story of Group 2: Successfully Completed Two Courses

Group 2 consisted of four participants. The participants in this group began by posting their original thinking with certainty, thus suggesting that their mathematical backgrounds may have been a bit stronger. In addition, they each participated in almost all of the minimum requirements for the course, posting their initial thoughts, and at least two responses to each of the Activity Blogs and Discussion Board Forum, with the exception of one participant who discontinued the course temporarily due to health reasons. She rejoined us in the second course.

They all posted more often than the first group. They posted more when they struggled with material and less often when they understood the material better. They were quite diverse in their actual posts, many focusing on pedagogy or less specific posts on how much they learned. We noted however that they did not make the specific mathematics they learned visible in their posts. We saw glimpses of these participants' learning from both the text and from their colleagues but no consistency in taking advantage of the mathematics in the collaboration. Again, they came into the program taking advantage of many of the more traditional supports offered in mathematical courses, introductory material and asking questions, but not the collaboration supports of the OAC model. This group also left the program without learning to take advantage of these aspects of the program.

The Story of Group 3: Successfully Completed Three Courses

Group 3 consists of four participants. All of them had completed three courses in our program and continued to the fourth course. Their interactions include many that we demonstrated in the introduction to this section. Each of them was willing to post both when they were certain and when they were not. They showed much more consistent evidence of taking advantage of many aspects of the collaboration that were available to them, including learning from other's thinking, asking and answering questions, and revoicing the mathematics of others or learning from other's revoicing. They did not post much about technology suggesting that this was not an issue for them or extremely beneficial to them. We note here that these participants came into the program able to take advantage of the majority of the supports, including the collaborative ones, and continued to do so throughout the courses.

When facilitating later courses in the sequence, which consisted solely of members from group 3, we noted that the participants had formed a community that took advantage of the collaboration around significant mathematics and were aware of doing so. We hypothesized that participants had learned how to take advantage of the supports provided by our OAC model. However what we found in analyzing the data was that participants who took active part in the learning of mathematics from the community stayed in the program longer than those who did not, as opposed to our original hypothesis that people learned how to participate in the community. In fact all of those who continued through the entire program with us took advantage of the majority of the supports provided by the OAC model from the beginning. Thus we determined that our next challenge is to support participants in learning to take advantage of the supports that we have found to be essential to the program while changing those aspects of the course that we did not find beneficial to our participants. Toward this end we have altered our program for the second cohort both in structure and in facilitation strategies.

Resulting Changes

Structural Changes

We have made three structural changes to our program. We discontinued the use of what we referred to as the Learning Exercises, changed the time frame and structure of the modules, and minimized the use of technology.

On the issue of the Learning Exercises, our original hypotheses were based on our experiences in face-to-face classrooms, in which students were introduced to new material in a class session and then completed homework assignments, thereby spending more time on the same material. In the following class session, the homework is addressed before moving on to the introduction of new material. Our intention was to provide this opportunity for our participants. Thus we created an online module based on this face-to-face experience. Each module, excepting the first, was structured as follows:

By Saturday night, you should:
- *Do the Learning Exercises from Module 1 and post to the Learning Exercises Discussion*
- Listen to the Module 2 Podcast
- Read Chapter 30 Sections 3–5 *and* Reread Chapter 31 Sections 1–2
- Attempt the Activities in the Module 2 Activity Blog
- Share your thoughts, questions, and issues with the readings or activities on the Module 2 Discussion Board.

By the following Saturday night, you should:
- *Participate in the Learning Exercises and Module 2 Discussion Boards.*
- Comment on the blog entries immediately above and below yours (and any others that pique your interest).

- Respond to any questions asked of you about your work on the blog or the discussions.

However, in every section of our courses, there were fewer interactions to the learning exercises from the previous work than to the original work for the week. We took this as more a sign of the timing of the exercises than the content of the material. Thus, in our second course we contained each topic to a single module. This action forced us to decide which activities would be most beneficial for the learning of our participants within this new time constraint and improved the focus of our modules. We found this also to be unsatisfactory as it generally takes more than one sitting with one's own thoughts for learning to happen, thus in our third course, we moved to a module which included a week for initial posting and a week for discussion *and revision*. Unfortunately, without designating a distinct time frame for revision, we lost the focus of this activity, which we considered crucial to both learning and the feeling of accomplishment one feels from that growth. Thus, after three semesters of experimenting, we have instituted a three-phase structure, *Initial Thinking, Discussion of our Thinking, Revision of our Initial Thinking*, allowing approximately three days for each phase. The new courses have modules structured as follows:

Initial Thinking BY TUESDAY @ MIDNIGHT
- Post your initial activities
- Use the discussion board to ask any questions that would support you in getting it.

Discussion of our Thinking BY SATURDAY @ MIDNIGHT
- Post AT LEAST TWO comments to others activities–the one directly before yours and the one directly below yours.
- Continue to use the discussion board to ask your questions and look for answers to your questions. Others will often ask what you are thinking about. Also, feel free to answer each other's questions. Often people struggling through things have better answers than someone who is already an expert (the teacher).

Revision of our Initial Thinking BY TUESDAY@ MIDNIGHT
- Post your revision with comments about what you learned from this Module. This is when we get to make sure we learned and feel like we can use it in the future. So, let's pay special attention to this portion of the module in this course.

In addition to these changes in the structure of the modules, we also experimented with the time frame of the modules. Looking back to the two structures above, you can see that when we had only two phases we allotted a week for the initial thinking phase and a week for a discussion and revision. When we moved to three distinct phases, we continued the two-week time frame allowing approximately five days for each of the three phases. However, two weeks was a little too long to keep participants attention on a topic and dragged the term out to 14 weeks, thus we settled on ten-day modules, allowing approximately three days for each phase.

Finally on the issue of technology, we began with the assumption that our participants would appreciate being introduced and supported in their learning of varied technologies that they could bring back to their classrooms. Thus we incorporated several choices of technologies for the participants to use in sharing their thinking with the group. Although this assumption was based on our previous work with teachers, our participants were interested in learning mathematics to pass their Praxis exams, thus there was very little talk about technology and a large majority of them demonstrated that the technology was an added burden, not the gift we intended it to be. Thus, we have now minimized the technology in the introductory course to technology that is needed to facilitate the course online. We do have options for those who are interested in experiencing varied technologies, but it is no longer part of the requirements of the course, nor do we provide activities in which technologies would be useful.

Facilitation Changes

Our current working hypothesis in facilitation is that if we intervene early and often supporting participants in learning to take advantage of the supports, we can retain more participants in the early stages and return to our lesser-facilitated model as the cohort progresses, as this appears to be the determining factor for continued participation in the program.

In the initial thinking phase, we still request that the participants share their initial thinking on the activity blog in a private setting that they know will become public. However, rather than require the posting of an entire activity set, we ask that they post one problem at a time, so that we are more likely to have an initial post when we open them up for public discussion. They are then asked to use the "edit" button when they complete each successive part of the activity. In addition, we ask that participants ask any questions that would support their learning in the discussion board. In this way, we are able to create a public space for getting questions and answers posted. We will then suggest early and often that participants check the discussion boards for answers to their questions before posting their own. This will save the participants' time in getting their questions answered, which will mean that they spend less time being frustrated.

In the public discussion phase with our group of nonspecialists, we are faced with the issue of teachers not having enough confidence to address areas in which they are unclear. In other words, they are unwilling to challenge an answer they think is incorrect, because they aren't sure they know what they are talking about. Thus we have moved from more general suggestions to more specific sets of criteria within each module to assist our participants in analyzing each other's thinking. The first excerpt demonstrates an early set of instructions for looking at each other's work.

> The requirement for the second half of the module is that you reply to at least two of your colleagues on the discussion board and two of your colleagues in the activity blogs. Here's what we're looking for in the responses:
> - Questions about how other's thought about things, either for your own learning or to push them a little farther in their own thinking—for instance, "can you give me an example of when different variables would help you decide to use a different graph?"
> - Answers to others' questions or suggestions for how to think about things.
> - Things you notice and wonder about groups of posts—for instance, posts that are in conflict with each other or posts that agree, but someone takes it farther, etc.
> - In other words, this is a chance for us to push each other's learning. If all we say is "good job" or "I like your presentation" then we aren't really making the most out of our collective wisdom.

In the following excerpt, you can see the specific mathematics and the focus on language about which we are asking participants to think.

> From now until Friday evening, your task is to read/listen to three or four of your classmates' posts. Please make sure that you read the post directly before yours and the one directly after yours. When you read/listen to their posts, try to determine which language they used, choosing from the ones above, or describing them in some way.
> - Reading from LEFT to RIGHT
>   - "x squared plus one"
>   - "negative two x plus six"
>   - "x squared plus 2"
> - Main focus on OPERATIONS
>   - "the sum of x squared and 2"
>   - "the product of 5 and 4 raised to the x power"
> - Can you determine who the MAIN CHARACTER is of each of these sentence/phrases?
>   - "negative 2 times x"

- "x times negative 2"
- "x is being multiplied by negative 2"

Do you see that the last one makes x the subject or main character of the story with things happening to it?

With the revised guidelines, we focus on which representations are used, what underlying mathematics is present, or how consistent the language is, rather than trying to figure out if the answers are right or wrong, In this type of discussion, it is easier to have confidence while it allows the facilitators to orchestrate discussion around the fundamental mathematical topics of the course. Returning to the first excerpt, you can see that the instructions are so generic that you cannot even tell that they come from a mathematical course.

We have found several benefits to this new interaction. First, asking the participants to focus on the mathematics ensures that participants receive feedback that supports their learning in ways that the original responses did not, mathematically. Second, having to look critically at someone else's work supported the teachers in hearing and seeing the mathematics differently. They were often able to return to their own work thinking differently about the mathematics. This phenomenon often showed up in their focusing on different topics in their revisions for instance. Finally, this focus on the mathematics by the participants ensured that every participant received mathematical feedback without the facilitator having to spend the time doing so, creating a break through in the sustainability issue.

In the revision phase, which we have just begun to institute, we have chosen to focus on specific topics, often fewer than in the original work, supporting the learning of one or two significant mathematical moments that participants can achieve and about which they can feel confident.

Conclusion

In the Moving to Mathematics Program, we set out to provide access to valuable and sustainable teacher education in mathematics. Upon embarking on this task, we began with assumptions from our experiences in online learning from both the undergraduate and graduate classes at the School of Education as well as online professional development at Math Forum at Drexel University. We have taken advantage of the online setting, which captures all interactions associated with the course, to continuously assess our work in the program. We have analyzed the participation of the group as a whole as well as the participation of individuals, in how they took advantage or failed to take advantage of the supports offered in the program all with the reality of sustainability persistently on our minds. We have learned three distinct lessons from the implementation and analysis of the archives of our program. First, participants who came into the program taking advantage of the majority of the affordances of the mathematical collaboration remained in the program and succeeded in passing the certification exam; those who did not come into the program taking advantage of the mathematical collaboration did not learn how to do so naturally as a result of their participation in the Program despite seeing others do so. Second, to provide a sustainable professional learning community for continuing education of practitioners, we need to find a way to move from individualized expert feedback to mathematically specific feedback among the participants themselves. And third, to continue to improve the learning opportunities for practitioners, we need to continue to learn more about the ways in which participants learn from each others' work.

Within the persistent tension between providing expert facilitation to retain our participants early in the program, thereby addressing our first lesson, and creating a sustainable model that allows affordable replication for the ongoing professional learning experiences of practitioners in the field, rather than the level of full-time university courses for which individualized attention is the norm, our second lesson, we have experimented with moving from an expert-facilitation model to one of distributed expertise throughout the collaboration. In our attempt to move from the high-touch expert facilitation to distributed facilitation by the participants, we have found it necessary to provide explicit instruction around looking at each others' thinking, through both describing and modeling the process of looking at the mathematical thinking of others. We have experimented with creating specific guidelines of the mathematics to observe and model this process on a sample of the thinking in the public discussion area. In future implementations, we can create the models of providing mathematical feedback using the archive of thinking we are now collecting, thus only having to create the models once rather than once for each section of each iteration of the course. We believe the next challenge, for ourselves and the research and practitioner community, is to support participants in learning to take advantage of the supports of the online mathematical collaboration, which we believe can be done by providing more individualized expert feedback early in the program to make visible the value of the participation more quickly while working toward supporting participants in learning to provide specific mathematical feedback to each other and learning how to take advantage of the now improved interactions among themselves.

In addition to attending to the facilitation in the collaborative environment, there is much to be learned in looking at the ways the participants take advantage of the participation. After one iteration of the program, we have learned that the transition from face-to-face to online is not a straightforward one, but that the affordances of the online environment, which allow for asynchronous (flexible and ongoing) access to not only the course materials but also everyone's attempt at making meaning of the course materials, can be advantaged.

Throughout the Moving to Mathematics Program, we have begun to develop a model of online mathematics collaboration intended to deepen teachers' conceptual knowledge in ways that allow them to transfer this knowledge to the classrooms. We believe we have taken steps in the right direction by supporting participants in learning to take advantage of the collaborative model and continuing to work toward increasing the level of participation as early on in the program as possible. This makes the learning accessible to more teachers and makes the experiences of those who do participate a more valuable one, while maintaining a sustainable amount of facilitation that allows for scaling of professional development for teachers in need of mathematical content knowledge.

NOTES

1. All posts will be identified by the first or first two letters of the family name of the author of the post. Dates and times of posts are included when they are necessary for the point being made.

REFERENCES

Altbach, Philip G., Liz Reisberg, and Laura E. Rumbley. 2010. "Tracking a Global Academic Revolution." *Change: The Magazine of Higher Learning* 42 (2): 29–32.

Ball, Deborah L., and Hyman Bass. 2000. "Interweaving Content and Pedagogy in Teaching and Learning to Teach: Knowing and Using Mathematics." In *Multiple Perspectives on the Teaching and Learning of Mathematics,* ed. Jo Boaler, 83–104. Westport, CT: Ablex.

Ball, Deborah L., Heather. C. Hill, and Hyman Bass. 2005. "Knowing Mathematics for Teaching: Who Knows Mathematics Well Enough to Teach Third Grade, and How Can We Decide?" *American Educator* 29 (3): 14–22, 43–46.

Billingsley, Bonnie, Anna-Maria Fall, and Thomas Williams. 2006. "Who is Teaching Students with Emotional and Behavioral Disorders? A Profile and Comparison to Other Special Educators." *Behavioral Disorders* 31 (3): 252–264.

Blackboard. 2010–11. Drexel University Online Learning Management System. Available at: http://drexel.blackboard.com.

CEC (Council for Exceptional Children). n.d. *Policy on Academic Subject Matter Content of General Curriculum and Special Educators.* Arlington, VA: CEC Available online at: www.cec.sped.org.

Cobb, Paul, Michelle Stephan, Kay McClain, and Koeno Gravemeijer. 2001. "Participating in Classroom Mathematical Practices." *The Journal Of The Learning Sciences* 10 (1–2): 113–163.

Greer, Diana, and Edward Meyen. 2009. "Special Education Teacher Education: A Perspective on Content Knowledge." *Learning Disabilities Research & Practice.* 24 (4): 196–203.

Individuals with Disabilites Education Improvement Act of 2004. 2006. Pub. L. No. 108–446. § 118, Stat. 2647.

Lampert, Magdalene. 1990. "When the Problem Is Not the Question and the Solution Is Not the Answer: Mathematical Knowing and Teaching." *American Educational Research Journal* 27 (1): 29–63.

Ma, Liping. 1999. *Knowing and Teaching Elementary Mathematics: Teachers' Understanding of Fundamental Mathematics in China and the United States.* Mahwah, NJ: Lawrence Erlbaum Associates.

No Child Left Behind (NCLB) Act of 2001. 2002, Pub. L. No. 107–110, § 115, Stat. 1425.

Silverman, Jason, and Ellen Clay. 2010. "Towards A Model for Supporting Teachers Development of Mathematical Knowledge for Teaching in an Online Environment." In *Proceedings of Society for Information Technology & Teacher Education International Conference 2010,* ed. David Gibson and Bernie Dodge, 884–891. Chesapeake, VA: AACE.

Simon, Martin. 2006. "Key Developmental Understandings in Mathematics: A Direction for Investigating and Establishing Learning Goals." *Mathematical Thinking and Learning: An International Journal* 8 (4): 359–371.

Tinto, Vincent. 2006–2007. "Research and Practice of Student Retention: What Next?" *Journal of College Student Retention: Research, Theory and Practice* 8 (1): 1–19.

Wooten, Brent, and Thomas Hancock. 2009. "Online Learning Offers Flexibility and Convenience for Teacher Education." *Momentum* 40 (1): 28–31.

Yackel, Erna, and Paul Cobb. 1996. "Sociomathematical Norms, Argumentation, and Autonomy in Mathematics." *Journal for Research in Mathematics Education* 27 (4): 458–478.

Part III

Reaching Underserved Populations

Chapter 8

The International Negotiation Modules Project
Using Simulation to Enhance Teaching and Learning Strategies in the Community College

Rosalind Latiner Raby, Joyce P. Kaufman, and Greg Rabb

The International Negotiation Modules Project (INMP) uses the International Communications and Negotiations Simulations (ICONS) computer-assisted simulation as a tool to enhance learning and teaching strategies about international issues and negotiations across the community college curriculum. Simulation in this context is more than merely playing a game or participating in a predefined exercise. Rather, it encompasses the entire class structure and affects all learning modalities. Since its inception in 1995, over 50 community colleges and 115 classes have participated from colleges that represent both rural and urban areas across California, Florida, Hawaii, Illinois, Maryland, New York, and Texas, and a community college in Northern Thailand even participated on occasion. The unconventional pairing of disciplines, the nontraditional use of integrated technology, and the diverse student body all enhance the overall quality of the simulation and the direct learning experience for students. Combined, this improves the quality of instruction in the classroom. International issues that depict real-life negotiation strategies and that specifically highlight the needs of community college students underscore the cross-institutional character of this project. This chapter examines (a) INMP as a viable model for linking technology and internationalization of the curriculum, (b) how the INMP is an innovative approach to teaching and learning at the community college, and (c) noted links between the INMP and faculty development. At the foundation is the fact that the INMP recognizes that international issues are an integral part of every community college discipline, and that the task of internationalizing the curriculum not only can but *also* be infused in all areas of the college environment (Raby 1999).

Community Colleges

In the United States community colleges serve an essential educational function and role. Standing between compulsory education and the post-secondary sector, they provide the first two years of college along with occupational training and developmental studies. Over 1,200 publicly supported community colleges provide academic and career programs along with basic skills development and a variety of lifelong learning services to the community (AACC 2011). These institutions not only offer options for university overflow but also offer a "second chance" for nontraditional students to achieve a higher education (Cohen 2009).

Community colleges offer short-term semi- and professional terminal courses as well as an academic curriculum that results in an associate degree in arts or sciences, and in some cases, the means to transfer to four-year universities. The curriculum is more advanced than secondary school, but generally offers the first two years of a baccalaureate instruction. There are also an increasing number of community colleges that are offering practical baccalaureate degrees. Arthur Cohen and Florence Brawer (2003, 5) define community colleges to "include public and private comprehensive two-year colleges and technical institutions, but exclude vocational schools and adult education centers and proprietary business and trade colleges." The skills-based training that is needed to grow economic and social capital is the skill-set that community colleges provide. More than half of all adults in US post-secondary take classes at community colleges (AACC 2011), and for many the community college remains their sole venue for higher education. As a result, an internationalized curriculum becomes the only opportunity these students have to gain international literacy skills.

Historical Connections

In 1995, the INMP adapted the University of Maryland ICONS project specifically for the community college environment (ICONS 2010. ICONS was created in the 1970s to find ways to use the then-new Internet technology in undergraduate political science international relations classes. From the beginning, the INMP was designed to be distinct from ICONS. First, it was created to be multidisciplinary, so that it could easily fit into any academic, career, or lifelong learning community college program and not just into international relations classes. Second, it was designed for a different student population from the one that attended the University of Maryland or other universities that were the presumed audience for ICONS. Finally, over time, other changes, which will be described in this chapter, had to be introduced to solidify the relevance of INMP to the community college.

The incorporation of information technology as an intricate component of the community college learning experience is seen as a way to combine reading, writing, and comprehension literacy needed in work environments. The deliberate goal to include a range of disciplines is consistent with the belief that a truly educated citizen needs to understand that international issues intersect all aspects of local community life and that internationalization is a core component of post-secondary learning. In short, the INMP is proving that international issues are not the purview of any one part of the curriculum but should fit in all, and that community college students especially benefit from getting a better understanding of these issues. At the time this approach was adopted, it was novel (Kaufman 1998a). Seventeen years later, there are still no other similar pedagogical tools.

The adaption of the INMP to community colleges has at its root the acknowledgement and purposeful use of the nontraditional and often diverse student body. Community college students bring to the classroom backgrounds and skills that enrich the simulation experience in ways not seen with traditional undergraduate populations (Kaufman 1998a). Furthermore, a synergy exists between current community college computer literacy requirements, internationalizing initiatives, and the INMP, which inherently internationalizes any course in both structure and learning experience outcomes. The information technology that is learned as a result of the INMP experience therefore assists community college students in both the quest for higher education and in a direct application in the current job market.

In total, more than 6,300 students have participated in the program. Student ethnicity varies with college location, with many classes consisting exclusively of low-income students, students of color, and nontraditional students. Also, depending on the college, there can be a large percentage of immigrant and international students. Most students concurrently take classes and work at least five hours a week, and the average age of students remains in their late twenties, which is the norm for community colleges. Although problems can exist with the use of simulations, the benefits, especially in the case of the INMP, far outweigh the drawbacks.

Over the course of almost two decades, the INMP simulation has become an effective teaching tool because it engages students and makes them active participants in the learning process. It is equally important as an effective resource for faculty development (Kaufman 1998a; Raby 2006). Internationalization begins with an individual faculty member, for without faculty advocates, there is no one to teach an internationalized curriculum or take advantage of innovative curricular programs. Educating all individuals—be it student, teacher, staff, trustee, or administrator—is the foundation upon which effective international education reform exists.

INMP Description

INMP places students in the role of decision makers who represent different countries and who are asked to negotiate on real-world global issues. The issues are chosen by the participating faculty to fit within the range of classes in which the simulation will be a major component. Past community college classes include anthropology, business, communications, economics, education, engineering, English, ESL (English as a second language), French language, geography (physical and cultural), health, math, political science, psychology, public speaking, sociology, Texas government, women's studies, and world history. The nonconventional pairing of disciplines allows the students to develop an expertise and to formulate positions and negotiating strategies in unique ways. For example, while an economics class that represents one country may stress the financial flows related to a social problem, another country represented by a health class may stress the human interactions and health-related dangers that could result from the same social problems. Students in both classes need to interact by communicating online and then, through that process, understand interconnections and real-life applications while also learning the subject matter by application.

Faculty ownership of the program exists from the beginning and is a key component to overall success. Each year, participating faculty choose elements of the upcoming simulation including the "country" or nonstate actor that their class will represent and particular scenarios themes/issues. Country/actor selection is dependent upon personal interest, course content, and student composition. This match allows for the use of incorporating both international student and immigrant student populations as a resource.

Over 17 years of the simulation, it has become apparent that not all countries work equally well. Countries that in real life have little or only minimal connection with one another have difficulty in the simulation where negotiation is based largely on real-life issues. Therefore, even after the countries are chosen, fine-tuning may be needed with the faculty negotiating amongst themselves to arrive at a mix of countries that meet classroom and faculty needs, and will also be active participants.

The choice of having each class play a nation-state or a nonstate actor is a distinct variation from the original ICONS simulation that had classes play only nation-states. This variation was chosen so that a combination of voices will more accurately reflect the way in which international discourse currently exists and reinforces the fact that negotiations occur at many levels. Moreover, many community college classes can relate to NGOs that support their curriculum. Examples of INMP nonstate actors have been the European Union, Human Rights Watch, United Nations Development Fund for Women, and the World Health Organization.

Prior to each simulation the specific topics to be negotiated are chosen by the participating faculty. Three broad themes, which typically cross economic, sociopolitical, and humanitarian issues, are narrowed to specific topics that are relevant to the range of courses for that particular year. For example, under the general category of "Human Rights" the simulations have focused discussions on eliminating world hunger, mobility patterns and immigration, and child soldiers. Under "International Trade" discussions have addressed the global recession, updating the Bretton Woods model, and narco-terrorism. Finally, under "Environment" discussions have addressed updating and implementing the 1997 Kyoto agreement, water scarcity, and genetically modified food. Since the curriculum is set by each individual community college, no changes are made to the overall course. Rather, the challenge is finding ways to highlight the chosen topics of the simulation to directly support links to an existing curriculum. As the faculty prepare their classes, they share ideas with one another and the links between classes become apparent. The unique mark of INMP is that it has always been able to find intersections between a range of disciplines so that the themes are consistent, but the topics are new for each academic year (Raby 2006). New faculty often work with more experienced faculty mentors to help find links between the chosen issues and the existing curriculum.

The actual simulation includes a combination of student individual and group research, drafting written statements, oral class discussion, and then negotiating ideas via Internet using both synchronous and asynchronous communication. For many students, this combination of activities constitutes their first introduction to information technology specifically used for the purpose of research and academic communication. The preparation for the simulation typically lasts up to six weeks while the simulation, or online negotiation, itself runs for four weeks.

During the simulation, students engage in direct but moderated communication with their own teams during class time and with other teams via e-mail. Extreme care is taken to preserve the secrecy of personal information about all participants, even if multiple classes from any campus participated. The real identity of the "country players" is never revealed. At the conclusion of the simulation, there is one 90-minute online real-time "summit" on each of the three themes. This is especially challenging when participating colleges not only span the United States but also sometimes other countries. However, the testimony of the success of the INMP is that students participate in these "summits" even if they take placeoccur in the early morning or late evening hours because they are eager to have the opportunity to interact directly with their colleagues. For the remainder of the semester, the INMP faculty debrief by continuing to refer to the simulation in support of their course curriculum.

Internationalizing Community College Curriculum

It has long been understood that the ways in which curricula are constructed and offered greatly influence what students learn. Internationalizing the community college curriculum occurs through both on-campus programmatic changes and off-campus education abroad programs (Raby 2008). Efforts to internationalize the on-campus curriculum infuse cross-cultural concepts, theories, and patterns of interrelationships into class content. A basic principle of internationalizing curricula is the acquisition of skills to perceive multiple perspectives, reconcile conflicting ideologies, and respect relative differences (Harari 1989; Edwards and Tonkin 1990). This is what Madeline Green (2007) refers to as an "international mind-set" and what Holly Emert and Diane Pearson (2007) refer to as an "intercultural mind-set and skills-set." To achieve this literacy, curricula must include more than just a simple awareness of basic cultural traits or geographic locales, for it needs to provide a context for active learning in which people begin to think in international and intercultural terms; where differences in response can be anticipated and understood merely as differences and not as right and wrong reactions; where one is constantly conscious of the different meanings and interpretations of the same words and expressions by people whose minds are conditioned by other languages. (Bhatia 1985, 1)

Thus, when a student or faculty is able to change their focus, behavior is altered, which influences what and how learning occurs. Individuals start saying things such as: "I never thought of that," or "I never knew I could apply it that way" (Fersh 1993, 7).

All community college disciplines (academic, technical, vocational, and occupational) are influenced by international relationships and therefore, *no* discipline is so provincial that it cannot be viewed from an international perspective. Courses with a comparative focus or those that address cross-border issues are believed to be *easily* internationalized and are the ones that are most often targeted by faculty (King and Fersh 1992). The reality is that internationalization of all disciplines only requires a simple introduction of new ways of viewing course content (Raby 2000). The INMP illustrates how fundamental internationalization is for all subjects.

The basics of community college internationalizing curriculum show a clear connection to the intent of this volume. Pedagogically, it is indefensible to not prepare any student to live, work, and transact in our global world. A college without an internationalized curricula is one that cannot prepare students adequately and hence does not meet a basic mandate of the community college that is to be student focused. Equally important is the fact that the community college remains, for many, the only means to acquire international literacy skills. Yet, despite three decades of effort, this form of pedagogy remains at the periphery of the institution and the level of internationalization remains "low" (ACIIE/Stanley Foundation 1996; Green and Siaya 2005; Green 2007). Moreover, the barriers to reform, which include leadership, faculty engagement, and economic choice, are well-known and still have not been fully addressed (Green 2007; Raby 2008). Hence, there remains a need for administrators, faculty, and students to embrace a philosophical shift that supports development opportunities to learn that there is more than one way to view and therefore teach a particular subject.

Methodology

Because the INMP was initially created by a grant from the Fund for the Improvement of Post-secondary Education of the Department of Education, the program was evaluated extensively during its first three years

(1995–1998). Qualitative and quantitative evaluation stressed student-learning outcomes. Part of the evaluation also included faculty evaluation of their own professional growth. Since 1998, no additional formal evaluation has been conducted.

However, since 1999, an informal focus group has been included as part of the annual fall semester faculty training workshop. Directed questions on issues of success, faculty pedagogical change and self-assessment, are traditional student learning outcomes and assessment are posed to each returning group of faculty. These informal focus groups are facilitated by Drs. Joyce Kaufman and Rosalind Latiner Raby who seek to encourage discussion among participants and record emerging opinions and feelings alongside descriptions of individual experiences. These discussions are used to chart educational reform to the INMP and to keep it current and relevant to the changing needs of community colleges.

Finally, in 2004, veteran faculty members were invited to help develop a set of learning objectives for the program. As part of this process, basic elements of evaluation, both traditional and nontraditional, were developed. Subsequent faculty participants have been encouraged to utilize these evaluative techniques within their own classes and to send to Drs. Kaufman and Raby summaries of their evaluations of student learning.

The formal evaluations conducted from 1995 to 1998, the informal evaluations from 1999 to 2011, and the directed student success emphasis from 2005 to 2011, have all consistently confirmed development of faculty pedagogy and student learning. Moreover, the contemporary evaluations are surprisingly similar to the formal evaluations of the late 1990s in that INMP students (a) learn and retain more than students in "traditional" classes, (b) substantially increase their knowledge of the issues and recognize relationships between abstract and concrete concepts that were central to discussions (not just concepts in one area such as economics or human rights), (c) are highly involved in the decision-making process and believe that they have contributed cognitively to it, (d) develop critical thinking skills, and (e) participate more fully in class (Torney-Purta and Pavlov 1998; Raby 2006).

Contemporary Pedagogical Contributions

The INMP has a particular effect on the construction of knowledge, which reinforces the notion that when students are directly engaged in their learning, they internalize a new vision of knowledge. The INMP, in particular, makes group work and discussion a central part of the program and is extremely effective for constructing knowledge among community college students who often need nontraditional approaches to learning for their success. The INMP is also a valuable conduit for internationalization of the curriculum as well as for directed professional development. There are three contexts in which these contributions will be discussed: (a) INMP as a viable model for linking technology and internationalization of the curriculum, (b) how INMP is an innovative approach to teaching and learning at the community college, and (c) noted links between INMP and faculty development.

Linking Technology and Internationalization of the Curriculum

At the foundation of INMP has always been integration of computer technology across the curriculum as a tool for research and communication. A critical programmatic objective is to enhance computer literacy in a way that is not intrusive but rather supportive of larger educational goals. In this way, students take charge of technology in the learning process, rather than to have technology control the student (Raby 2000). Realization that computer literacy is an important skill for both college-bound and work-oriented students continues to strengthen technology as an integral aspect of the curriculum and learning experience.

Time has not lessened the need for, nor the impact of, the integration of computer technology into a range of courses. Indeed, the growth of the INMP parallels the escalating use of technology and computer-assisted communication within post-secondary education around the world (Lim 2004; Shakirova 2007). During the first decade of the INMP application, community colleges that had the most successful experiences were those with the easiest access to technology; conversely, the greatest frustration levels were experienced by those faculty and students whose access to the technology was blocked or limited. Indeed, from 1995 to around 2005, technology was a scarce resource at many community colleges. Early faculty participants had to compete with colleagues outside their department and sometimes with their own departmental colleagues for computer time/access. What emerged was a "zero-sum" situation, in which a promise of limited resources to one faculty essentially denied it to others (Raby and Kaufman 2000). Students of this era had limited if any experiences with their own technology skills (Gorard and Selwyn 1999), and that was confirmed among INMP students as well, who more often represented low-income students. Especially during the first decade of this program, few community college students had personal computers, and personal Internet use was even less common. Hence, for many students, this instruction was among their first introduction to a field that has since become the norm.

Since 2005, increased access to and the growing sophistication of technology have made resource competition and overall access obsolete on the whole. Yet, despite increased access, evidence of a digital divide still exists in higher education (Eynon 2009). In the community college, there remain few classes that purposely integrate technology into the curriculum despite the plethora of technology applications in our daily lives. Even veteran INMP faculty report limited application of technology beyond their INMP class section. Only one INMP faculty noted inclusion of integrated technology into the teaching of all classes because of the INMP experience (Faculty Evaluation, Butte College, CA 2000).

The benefit of INMP is that it continually focuses faculty on finding ways to encourage students to use the Internet, and in recent years, to use various forms of social media, as a directed tool for their work. Most importantly, INMP validates that technological innovations introduced into the classroom must have a context, for introducing the use of technology is not sufficient unless it can be tied into and used to support the substance of the course. Although the computer software gives students the tools for research and negotiation, it remains the learning that takes place within the context of substance that shows growth and academic success. At a discussion at the November 2010 INMP faculty development workshop, faculty confirmed that technology skills learned in INMP can easily be applied in other classes and even in the work place. Thus, technology becomes an important tool specifically used to support other areas of the students' lives.

Innovative Approach to Teaching and Learning

The INMP focuses on four approaches that are interconnected in the learning process. The continued popularity of the INMP correlates with the now confirmed recognition in education that the individual student constructs his or her own knowledge (Wilkenfeld and Kaufman 1993; Torney-Purta 1996). An important aspect of the method of knowledge construction is that a student often enters a class with preconceived knowledge. It is only through active processing of new cognitive structures that this knowledge takes new meaning and becomes ingrained as part of the student's consciousness (Torney-Purta and Pavlov 1999). Through this process, INMP has proven that international issues are an integral part of every community college discipline, and that the curriculum not only can but also be internationalized in all areas of the college environment (Raby 1999).

Acquire Factual Knowledge and Develop Critical Thinking Skills

Initially, students learn about the country that they represent and that country's position on particular international issues. Later, students learn about the same issues from other countries' perspectives, so that they could negotiate in a realistic fashion (Kaufman 1998b; Torney-Purta and Pavlov 1998). It is clear from the ability of community college students to participate in INMP that this objective continues to be met in each and every course.

> I've come to realize that the Business section of the LA Times is not so boring after all and is actually very interesting. I have been able to carry intelligent conversations with my own opinions when talking about the pros and cons of open trade, NAFTA and GATT. (Student Evaluation, Mt. San Antonio College, CA 1997)

> The process of reading articles about the Middle East and any article pertaining to the countries involved in the INMP have created an outstanding discussion in class. Plus, I was able to explain Persuasive Theory with respect to the speeches, et cetera from the US or other countries using today's news as examples. And they got it! (Faculty Evaluation, College of Sequoias, CA 2011)

At the conclusion of INMP, during the debriefing stage, the students analyze and assess the experience, applying their "hands-on" experience to the theories that they had studied in class. Consistently, evaluation indicates that new knowledge acquisition and critical analysis did occur in the classroom.

Illustrate Interconnections among Issues, Develop a Global Perspective, and Enhance Understanding of Cultural Differences

On the cognitive level, the nature of the representation of knowledge is enhanced as students assess connections between concepts and with acquisition of new knowledge, these linkages become more numerous and significantly stronger. The realization that decisions cannot be made in isolation as well as the global influences across disciplines not only changes students' perceptions but also affects the manner in which they look at other students and members of their community (Kaufman 1998b). Indeed, student evaluations over the decades consistently include statements that students learned through INMP to appreciate the differences between cultures and to view their local and global communities differently. Moreover, participating international and immigrant students note how welcome their experiences are in allowing classmates to gain new skills and how the experiences has fostered self-esteem skills. Even when students were not officially enrolled in the class, many former INMP students become "advisors," helping the members of the class understand more fully the country, culture, and context that they were representing. A South Korean international student wrote: "Through this experience I really felt that I could offer a little of the problems that South Korea faces as well as the world" (Student Evaluation, Long Beach College, CA 1998).

> I learned that each country had its own way of making themselves powerful and using that source to negotiate with other countries. What was interesting was the smaller countries still had a lot to offer, and in some cases the smaller countries were more powerful than the larger countries. (Student Evaluation, West Los Angeles College, CA 2005)

Throughout the decades, student evaluations indicate evidence of the students' changing perspectives as a result of the INMP.

Foster Communication Skills That Can Be Applied in the Context of Real-World Interactions

Understanding policy decisions, how decisions are generated, and how students can use these decisions to support their own negotiation strategies occurs on different levels throughout a simulation (Farrelly et al. 1999). Such collaboration ceases to exist without effective communication. In the INMP, on the individual level, students communicate their own ideas to other students within the same class. Students first negotiate within their own study groups and then within their own class team to arrive at a single cohesive position. They then negotiate with teams from other classes to achieve INMP goals. Situations in which students move back and forth between written and oral expressions are of special value in the process of knowledge construction. INMP encourages both modes; written messages sent during the simulation and face-to-face group discussion within their own teams.

> I learned how to work together as a group to set our goals and to deal with [those goals] with other trading partners. (Student Evaluation, East Los Angeles College, CA 2002)
>
> The most valuable part of this experiment is allowing me to express my opinions on different issues and to hear the view points from other students. Many students had different viewpoints that help us think and challenge us. Education involves communication. Without communication, being educated is useless. (Student Evaluation, Jamestown College, NY 2004)
>
> I do believe that role-playing allowed a particular student to reach further capabilities in herself that she had not explored (with the first thing being confidence!). (Faculty Evaluation, College of Sequoias, CA 2011)

Those negotiation and communication skills learned as a result of the INMP are invaluable when applied in the work place, as part of further schooling, or at home.

Acquire Skills That Can Be Used in the Workplace

The INMP was structured so that students were required to work together in groups to solve real-world problems and apply in practice ideas that they learn in theory. During the simulation, they also develop a familiarity and comfort level with global economic issues and a context within which they can address such issues in the workplace. The comments of the students themselves identify the level of success in achieving this objective:

> I guess I can say that from this project, I learned a little about life. That is, the value of being prepared. (Student Evaluation, Butte College, CA 1998)

> I learned some economic concepts and business details. It really helped me to develop my knowledge, especially [since] my major is business. (Student Evaluation, Los Angeles Pierce College, CA 2000)

> This activity opened my eyes to a new "economic" perspective that I had never paid attention to before. I was also introduced to the Asian way of thinking that is valuable knowledge if one is to live in a truly global community. (Student Evaluation, Leeward College, HI 2006)

> The confidence gained by one of my students helped her become promoted to Manager of the local Starbucks. (Faculty Evaluation, College of Sequoias, CA 2011)

INMP and Faculty Development

INMP emphasizes active and cooperative learning for participating faculty members. Faculty members choose which countries their classes represent, help choose the simulation topics, and are active participants in both altering their curriculum and teaching methods. Success includes the ability to look at a class from a new and often different perspective and to be open to new ways in which to teach that class. For example, a class on anger and conflict management (Faculty Evaluation, Cañada College, CA 1997) changed from a microlevel focus on the individual to also include a macrolevel focus of individuals at the international level, and how negotiation can be an important conflict resolution tool at any level. An English professor (Faculty Evaluation, Los Angeles Valley College, CA 1999) initially had opposition from students who could not understand how the INMP could help improve their writing and grammar skills. Yet, at the conclusion of the class, they, along with the faculty, noted that they were doing more research, writing, and analysis than they would have been expected to do otherwise in a more traditional introductory English class. Finally, an engineering faculty member who was initially resistant to international applications of course concepts, enthusiastically found a commonality in "the foundation of building bridges that remains the same across nations" for the introductory engineering class (Faculty Evaluation, Mission College, CA 2009).

Teaching methodologies are positively affected by the INMP as faculty members assume the role of facilitator while students become directly involved in and responsible for their own learning. Although not initially comfortable for all faculty members, many learn to love allowing their students to take responsibility for their education (Faculty Evaluation, Leeward College, HI 2008). The use of collaborative groups facilitates this process, as students need to work together to do research and to draw and act upon conclusions. Resulting interactions are similar to other technological forums where "discussions arose a passionate determination to create a technology infused environment where students actively engage in their learning. And collaboration, we knew, would have to be a big part of the equation" (McCombs 2010, 11). Similar transitions of faculty learning to teach a familiar subject differently is not limited to US community colleges (Chesney and Marcangelo 2010).

Significant alteration to the way in which faculty teach as well as what they teach is an inherent part of the INMP. Faculty keep the structure of their course and content the same but need to modify their course to allow the INMP to support the subject content and to encourage students to participate in a way that is not typically conducted. Each faculty begins with internal revision of their curriculum and pedagogy. For some, these revisions are consistent with what they had been doing and require minor modifications beyond simply incorporating the scenario. For others, however, INMP is a radical departure that requires major rethinking of their classes.

> I teach Texas State and Local Government and had to work very hard to demonstrate to students links between global issues and our state. The experience turned out to be a great learning challenge for me and them ... I now teach the course very differently in order to stress to the students the importance of understanding that there is often a direct impact of national and international policies on the state of Texas, a linkage that students had not been making previously. (Faculty Evaluation, Austin College, TX 1998)

It is important to note that not all faculty members enjoy INMP. However, the vast majority of faculty members return for a second term and often remain for multiple years. As faculty stay with the program, they become very committed to internationalization of the curriculum. Many acknowledge that INMP has impacted how they teach their other courses as well (Kaufman 1998b; Torney-Purta and Pavlov 1999; Faculty Evaluations, Annual Workshop 2010).

A unique situation occurred in 2011 when the first education abroad program became part of INMP. INMP was introduced into a political science class that was part of a community college semester education abroad program in Italy. Issues unique to education abroad complicated and enhanced the INMP experience and ended positively.

> My students are feeling a bit confused and overwhelmed. Part of the problem is that they're scampering off to distant capitals every weekend. They're also on information overload as they try to process all the usual IR theory and prep for the simulation within the shortened, 12 week semester (Faculty Evaluation: Santa Rosa College, CA 2011).

Despite the concerns, the fact that the students represented Italy, which was where the students were studying, allowed them to view the country in a different and more complete way. The immigration issue was particularly timely given Italy's current dilemmas in dealing with the flood of refugees from North Africa. Students commented that it was easier for them to role play, since they were residing in the country they represented and had a greater motivation to follow the local news coverage of unfolding events (Faculty Evaluation: Santa Rosa College, CA 2011). This college will include INMP again in their education abroad program next year.

Challenges

Annual orientation and evaluation workshops are conducted by INMP staff for participating faculty to help them reflect upon what transpired during the previous year and to plan for subsequent years, incorporating changes as necessary. For example, how to address the problems of limited access to technology, class expectations that were unclear to students, and nontraditional class structure were concerns echoed in the early years that were not noted as problems subsequently (Kaufman 1998b). However, three challenges remain consistent across the decades. Since these challenges are known, they are addressed during the workshops, so that faculty can be informed and hence work to overcome these challenges.

First is a need to keep students enrolled in the class and prevent a large attrition due to the fact that the course is so different from what students normally expect. This is especially important in our economically challenging times when student enrollment is critical. Although some faculty feel that a larger-than-normal number of students drop the INMP class, all agree that those who stay are more committed and excited about what they are learning: "Because of the workload, I have had nine students drop the class so far. Unfortunately, I was too honest at the start in telling them we had a lot of work to do right away and I scared them! The students still involved in the course have become, how can I say this, 'immersed' in their assignment!" (Faculty Evaluation, College of Sequoias, CA 2011). Yet, another faculty member that same year noted, "a higher retention rate than would otherwise exist because in my college, INMP has been offered for years and students choose the section because of the INMP experience" (Faculty Evaluation, Jamestown College, NY 2011). In the nearly two decades of offering INMP, the only complete failure was the introduction of INMP in 2011 into a remedial English class in which students were two years below basic skills. Although INMP has worked very well in high-level ESL classes, the students at this level just could not read nor write well enough to communicate throughout the simulation process.

The second challenge concerns assessment of student performances. In this era of student outcomes and learning assessment, documentation of student performance is critical. Some traditional assessment techniques in recent years include pre/posttests (Faculty Evaluation, Jamestown College, NY 2008), portfolios (Faculty Evaluation, Sacramento City College, CA 2008), position/research papers (Faculty Evaluation, Ohlone College, CA 2010), and oral presentations (Faculty Evaluation, Brevard College, FL 2008).

However, INMP is difficult to assess using strictly traditional means. Hence, faculty have to make a concerted effort to determine how best to evaluate student learning in this nontraditional setting. Many faculty share anecdotal evaluations at the annual workshop that provide best practices on how to assess issues that are unique to institution/class and to highlight particular achievements. Some nontraditional benefits are ongoing communication with students from the "Mainland" (Faculty Evaluation, Leeward College, HI 2003), ongoing communication with students from areas outside of the rural community in which the college resides (Faculty Evaluation, Jamestown College, NY 2011), and the acquisition of leadership skills among a largely minority, poor student body (Faculty Evaluation, Austin College, TX 2005).

The final challenge is that there needs to be initial faculty interest in internationalizing the curriculum and ongoing administrative support. The current economic crisis has polarized faculty into trying to protect their own areas (Sutin et. al 2011). As a result, unless it comes from "top down," little interest and even less economic support is given to internationalization of curriculum despite the fact that such changes are occurring on a widespread basis at the university level. This weakness at the community college level is seen in many ways. First, interested faculty members have difficulty convincing their departments and colleges to allow participation in the INMP program. Second, there is little institutionalization of international efforts across the curriculum. If adopted, it typically represents an individual faculty interest. Finally, although many INMP faculty have been participating for over a decade, few have convinced colleagues at their college to also participate. Hence, when these faculty retire, all-too-often, so does INMP at that campus.

Conclusion

There is now a history that is almost two decades long in which INMP continues to be an innovative approach to teaching and learning at the community college. This program significantly alters community college curriculum by adding an international dimension across a range of disciplines and in reforming teaching methodologies, curriculum design, and enhancing computer literacy..

As implemented in the community colleges, INMP takes advantage of the nontraditional nature of the learners and their special skills and interests. It incorporates significant advances to a proven simulation program by developing negotiation scenarios appropriate to applied areas of international discourse. It expands the ways in which technology is used across the curriculum and alters significantly the ways in which faculty members teach. Both students and faculty members who participate in the INMP benefit from the experience academically and personally. Finally, in that the INMP blends together an emphasis on raising technology and international literacy skills, it fulfills an important need for contemporary community colleges' missions.

References

AACC (American Association of Community Colleges). 2011. *AACC Homepage.* Washington, DC: AACC. Available online at: http://www.aacc.nche.edu.

ACIIE/Stanley Foundation. 1996. *Retreat Educating for the Global Community: A Framework for Community Colleges.* Muscatine, IA: Stanley Foundation Publications.

Bhatia, Vishnu Narain. 1985. "The Use of the Curriculum in Internationalizing the University," *Journal of the AIERA* Spring 5 (1): 1–10.

Chesney, Sarah, and Caroline Marcangelo. 2010. "'There was a Lot of Learning Going On' Using a Digital Medium to Support Learning in a Professional Course for New HE Lecturers." *Computers & Education* 54 (3): 701–710.

Cohen, Arthur M. 2009. "Community Colleges in the United States." In *Community College Models: Globalization and Higher Education Reform*, ed. Rosalind Latiner Raby and Edward J. Valeau 39–48. Dordrecht, The Netherlands: Springer.

Cohen, Arthur M., and Florence B. Brawer. 2003. *The American Community College.* 4th ed. San Francisco: Jossey-Bass.

Edwards, Jane, and Humphrey R. Tonkin. 1990. "Internationalizing the Community College: Strategies for the Classroom." *New Directions for Community Colleges* 1990 (70): 17–26.

Emert, Holly A., and Diane L. Pearson. 2007. "Expanding the Vision of International Education: Collaboration, Assessment, and Intercultural Development." *New Directions In Community College Series* 2007 (138): 67–75.

Eynon, Rebecca. 2009. "Mapping the Digital Divide in Britain: Implications for Learning and Education." *Learning, Media and Technology* 34 (4): 277–290.

Farrelly, Francis, Sally Joy, and Sandra Luxton. 1999. "Marketing Theory and Practice On-Line: A Development Towards International Collaboration." *Higher Education in Europe* XXIV (2): 287–295.

Fersh, Seymour. 1993. *Integrating the Trans-National/Cultural Dimension (Fastback # 361: No. 104)*, Bloomington, IN: Phi Delta Kappa Educational Foundation.

Gorard, Stephen, and Neil Selwyn. 1999 "Switching on the Learning Society? Questioning the Role of Technology in Widening Participation in Lifelong Learning." *Journal of Education Policy* 14 (5): 523–535.

Green, Madeline F. 2007. "Internationalizing Community Colleges: Barriers and Strategies." *New Directions In Community College Series* 2007 (138): 15–24.

Green Madeline F., and Laura Siaya. 2005. *Measuring Internationalization at Community Colleges.* Washington, DC: American Council on Education.

Harari, Maurice. 1989. *Internationalization of Higher Education: Effecting Institutional Change in the Curriculum and Campus Ethos,* Occasional Report Series on the Internationalization of Higher Education, Report No. 1. Long Beach, CA: Center for International Education, California State University, Long Beach.

ICONS. 2010. *ICONS Home Page.* College Park, MD: Center for International Development and Conflict Management Department of Government and Politics, University of Maryland. Available online at http://www.icons.umd. edu.

Kaufman, Joyce P. 1998a. "Using Simulation as a Tool to Teach About International Negotiation." *International Negotiation* 3 (1): 59–75.

Kaufman, Joyce P. 1998b. *The International Negotiation Modules Project: Integrating International Simulation into the Community College*. Fund for the Improvement of Postsecondary Education (FIPSE) Grant Final Report. Whittier, CA: Political Science Department, Whittier College.

King, Maxwell C., and Seymour H. Fersh. 1992. *Integrating the International/ Intercultural Dimension in the Community College*. Cocoa, FL: Association of Community College Trustees and Community Colleges for International Development, Inc.

Lim, Cher Ping. 2004. "Engaging Learners in Online Learning Environments." *TechTrends* 48 (4): 16–23.

McCombs, Brenda. 2010. "Culture of Collaboration." *Learning & Leading with Technology* 38 (3): 10–13.

Raby, Rosalind Latiner. 1999. *Looking to the Future: Report on International and Global Education in California Community Colleges*. Sacramento: State Chancellor, California Community Colleges.

Raby, Rosalind Latiner. 2000. "Navigating the Digital Divide: Using Technology to Internationalize Community College Curricula." *International Journal of Educational Policy Research and Practice* 1 (3): 389–404.

Raby, Rosalind Latiner. 2006. "Using Technology to Internationalize the Community College Curriculum." *IIE International Networker*. New York: IIE Publications.

Raby, Rosalind Latiner. 2008. *Expanding Education Abroad at U.S. Community Colleges*. IIE Study Abroad White Paper Series, Issue No. 3, September 2008. New York: Institute for International Education Press.

Raby, Rosalind Latiner, and Joyce Kaufman. 2000. "The International Negotiation Modules Project: Using Computer-Assisted Simulation to Enhance Teaching and Learning Strategies in the Community College." In *Cases of Information Technology in Higher Education*, ed. Lisa Ann Petrides. Hershey, PA: Idea Group Publishing.

Shakirova, D. M. 2007. "Technology for the Shaping of College Students' and Upper-Grade Students' Critical Thinking." *Russian Education & Society* 49 (9): 42–52.

Sutin, Stewart E., Daniel Derrico, Rosalind Latiner Raby, and Edward J. Valeau, eds. 2011. *Increasing Effectiveness of the Community College Financial Model: A Global Perspective for the Global Economy*. New York: Palgrave Publishers.

Torney-Purta, Judith. 1996. "Conceptual Changes Among Adolescents Using Computer-Networks in Group Mediated International Role Playing." In *International Perspectives on the Design of Technology Supported Learning Environments*, ed. S. Vosniadou . Hillsdale, NJ: Erlbaum.

Torney-Purta, Judith, and Vladimir Pavlov. 1998. *Evaluation Report: International Negotiations Modules Project: Integrating International Simulation in the Community College*. FIPSE Grant Final Report. Baltimore: University of Maryland.

Wilkenfeld, Jonathan, and Joyce Kaufman. 1993. "Political Science: Network Simulation in International Politics." *Social Science Computer Review* 11 (4): 464–476.

List of Qualitative Sources

Faculty Evaluations (From INMP faculty reports 1997–2011): Cañada College, CA 1997; Austin College, TX 1998; Los Angeles Valley College, CA 1999; Butte College, CA 2000; Los Angeles Pierce College, CA 2000; Leeward College, HI 2003; Jamestown College, NY 2004; Austin College, TX 2005; Leeward College, HI 2006; Brevard College, FL 2008; Jamestown College, NY 2008; Leeward College, HI 2008; Sacramento City College, CA 2008; Mission College, CA 2009; Annual Workshop 2010; Ohlone College, CA 2010; College of Sequoias, CA 2011; Jamestown College, NY 2011; Santa Rosa College, CA 2011.

Faculty Focus Group Evaluations from November 2009 and November 2010 Workshops at Whittier College, CA.

Student Evaluations (from INMP faculty reports 1997–2006): Mt. San Antonio College, CA 1997; Butte College, CA 1998; Long Beach College, CA 1998; Los Angeles Pierce College, CA 2000; East Los Angeles College, CA 2002; Jamestown College, NY 2004; West Los Angeles College, CA 2005; Leeward College, HI 2006.

Chapter 9

Using ICT as a Vehicle for Nonformal Learning and Women's Empowerment in Rural Tanzania

Dorothy Ettling and Maria E. Marquise

According to the United Nations Development Fund for Women (UNIFEM), women's empowerment is "gaining the ability to generate choices and exercise bargaining power, developing a sense of worth, a belief in one's ability to secure desired changes and the right to control one's life" (Cheston and Kuhn 2005, 12). It is well recognized that empowerment of women is an important key to opening the new doors of development in any society. Women's ability to influence or make decisions that affect their lives and their futures is considered to be one of the principal components of empowerment by most scholars (Cheston and Kuhn 2005). However, empowerment is a challenging process. Susy Cheston and Lisa Kuhn (2005) state, "In order for a woman to be empowered, she needs access to the material, human, and social resources necessary to make strategic choices in her life. Not only have women been historically disadvantaged in access to material resources like credit, property, and money, but they have also been excluded from social resources like education or insider knowledge of some businesses" (12).

Utilizing information and communication technology (ICT) is a major source of new education and insider knowledge and can be a catalyst for women's empowerment. In discussing the role of education in development activities, Jane Parpart (2000) contends that control over knowledge is often an essential element of local power structures. It reinforces local hierarchies and is often highly gendered. Participatory methods, with their stress on inclusiveness and voice, threaten this hierarchy of control over knowledge. Many existing technologies have the potential to benefit women but, for a host of reasons, have never been embraced or adopted. Thus, developing and distributing technologies that meet women's needs must focus on key steps of the process that carry the technology from conception through use and widespread adoption in the field (Gill et al. 2010). There are surprisingly few documented examples of game-changing technologies for women. More research is needed to assess successes and failures and identify promising practices to inform other efforts to reach women with technologies (Gill et al. 2010).

The International Center for Research on Women notes, "The potential to advance women economically may be the most exciting transformative feature of technology" (Gill et al. 2010, 7). This chapter presents the process and the fruits of a web-based dialogue among rural women in Africa and the United States. The dialogue was initiated in 2003 as a means of cross-cultural exchange and expanding leadership capacities. It grew over the years into a significant opportunity not only for the sharing of ideas but also as a locus for evidence of personal and social empowerment in the women's lives.

Background

Women's Global Connection (WGC), a nonprofit organization formed in the United States, collaborates with women's cooperatives in Tanzania, Zambia, Peru, and the United States. WGC's intention is to promote the learning and leadership of women through capacity-building activities that assist them in addressing economic development and social issues in their communities. Amartya Sen (1992, 49) first articulated the idea of empowerment in relation to capacity building, stating "capability is primarily a reflection of the freedom to achieve valuable functionings." Martha Nussbaum (2003, 11) furthered this concept by claiming that women's "capacities to function" were women's "rights." The capability approach requires that we address human development not simply as abstract ideas but as lived capacities at the level of everyday life. This approach focuses on what each and every person is able to do and be, their "valuable doings and beings," in making meaningful choices from a range of options, hence, having the freedom to choose a life they have reason to value (Walker 2005).

Three essential pillars have supported all of WGC's collaborative processes of capacity building: local ownership, social empowerment, and sustainability. These served as benchmarks for WGC when working with

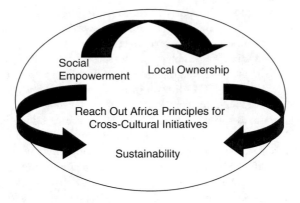

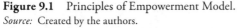

Figure 9.1 Principles of Empowerment Model.
Source: Created by the authors.

the women and are the foundation for a model of personal and social empowerment that has emerged over the years. It is pictured like this (see Figure 9.1).

Local ownership assures that women, in particular, gain access to resources, claim their power, and shape their own lives. In-country participants are expected to be active partners in planning and implementing activities that are culturally sensitive.

Social empowerment requires that participants are able to replicate the capacity building activities with others.

Sustainability insists that each of the initiated projects can be viable and sustainable into the future without WGC presence. Emphasis is put on developing local and national networks that strengthen the project's long-term survival. These pillars offered a reality check for the collaboration, when projects were envisioned that surpassed the scope or the support of the local partners. They remain important touchstones.

Through on-site immersion trips and web-based dialogues, WGC created lasting partnerships with women from Bukoba, Tanzania; Mongu, Zambia; and San Antonio and Houston, Texas. In each of these four locations, WGC collaborated with women who struggled with the effects of poverty but wanted to change their lives and their communities through capacity building for personal empowerment and economic development. As part of their goal, they chose to engage in a supportive web-based dialogue with women from other cultures. The Cross Cultural Dialogue was initiated in 2003 when the WGC director visited Bukoba, Tanzania, and Mongu, Zambia, and invited two small groups of women to engage in a leadership program through facilitated discussion on WGC's interactive website. None of the women had ever used a computer or typed messages. English was a second language for all of them, and they communicated daily in their native language. Yet they were eager to learn the new technology and invest in this dialogue. The intention was simply to share aspects of their lives with other women and in the process strengthen their own leadership capacity. Over a period of three days, the WGC director introduced them to the computer in a small Internet café with one computer, and within a short time, they were exchanging messages and beginning what would become a long-term relationship. That first year's dialogue was facilitated by a WGC team member from the United States. Obviously only a small group of women from each country participated, but they gained much from the interaction and shared the fruits of their experience with other women in their local area. This dialogue offered the humble beginnings of being connected globally and continues to this day with over 1,500 postings.

During that first year, the dialogue gradually broadened to include planning for the WGC immersion trip. At the end of that year, five women from the dialogue participated in an international conference in San Antonio. Three women from Zambia and two women from Tanzania interacted with women from over 30 different countries. By this time, there was a deepened sense of collaboration, nurtured through regular communication. More women in Mongu and Bukoba were introduced to computers. Interaction with WGC staff and volunteers was a means of ongoing support and accountability as well a source of new information. This chapter documents the women's perception of personal and group change by presenting quotes from the web-based blog at www.womensglobalconnection.org. The voices of the women are highlighted within the context of a theory on technology innovation and several theories on women's empowerment. Qualitative software (NVivo 9) was utilized in analyzing the data and minor grammatical and punctuation edits were added to facilitate reading.

Women's Voices through an ICT Lens

Everett Rogers has formulated a conceptual theory of "diffusion of innovation" (Richardson 2010). In it, he explains five characteristics necessary for an innovation to be accepted and useful in a new environment: (a) relative advantage (degree to which the innovation is perceived as a better idea), (b) compatibility (degree of consistency with one's experiences and needs), (c) complexity (perceived difficulty with using the innovation), (d) observability (degree to which one can see results using the innovation), and (e) trialability (degree to which the innovation can be practiced). Using

Rogers's characteristics as a lens, one can examine the ongoing dialogue of the women in the WGC blog to search for evidence of their perceptions of web-based technology as a valuable tool for personal and social impact. Rogers also identifies ways new users respond to an innovation (Richardson 2010). Some adopt the innovation immediately, while others watchfully wait and delay adoption. A third group will modify the use of the innovation to their needs and a fourth group will begin to utilize the innovation but shortly discontinue its use for one or another reason. A final group will never utilize the innovation. Rogers claims that an important key in adoption is the individuals' perception that this innovation is advantageous and is compatible with existing values and norms. These perceptions are especially relevant in this Tanzania case, since rural women beyond secondary school age are traditionally excluded from learning computer-based technology. This cultural bias toward adult learning makes it even more difficult for the women to be early innovators. The following quotes illustrate the women's perceptions of themselves as they moved through the process of utilizing an entirely new form of technology. First presented are several early entries from women in Africa. The Cross Cultural Dialogue offered a space for the women to reflect on and give voice to their own reality and their desire to take leadership in that reality.

> It's good this space, because I can share with you what is going on in my life and work. What I've experienced is that the Chronically Ill patients some of them die and others are still registered in the program. In another hand, there is an increase in the orphans, and we find some homes are orphan headed homes. So as a result I feel touched some times when I'm in the communities, because I met the people who are needy and who need our help. I grew also as a half orphan from 1959 when my Mother died. I was seven years old, this makes me feel bad and I feel the pain the children are going through and it's not easy when you are so young and have to live without a parent. (Lilian I. Mutoka, comment, *Cross Cultural Dialogue* [blog], September 17, 2003, 9:02 a.m.)

> Dear Paula Caffer. Thank you for your response. Yes, men don't recognise what we are doing as women leaders. But we don't have to give up. We have to be with that art of controlling our activities with self-confidence. Let us use confidence as a weapon to protect us and to make us strong. Thank you. Rachel. (Rachel Ndyamukama, comment, *Cross Cultural Dialogue* [blog], February 21, 2004, 1:02 a.m.)

> Dear Women, You are a leader, she is a leader, and I am a leader. Every woman is a leader wherever she is. I have come to realize that I am a leader like other women. I have come to realize my talents by working with various groups, encouraging them on working hard in order to improve their income and live better life than before. My culture has been too harsh

particularly to women by not sending girls to school instead giving them casual works, and they are given no chance to speak out their opinion. This has given me more experience of how to help women to overcome their problems. (Regina Majaliwa, comment, *Cross Cultural Dialogue* [blog], February 11, 2004, 5:47 a.m.)

This [Cross Cultural] forum has brought us close to one another to discover that issues affecting women are all the same and what make them complex is the environment we live in. They are very complex in Africa and together we will overcome. (Sanana M. M. Lewanika, comment, *Cross Cultural Dialogue* [blog], August 3, 2004, 9:51 a.m.)

The Conference has given me and my two colleagues new dimensions in the area of our work, I hope as time goes by, we will be able to share with all of you our new ideas. (Sanana M. M. Lewanika, comment, *Cross Cultural Dialogue* [blog], August 16, 2004, 7:21 a.m.)

At the same time, the women were aware of the problems with the use of this technology, particularly in regards to required time and cost.

On the first day everything looked strange because it was our first time to see and use the computer but as time goes on I am now typing some sentences with assistance. Thank you very much for uplifting women at local level. It is not easy to spend enough time on the computer for there are a lot of people waiting to use them at the cafe and so it will take a lot of time for other women to get a chance to use it. Regards from all women. (Regina Majaliwa, comment, *Cross Cultural Dialogue* [blog], October 16, 2004, 4:15 a.m.)

It wasn't long before the women began to see benefits from an Internet connection. This coincides with Rogers's idea, noted above, of compatibility. The opportunity to give feedback to their US partners, to send photographs over the internet, and to see women learning were all motivators to strengthen the ICT utilization.

I am sending to you some Photographs of women who form the co-operative of village women groups in Bukoba. The photographs were taken on the 8th Feb 2005 (Tuesday) on every second Tuesday of the March; there is a meeting for all group leaders and group members who have a turn of receiving money collected from the Mary-Go- Round. At the same time those who identified problems like school fees, hospital bills we borrow a loan from 5 USD to 30 USD (Regina Majaliwa, comment, *Cross Cultural Dialogue* [blog], February 15, 2005, 10:26 a.m.)

Dear Lucy,

How are you? I hope you have received my message. I once again thank you for the gift. We are busy learning computer programs. Paula is doing a good job to make sure that all women get a chance to use a computer. It is a golden chance to us. We thank you for your contribution to enable us to reach to this stage. We welcome you here to see the changes after acquisition of this new technology. Thanx a lot more. Regina. (Regina Majaliwa, comment, *Cross Cultural Dialogue* [blog], August 7, 2005, 11:36 p.m.)

Greetings from the all members of the group. We are missing you. In our last monthly meeting we arranged our timetable for computer learning. We are going to teach each other from what we have gained from you. With Love, Rachel. (Rachel Ndyamukama, comment, *Cross Cultural Dialogue* [blog], September 10, 2005, 5:39 a.m.)

The next few years, 2006–2008 ushered in new levels of interaction. WGC held another international conference in San Antonio, Texas, in 2006 and several women participated. As the women's confidence grew, supported by online dialogue and face-to-face contact, the Bukoba women stretched toward new horizons. In 2006, the Bukoba Women's Empowerment Association (BUWEA) established itself as a registered cooperative in Tanzania, and the skills of the women increased significantly.

Hellow Regina and all St. Cecilia members How are you? I arrived safely as my explanation in my e-mail. Tomorrow evening I will have my presentation. This conference will have more participants than the past one. I hope we will gain much. Rachel. (Rachel Ndyamukama, comment, *Cross Cultural Dialogue* [blog], May 17, 2006, 10:25 a.m.)

We have good news from Bukoba. We received the certificate of registration of BUWEA. We have attached its copy with this letter, it is a long process. Thanks for the workshop you have conducted to Bukoba women. We have gained a lot. As a treasurer of BUWEA I have increased my knowledge of keeping my accounts book. This knowledge I got will be beneficial to my family, and the all group. Women are able to learn. We are empowered. (Regina Majaliwa, comment, *Cross Cultural Dialogue* [blog], May 27, 2006, 5:24 a.m.)

The use of the Internet enabled BUWEA to make contact with other resources, both local and beyond. A posting from WGC staff introduced the women to Professor Rutatora of the Sokoine University of Agriculture. This led to a significant partnership between BUWEA and the university, which has lasted till now.

Thus, BUWEA women began to seek out new sources of assistance to improve their agricultural and business expertise and to secure additional funding. This matches Rogers's point about observability, the degree to which one sees results from the use of the innovation.

Thank you for the message. We are in touch with John and he is trying to look for some other two more links that he told us that he is going to send us so that we can fill them too. I shall inform you when we get the forms soon this week. We met Peter on 16th July he said our application is being considered. He said our paper was thoroughly done well. He said that they are slow but sure. He also instructed the Director of G.P. at Karagwe to include our group in the programme of August's conference which will take part in Karagwe. I shall call Maimuna and see if we can meet when she comes to Bukoba. I shall keep you informed. Regards. (Regina Paula Caffer, comment, *Cross Cultural Dialogue* [blog], April 10, 2007, 11:05 a.m.)

We have started using the mobile phone connected to the internet where we use the lop top. This was purchased from the money we got from selling Soya products. It coasted us 105,000/= Tsh. (Regina Majaliwa, comment, Cross Cultural Dialogue [blog], July 25, 2007, 1:11 a.m.)

Hellow Women at WGC. How are you? I am happy to share with you today. I was silent for long time. Now I am on line because we have internet connection in our office. I am happy with it because it is our fruits from our Soya sales. BUWEA now is progressing, We have introduced SACCOS in our group. From SACCOS we get small loans for generating our home based project. We are selling our soya and the local market is available. (Theodosia Rugangira, comment, *Cross Cultural Dialogue* [blog], February 20, 2008, 8:46 a.m.)

New sources of knowledge were opened up for the women as they grew in their use of the Internet. Sites offering content on agriculture and nutrition were useful, especially when the information was presented in an accessible manner. The following quote demonstrates how the women were growing more aware of their marketing needs as well as the quality control of the products they produced through their cooperative.

How are you and your family?
    Regina and Rachel are in the cafe. Thank you for the information on the E-AGRICULTURE. It is very interesting. We will keep being aware on what is going on. We are going on with Soya marketing. WE have packeted in plastic bags. Each packet is about half kg. We are selling it at 400 T.shs. We are still looking for more market since people are not used to soya products. Once they have started they seem to like it. In the farm, corn, beans and cassava are growing. There is enough rain in this season. We expect to harvest in January and make preparations for Soya. Some BUWEA members have sold piglets and are making some savings through the so call SACCOS. Mr. Rwangobe is a consultant for the SACCOS. He is training Consolatha and Rachel how to keep records. They have started to save 2000 T.Shs. This is recorded in their Passbooks. This is recommended by District Cooperative officer. They are the ones helping BUWEA and other groups. About improving quality on baskets, we are working on that. We have selected a few basket weavers to specialize in weaving in order to get the best quality. We hope next time we shall have good baskets which

can compete with other baskets from elsewhere. We have received a thanks-giving letter from Peter together with other Global Partners from Africa. We hope this will be a good indication of working together. Greetings from The Group. Regina and Rachel. (Rachel Ndyamukama, comment, *Cross Cultural Dialogue* [blog], December 7, 2007, 4:06 a.m.)

An important aspect that influences the adoption of an innovation, noted by Rogers, is the degree to which the innovation can be modified to meet the needs of the users. Following are examples of the women's creative capacity to utilize the innovation in ways that met their available resources and addressed the compelling social problems of their community.

Our plans for the Learning combine all types of learning which will be available. We expect to use the cell phone for the Internet communication and not to provide Internet service to the customers. That is very expensive and difficult for us to manage. (Regina Majaliwa, comment, *Cross Cultural Dialogue* [blog], August 13, 2008, 1:58 a.m.)

We have opened our Learning centre on 1.August.2008. The location is within Bukoba Town so it is easy for any BUWEA member to get access on computer by using our two Laptops. We have and internet access by using TTCl cellphone. Internet connection is very expensive, for communication. Our cellphone is doing fine. (Rachel Ndyamukama, comment, *Cross Cultural Dialogue* [blog], August 6, 2008, 6:11 a.m.)

Hellow Eric.

Bukoba women are very excited with the work done by Dr. Patricia and all the team that visited Bukoba. They have done wonderful work to empower Bukoba women. Water project is a big support to our social development. It will minimize time taken by women going to and from wells fetching water for their home use. The government through Bukoba District commissioner and water Engineer promised to work with you in the availability and sustainability of water project. The visit has borne much fruits. We thank WGC and WGN for your collaborations. (Rachel Ndyamukama, comment, *Cross Cultural Dialogue* [blog], July 9, 2009, 2:54 a.m.)

Hellow Sanana, Batrice and Lilian

I am glad to hear you through cross cultural. Congratulation for the development of Masupanzila. I hope you are doing fine in rice growing. In BUWEA, we are progressing well with our different projects. Our concentration now is soya growing, processing and marketing. Changes of weather is our great challenge to farming. We hope in the coming days the pumping machine will start to work as a support from our Government. We are working for achievement of our goals; We love you all, and we remember you especially for those good days we stayed together at San Antonio and Kenya workshops. Hai to Masupanzila group. With love. (Rachel Ndyamukama, comment, *Cross Cultural Dialogue* [blog], September 17, 2009, 4:12 a.m.)

During the last two years, BUWEA has continued to develop. Web-based technology has become a part of their life and their projects. Women in surrounding villages come to Bukoba town and are introduced to computers through the Learning Center. In some ways, this technology is still remote from daily, life because it is not accessible in the village. Yet there is a tremendous sense of empowerment in the learning. It is simply a matter of time for ICT to be as common in Africa as it is in the developed world. Information and knowledge cannot be kept as a prerogative of the privileged.

> Easter Greetings Thanks for your appreciation. I am in third year now at the Open University of Tanzania taking Business studies, and as BUWEA secretary, using BUWEA computer for communication with women has developed my skills and Technology. Thanks WGC for your support. Rachel. (Rachel Ndyamukama, comment, *Cross Cultural Dialogue* [blog], April 13, 2009, 11:27 a.m.)

> Hello I hope everything is well for all our supporters and friends in the States. On Friday, BUWEA sponsored a Soy Promotion Event and invited experts and teachers from the local community to attend to receive education and resources regarding our soy flour. It was highly successful and Regina has asked me to say this about the event: Greetings from BUWEA. We have just finished the Soy Promotion, it was on the 26th of March. It was a day of advertising soya products that BUWEA sells. The guest of honor was Mr. Kamote Samweli the District Commissioner, he gave many thanks to WGC initiatives to the group. He remembers you well. Terri played a very good role from the time of preparation to the peak, where she read a Swahili speech to the guest of honor, it was about the school feeding program which impressed all participants. It was arranged well and of course the message was delivered.
>   We invited several people as follow:
>   1. Nursery school teachers from 2 schools, Bukoba urban and rural.
>   2. Education, community development, and health and agriculture departments.
>   3. Newspapers, radio stations.
>   World Vision, who has been a constant support to the soy project, attended and offered to buy packets of soy porridge for village schools. We hope all these advertisements won't die off but deliver many fruits. (Tere Dresner, comment, *Cross Cultural Dialogue* [blog], March 29, 2010, 7:53 a.m.)

Women's Voices through an Empowerment Lens

Originally, empowerment carried a strong connotation of imparting or bestowing power upon someone for a particular purpose (Cheater 1999).

With feminism, "empowerment has gradually taken on the reverse of the original meaning: now it is self-empowerment and comes not from above, but from below" (Pieterse 2003, 112). The literature also points to empowerment as a process of change rather than a static condition (Kabeer 1999a; Jejeebhoy 2002; Malhotra, Schuler and Boender 2002). It includes ongoing steps of awareness and understanding and is evidenced in changed behavior. Naila Kabeer (1999b, 437) offers a definition of empowerment that can be applied in the context of innovative technology: "The expansion in people's ability to make strategic life choices in a context where this ability was previously denied to them." Defined as such, empowerment is an integral part of the development process in any group or local society. The ability to make strategic life choices and the capacity for self-determination are prerequisites in the process of drawing out individuals' latent capabilities to empower themselves and thereby enrich the community (Kabeer 2001).

Kabeer (2001) further argues that empowerment contains three interrelated dimensions: resources (access and future claims on material, human, and social resources), agency (the ability to define one's goals and act upon them), and achievements (well-being outcomes). Much of the literature on the concept of empowerment stresses this second aspect of choice and personal agency. This element of agency necessitates that the women, themselves, must be significant actors in any process of change that is being described or facilitated (Sen 1992; Murphy-Graham 2008). Yet research clearly warns that gender inequalities will not just disappear through giving voice to women or simply including them in development activities. It is imperative to think in new ways about participation and empowerment, particularly for women. They must be able to define self-interest and choice, and consider themselves as not only able, but also entitled to make choices (Mehra 1997; Kabeer 2001). Women's own aspirations and needs are complex, and often contradictory. For example, their immediate need for an income can in many cases only be fulfilled by challenging entrenched inequalities of which they may be only partially aware and which they may be ill-equipped to challenge, even with the support of outside forces (Nussbaum 2003; Cheston and Kuhn 2005; Kabeer 2005). Dorothy Ettling, Allison Buck, and Paula Caffer (2010, 49) claim that women working for economic sustainability and social change in their local communities, especially economically poor women in developing countries, need: "a) recognition of their capacity for leadership; b) encouragement to exercise this leadership in their local communities; c) psychological, educational and material support to encourage these important efforts; and; d) successful role models of other women in similar situations."

Above all, Ettling et al. (2010) see collective, grassroots participatory action–the *power* to work *with* others–as the key to women's empowerment. It is better understood as an all-encompassing experience in which a whole range of economic and social activities including group organization, agriculture, and income generation initiatives, education, integrated healthcare and so on, would work synergistically toward the common goal of empowering the poor (Mayoux 1998; Kabeer 1999a; Dessy and Ewoudou 2006).

Dorothy Nkuba (2007) in a recent study investigated the opportunities and challenges the Bukoba women faced as they participated in capacity building and entrepreneurial activities, primarily under the auspices of the BUWEA's collaboration with WGC. Her premise was that when women are empowered, they will have improved self-confidence, improved self-esteem, improved nutrition, contribute to children's education, improved family income, gain more recognition, and be involved in decision-making beyond the household (Torri and Martinez 2011). She found that the women *kujikwamua*, a Swahili phrase meaning to take a step and move forward to get out of the unsatisfying situation. The phrase was applied in all unsatisfying situations essentially as their cry for freedom (Nkuba 2007).

Based on the principles mentioned earlier in this chapter, WGC adhered to a model of empowerment that was rooted in a feminist approach and included the aspect of microfinance activities (Carney 2002; Cheston and Kuhn 2005; Nkuba 2007). In this context, Cheston and Kuhn (2005) note that several indicators of impact are considered relevant to women's empowerment in many cultures: women's increased participation in decision making, women having more equitable status in the family and community, increased political power and a sense of women's rights, and increased self-esteem. WGC took these aspects as guideposts and laid out six personal and social impact outcomes that seemed appropriate to the Bukoba women and piloted a survey with the women to ascertain content validity. The survey, the Women's Economic Development Personal and Social Impact Survey (WEDIS) was constructed on these six indicators: (1) the ability to apply new knowledge, (2) the ability to utilize technology, (3) involvement in major family decision making, (4) political and legal awareness and increased participation in public action, (5) increased physical mobility/social interaction, and (6) increased ability to manage economic resources.

The WEDIS survey was first administered to 48 women and then to 50 more in the Bukoba region during a period of 12 months in 2008–2009. The data from this preliminary research pointed to an overarching sense of women's empowerment (Buck and Teachout In press).

Congruent with the survey data, documentation from the WGC web-based dialogue evidences that the capacity building activities throughout the seven years strengthened the self-confidence of the women as well as their ability to engage in new ventures. It also appears that the acquisition of new skills offered the women a stepping stone to collaborative economic activity and provided the necessary motivation to unite them at the collective level. A deeper significance of empowerment is that it indicates a shift in thinking about power, which is both subtle and profound. Mark M. Pitt, Shahidur R. Khandker, and Jennifer Cartwright (2006) concur with this when studying women and microfinance opportunities. They found that "women's participation in micro credit programs helps to increase women's empowerment. Credit programs lead to women taking a greater role in household decision making, having greater access to financial and economic resources, having greater social networks, having greater bargaining power vis-à-vis their husbands, and having greater freedom of mobility" (817). This appears to evidence a new sense of personal power.

The following quotes offer a glimpse into the ways the women revealed their sense of growth. Their words are set in the context of the six indicators that WGC uses to assess personal and social empowerment. The preliminary quote is characteristic of their perception of themselves shortly after they began interacting with WGC. The writer recognizes that the group already has a vision of what it wants to accomplish; courage and determination are evident.

Ability to Apply New Knowledge

One indicator WGC identifies as a sign of personal empowerment is the ability to apply new knowledge.

> Thank you for your message to Regina and the group.All members were happy of having a workshop with Val. We are going to give this information to other women groups whom we are collaborating with. At your arrival we will all be prepared. Thank you.We have already introduced our business to Val through Starting Business. We will continue the discussion with her. (Rachel Ndyamukama, comment. *Cross Cultural Dialogue* [blog], April 2, 2004, 10:16 a..m.

Shireen Jejeebhoy (2002) reminds us that since empowerment is a process, and not a static state, it must be measured over time. The following quotes are from the same individual and cover a span of four years. They thus illustrate an increasing grasp of the import of new knowledge.

> Greetings to all my dear women on the Globe and Happy Easter! I haven't been on line for so long because I was away working in villages where there is no Internet access. Women are happy there appreciating the way they

live but of course they love so much being empowered on development on different fields for a better change. (Paschasia Rugumira, comment, *Cross Cultural Dialogue* [blog], March 26, 2004, 3:40 a.m.)

Hellow Women at WGC.

In am glad to be with you on line. Greetings from Buwea Women. Women are anxious to receive the team and to attend the workshop. Thanks for empowerment of Buwea women. WE have developed our project and others have started new projects. This makes possible our children to go to school. The knowledge we get from workshop has made to prepare our balanced diet. We thank all. You are welcome. (Paschasia Rugumira, comment, *Cross Cultural Dialogue* [blog], April 19, 2004, 4:37 a.m.)

Ability to Utilize Technology

Earlier quotes documented the development of the women with regards to ICT. The following quotes show a sense of enhancement with other skills in farming, record keeping, and food preparation. All of these are perceived as a new level of technical advancement by the women.

Hope you are all fine going on well with your day to day activities. I have been away for quite some time, working with women in villages a bit far from my home. We have a Programme where we want to empower women improve their small farms. Women and men by far are encouraged to use organic manure aiming at Organic Farming. This means is less expensive and cost effective. I have tried my level best to read and learn from what all of you mothers have been communicating. Your words are very much encouraging and have learnt much more. As a group we are now preparing for July conference, at the same time preparing for the visitors coming to Bukoba-Tanzania. (Paschasia RugumiraTheodosia Rugangira, comment, *Cross Cultural Dialogue* [blog], 26, March 2004, 7:54 a.m.)

We are all fine.

We are applying the knowledge we got from your workshop in our everyday life. I am at my home. I prepare soya bites like chapati for breakfast for my family. I also apply bookkeeping knowledge I got from you for keeping records of my projects, that is chickens and cows. It enables me to detect whether make profit or loss at the end of the month. Congratulations to the facilitators. Most of women in the group now know how to keep records for their business. Your workshop has brought good fruits to women. Best wishes in your studies. (Eugenia Rwezahura, comment, *Cross Cultural Dialogue* [blog], May 31, 2007, 7:43 a.m.)

Hellow Paula.

Greetings from BUWEA Ladies and my family.

We are very anxious to receive you in Bukoba with Tracy. Our BUWEA office is opened we are working in it now. We are selling varieties of goods from BUWEA products. You will be impressed when you come, there are changes. On Saturday we will have short meeting with Peter of Global Partners with his delegation. Thanks for the information on how to apply to the African Women Development Fund. We are going to write our proposal and send it. Tomorrow we have short meeting in our office and I will take models of mobile phones of some women and send them to you. (Paschasia Rugumira, comment, *Cross Cultural Dialogue* [blog], March 26, 2004, 3:40 a.m.)

Dear Sr Dorothy and Tere,
We feel proud for sharing BUWEA experience In San Antonio workshop through SKYPE communication. It is a new technology which we haven't applied before so now we are advanced and our voices had heard among various women. We are doing fine with Teri. Last week we had poor internet connection due to rains, With Love Rachel. (Rachel Ndyamukama, comment, *Cross Cultural Dialogue* [blog], September 11, 2007, 3:56 a.m.)

Involvement in Family Decision Making

Jo Rowlands (1997, as cited in Murphy-Graham 2008) argues that "the development of self-confidence and self-esteem are central to the empowerment process" (40) and argues "that an essential component of empowerment is for the individual to move out of the gender assigned roles that her context and culture have given her" (41). This can constitute a direct challenge to cultural role traditions. African women carry the primary responsibility for maintaining the home.

In this capacity, they are generally subservient to their husbands, as he controls any monetary resources the family has. Nkuba (2007) found in her study on rural Tanzania that along with food and household survival, women are also concerned about their children's education, health care, and nutritional status, all important for the well-being of their families. She also found that the women expressed a need to reduce their dependence on their husbands and become more self-reliant. She noted that their home businesses, which were initiated through capacity building and microloans from BUWEA, provided an opportunity for this increased sense of independence and control over family resources. In general, in the Cross Cultural Dialogue, the women spoke very little about their relationship with their spouse. There are a few references to the changes that were taking place as the women developed new capacities and took on new roles.

Dear Dorothy.
I hope you are doing fine your activities with a lot of efforts on poverty eradication especially on women. Your efforts are bearing fruits in Bukoba.

Most women are coming to us with baskets asking if there is another order. They wanted to improve their family farms by keeping animals. Their Mary go round (Monthly contributions) have gone up from 20 cents of a dollar to half a dollar in some groups especially those who are making baskets. This is great, the reach out Africa programme is now taking off with more groups being formed. My husband has given us a room to be used as an office. We have a number of data to be recorded and installed. We have started with two days in a week Wednesday and Friday where women come to present their baskets and attending the internet cafe. We shall keep you informed of the progress. May God keep you heart. (Regina Majaliwa, comment, *Cross Cultural Dialogue* [blog], October 16, 2004, 4:00 a.m.)

After two weeks, weeding will begin, we are planning to work with 10 women. I am glad to inform you that women are very happy with the exercise. More men are asking for consideration for their wives to take part in the project. This is an achievement for BUWEA and W.G.C. We hope more changes will come. (Regina Majaliwa, comment, *Cross Cultural Dialogue* [blog], February 25, 2007, 12:45 a.m.)

Thanks for your idea of using women. It has been impressive to all of us. We thought it could be difficult for women to leave their homes and stay away for 4–7 days, But after planting, more women they can get money, after work. Men allow their wives to participate, this is wonderful and a very good step to women's progress. We never thought, of men married to grassroots women could let them go out to earn some money. But with BUWEA things are changing. We take took a Video cassette where women give their opinion about BUWEA and W.G.C. Also men have something to say about this. (Regina Majaliwa, comment, *Cross Cultural Dialogue* [blog], February 25, 2007, 1:14 a.m.)

Political and Legal Awareness and Increased Participation in Public Life

Rowlands (1997, as cited in Holmarsdottir et al. 2011, 17) talks about "power from within" when speaking of the empowerment of women. She calls it the spiritual strength and uniqueness that resides within and makes us truly human. Its basis is self-acceptance and self-respect, which extends, in turn, to respect for and acceptance of others as equals. An increased awareness of gender equality can spur women to assume a more public role, both in their businesses and in community activities.

Dear Dorothy
    How are you.
    We are working on our farms both family farm and commercial farm. They are all planted. We are very happy to have the opportunity of attending the December conference in Kisum. Two members will attend Lena and

Regina. We are planning to take a few samples of baskets with us. We took your advice of taking a D.V.D thanks a lot. We are taking pictures using the camera from W.G.C, we are sending a few pictures and we shall continue to send. We are taking the opportunity of meeting Government authorities and managed to get seeds for our farms. We got 100 worth T.shilling 250,000. We distributed them to BUWEA members. (Regina Majaliwa, comment, *Cross Cultural Dialogue* [blog], October 14, 2006, 7:38 a.m.)

Dear Dorothy. How are you.

Greetings from BUWEA. We had elections taking place in constituencies and I am glad to tell you that 10 women took part and applied for several positions. Out of 10, 8 members got through. For the first time more women participate in the election, I mean grassroots women. It is an achievement through W.G.C. Things are changing and grass root women are gaining confidence. Below are members and their positions:

- Consolata Emmanuel-District Executive Councilor
- Regina Steven-District Executive Councilor
- Audacta Ruta-District Executive Councilor
- Eugenia Rwezahura-Ward Executive Committee
- Lucia Kimbisa-Ward Executive Committee
- Annastela Doruzi
- Regina Majaliwa-District Loan Committee
- Adventina Byera-Branch Executive Committee We hope to hear from you soon. (Regina Majaliwa, comment, *Cross Cultural Dialogue* [blog], June 4, 2007, 1:53 a.m.)

Increased Social Interaction

Empowerment of women is not solely an individual process. Rowlands (1997) states that although individual empowerment is one ingredient in achieving empowerment, concentration on individuals alone is not enough. Changes are needed in the collective abilities of individuals to take charge of identifying and meeting their own needs—as households, communities, organizations, institutions, and societies. The women's groups that WGC works with in Tanzania and Zambia always envisioned themselves as making a difference in their communities. Their capacity to have a broader influence increased with the acquisition of new skills and their sense of collective power.

I am here in Canada at Cody International Institute of St Francis Xavier University on a Community Based Development Diploma program, part of my studies here is an independent study on the causes and effects of poverty on women in Zambia. I am almost finishing my research but still remaining with a few mandatory and elective courses. I hope to use the knowledge in empowering the women at home in coming up with sustainable developmental activities in our own communities. I will be graduating on the 10th of December 2005 and be back home thereafter. I would like to thank you and all the Women out there for sacrificing your time, energy and resources to make it better for women and children in Africa. It is for a noble cause and I only pray that the Lord bless you mightily. (Sanana M.*M.* Lewanika, comment, *Cross Cultural Dialogue* [blog], September 24, 2005, 6:55 a.m.)

Hellow Eric

Bukoba women are very excited with the work done by Dr. Patricia and the all team visited Bukoba. They have done wonderful work to empower Bukoba women. Water project is a big support to our social development. It will minimize time taken by women going to and fro wells fetching water for their home use. The government through Bukoba District commissioner and water Engineer promised to work with you in the availability and sustainability of water project. The visit bears much fruits. We thank WGC and WGN for your collaborations. (Rachel Ndyamukama, comment, *Cross Cultural Dialogue* [blog], July 9, 2009, 2:54 a.m.)

In the following quote, the women from Bukoba, Tanzania are reaching out to encourage a new collaborative partner in WGC, a women's group in Chimbote, Peru. They realize that they can be a source of support and mutual learning across thousands of miles through this web-based connection.

Hellow Sandra. Greetings.

I am Rachel Ndyamukama, BUWEA Secretary. I am very happy to hear about the Women's school of leaders. I congratulate you for learning and personal productive economic activities. You have shown a good image for women empowerment. BUWEA women are doing the same. In July we had opportunity of meeting WGC team. We learnt much from them. One of it is Soy milk processing. We are now processing 14 lts a week. We have a market. Most of our customers like Soy milk with vanilla. Now we are participating NANENANE trade fair which in our place belongs to promotions for farmers products. We hope our sales will increase. BUWEA involves in different activities like Soy farming, handcrafts, poultry, keeping animals like cattle, goats, and pigs. We expand our knowledge through workshops and seminar. Sandra, we are travelling on the same journey. I invite you for communication, sharing and learning from each other. Much love to your group. (Rachel Ndyamukama, comment, *Cross Cultural Dialogue* [blog], August 5, 2010, 2:52 a.m.)

Increased Ability to Manage Family Resources

A crucial indicator in women's empowerment in developing countries is the capacity to have some say in the use of family resources. Nussbaum (2003) points out that women's preferences often show distortions as a result of unjust background conditions. Agency and freedom are particularly important goals for women, who have so often been treated as passive dependents. When a woman can participate in the microlending program and start her home business, she achieves a new status. Nkuba (2007) claims that when a rural woman improves her family income, she minimizes the humiliation of begging her husband for money for a small family expenditure such as soap. This makes her more confident, aware and assertive. The following excerpts highlight the sense of accomplishment that BUWEA women felt as they managed their businesses.

> Hellow Women of the G. connection. How do you do? We invite you to attend the September Basket sale in San Antonio. Your support will touch African Women at grassroots level particularly from Bukoba, who expects an earning from those baskets. Whatever is collected from there reaches a woman directly. She can decide what to do with the money e.g. to buy essential commodities like soap, sugar, as a support for HIV patient and orphans in their neighborhood. This is another way of empowering BUWEA. Please join us. We shall be grateful to have your support. (Regina Majaliwa, comment, *Cross Cultural Dialogue* [blog], September 18, 2005, 3:56 a.m.)

> Dear Sr. Naomi
> Greetings, I hope you had a good Easter holiday. Good news from BUWEA. Two women out of three who received a grant for buying cows, have got two female calfs. I visited them last week, they are doing well with both farms and animals. Thanks to WGC Donors. Below are pictures of women with calfs:
> 1. That is Domina Paulo from Lugwi village with a baby cow she has given it a name to shukuru which means THANKS. Her farm is among the best farms in the village She is selling milk with bananas.
> 2. That is Costansia with a baby cows she is from Itahwa village. It is her first time to milk a cow. She is having milk for her family and selling some. She is very happy with the project. The name of the new cows is Tumain which means hope. We hope both cows will and get more cows. (Regina Majaliwa, comment, *Cross Cultural Dialogue* [blog], March 31, 2008, 1:39 a.m.)

> Recently BUWEA sat down and compiled a list of women who we believe have succeeded and had much growth in their businesses. Of course, all of our women are success stories simply for their perseverance, strength, creativity in problem-solving, and resilience in hard times, but here are the members whom we feel we have seen much growth in March 2010. (Terri, comment, *Cross Cultural Dialogue* [blog], March 4, 2010 7:55 a.m.)

Conclusion

The effort of Women's Global Connection to facilitate women's empowerment is a "work in progress." When we review the collaborative process of using ICT with the Bukoba Women's Empowerment Association in

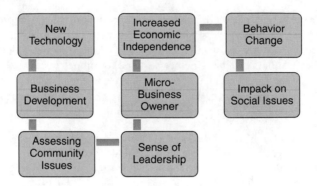

Figure 9.2   Facets of Empowerment.
Source: Created by the authors.

Tanzania, several steps stand out. Technology is vital, but not in isolation. Factors of relationship, capacity building, and leadership development are also crucial. These are linked to each other, not as a progression, but as intermingling facets of the broader picture of personal and social empowerment. Figure 9.2 depicts that linking.

In conclusion, at the end of seven years of collaboration with the women of Tanzania, the WGC team is most aware of the many lessons learned about the role of ICT in strengthening the empowerment of women. We know, primarily, that ICT development happens best in the context of personal relationship. In high context cultures, such as African countries, where oral, face-to-face interaction supersedes written communication, this is particularly relevant. Through a combination of on-site and online communication, the women's capacity has grown and evidences of new leadership abound. We are confirmed in the principles of local ownership, social empowerment, and sustainability. Without the participants' consistent collaboration, the new technology would likely have set idle, no matter how innovative it might have been. The foundation of this collaboration is a commitment to the time and the effort in building authentic relationships. We understand better the struggles and the courage of these rural environments. We have made lasting friendships and benefitted immensely from the generous welcome we received in both countries. But our efforts toward mutuality did not diminish the reality of structural inequalities and the lack of access to critical resources. Our experience demonstrates that these divides can be bridged and collaborations can be formed. Today, BUWEA women are more aware of their role as women entrepreneurs and as creators of their personal and family destiny. Capacity building, along with the introduction and implementation of ICT, played a major role in that empowerment. Women's Global Connection hopes to continue to be a partner in that endeavor.

> We had meeting with Dr.Baikukya of African Research Institute. He wants to connect BUWEA with other Soy producers in Africa. We discussed on how we can become seed growers to other countries since we have more land. We are happy and hopeful. (Rachel Ndyamukama, comment, *Cross Cultural Dialogue* [blog], November 8, 2010, 1:20 a.m.)

References

Buck, Alison, and Mark Teachout. *Evaluating the Impact and Sustainability of Capacity Building Efforts in Tanzania and Zambia.* In press.

Carney, Diana. 2002. *Sustainable Livelihoods Approaches: Progress and Possibilities for Change.* London: Department for International Development.

Cheater, Angela, ed. 1999. *The Anthropology of Power: Empowerment and Disempowerment in Changing Structures.* New York: Routledge.

Cheston, Susy, and Lisa Kuhn. 2005. "Empowering Women Through Microfinance." New York: United Nations Development Fund for Women (UNFPA).

Ettling, Dorothy, Allison Buck, and Paula Caffer. 2010. "A Pathway to Women's Empowerment." *Journal of Knowledge, Culture and Change Management* 9 (12): 49–61.

Gill, Kirrin, Kim Brooks, Janna McDougall, Payal Patel, and Aslihan Kes. 2010. *Bridging the Gender Divide: How Technology Can Advance Women Economically.* Washington, DC: International Center for Research on Women.

Holmarsdottir, Halla B., Ingrid B. Mollerekne, Heidi L. Augestad. 2011. "The Dialectic between Global Gender Goals and Local Empowerment: Girls' Education in Southern Sudan and South Africa." *Research in Comparative and International Education* 6 (1): 14–26.

Jejeebhoy, Shireen. 2002. "Convergence & Divergence in Spouse's Perspectives on Women's Autonomy in Rural India." *Studies in Family Planning* 33 (4): 299–308.

Kabeer, Naila. 1999a. *Institutions, Relations and Outcomes: A Framework and Case Studies for Gender Aware Planning.* New Delhi, India: Kali for Women.

Kabeer, Naila. 1999b. "Resources, Agency, Achievements: Reflections on the Measurement of Women's Empowerment." *Development and Change* 30: 435–464.

Kabeer, Naila. 2001. "Conflicts Over Credit: Re-Evaluating the Empowerment Potential of Loans to Women in Rural Bangladesh." *World Development* 29 (1): 159–164.

Kabeer, Naila. 2005. "Gender Equality and Women's Empowerment: A Critical Analysis of the Third Millennium Development Goal." *Gender & Development* 13 (1): 13–24.

Malhotra, A., S. Schuler, and C. Boender 2002. Measuring women's empowerment as a variable in international development. www.aed.org/Leadershipand-Democracy/upload/MeasuringWomen.pdf (accessed 13 December 2005).

Mayoux, Linda. 1998. "Participatory Learning for Women's Empowerment in Micro-finance Programmes: Negotiating Complexity, Conflict and Change." *IDS Bulletin* 29 (4): 39–50.

Murphy-Graham, Erin. 2008. "Opening the Black Box: Women's Empowerment and Innovative Secondary Education in Honduras." *Gender & Education* 20 (1): 31–50.

Nkuba, Dorothy. 2007. "Rural Tanzanian Women's Agency: Experiences and Responses to Socio-economic Challenges." PhD diss., Graduate School of Education and Research, University of the Incarnate Word, San Antonio, Texas, USA.

Nussbaum, Martha. 2003. "Capabilities as Fundamental Entitlements: Sen and Social Justice." *Feminist Economics* 9 (2–3): 33–59.

Parpart, Jane. 2000. "The Participatory Empowerment Approach to Gender and Development in Africa: Panacea or Illusion?" Paper presented at the Africa seminar at the Centre of African Studies, University of Copenhagen, 7 November 2000.

Pieterse, Jan Nederveen. 2003. *Globalization and Culture: Global Melange.* Lanham, MD: Rowman & Littlefield Publishers, Inc.

Pitt, Mark M., Shahidur R. Khandker, and Jennifer Cartwright. 2006. "Empowering Women with Micro Finance: Evidence from Bangladesh." *Economic Development & Cultural Change* 54 (4): 791–831.

Richardson, Jayson W. 2010. "Challenges of Adopting the Use of Technology in Less Developed Countries: The Case of Cambodia." *Comparative Education Review* 55 (1): 8–29.

Rowlands, Jo. 1995. "Empowerment Examined." *Development in Practice* 5 (2): 101–107.

Rowlands, Jo. 1997. *Questioning Empowerment: Working with Women in Honduras.* Oxford, UK: Oxfam.

Sen, Amartya. 1992. *The Political Economy of Targeting.* Washington, DC: World Bank.

Torri, Maria-Costanza, and Andrea Martinez. 2011. "Gender Empowerment and Equality in Rural India: Are Women's Community-Based Enterprises the Way Forward?" *Journal of International Women's Studies* 12 (1): 157–176.

Walker, Melanie. 2005. "Amartya Sen's Capability Approach and Education." *Educational Action Research* 13 (1): 103–110.

Women's Global Connection. 2011. *Women's Global Connections: Cross Cultural Dialogues.* San Antonio, TX: Women's Global Connection. Available online at: http://www.womensglobalconnection.org.

Chapter 10

Blended Learning for Female Empowerment
A United Arab Emirates Case Study

Rana M. Tamim

Introduction

Various statistics reflect a worldwide continuous increase in ownership and use of computers and computer-related communication tools with almost 361 million Internet users worldwide (Internet World Stats 2011). With their growing economies, the Gulf Council Countries are not very different with regard to technology use and advancement compared to other regions in the world. On the contrary, in light of the visionary leadership in the region, the development and change pertaining to technological readiness, infrastructure, and utilization of technology is quite impressive. A good example is the United Arab Emirates where it was reported that 69 percent of the population in 2011 were Internet users (Internet World Stats 2011).

One of the main areas that have been highly influenced by the continuous progression and widespread use of computer technology and the Internet throughout the world is distance education (DE). Although it was not highly valued in earlier times, DE has started gaining worldwide attention especially with emerging research that indicates its success and efficiency. It is considered to offer many advantages including accessibility, cost-effectiveness, and opportunity for learning anytime anywhere.

An influential meta-analysis conducted by the systematic reviews team at the Centre for the Study of Learning and Performance (CSLP) at Concordia University, Montreal, Canada, synthesized findings from 232 studies addressing how DE compares to classroom instruction (Bernard et al. 2004). The review included 599 effect sizes addressing students' achievement, attitude toward instruction, and retention. Findings indicated that DE and classroom instruction are similar with regard to the three different outcome measures with a wide variability in effect size. More importantly, the results revealed that pedagogy accounted for a larger percentage of variance as compared with media study features, thus highlighting the importance of instructional design in the success of both DE and classroom instruction.

With all this advancement and change, a substantive body of literature has addressed the impact of technology use on students' performance and achievement in various contexts and environments (Bernard et al. 2009; Schmid et al. 2009; Tamim et al. 2011). However, a more important and less targeted issue is technology's ability to empower minority groups in different settings and females in particular cultures. At the present time, researchers advocate for blended or distance education for female empowerment (Janaki 2006) with limited research that supports this idea. This chapter presents findings from a case study of a new United Arab Emirates (UAE) university that uses blended learning in delivering its programs, and its role in addressing UAE adult female learners' needs, allowing them to support their personal growth and achieve academic and professional goals while enabling them to meet their family and social commitments.

The purpose of the current study was to investigate how the blended learning course delivery mode addressed the needs of female learners in the UAE. The decision was to undertake an in-depth investigation and analysis from the perspective of female learners enrolled in formal academic programs at Hamdan Bin Mohammed e-University (HBMeU).

The United Arab Emirates

The UAE is a young country that comprises seven emirates: Abu Dhabi, Ajman, Dubai, Fujairah, Ras al-, Sharjah, and Umm al-Quwain, with Abu Dhabi being the capital. It is located on the shores of the Arabian Gulf in the Middle East and became a federation in 1971 (Morris 2005). Prior to becoming a federation, it was known as the Trucial States and the economy depended mainly on nomadic animal farming, agriculture, pearling industry and trade, fishing, and seafaring. The formation of the federation coincided with the increase in oil production and oil exports, and although the UAE was among the less developed countries 30 years ago, it has gone through a gigantic leap that enabled it to achieve developments comparable to industrialized nations without having to go through the development "stages" that other countries tend to traverse (Shihab 2001).

The UAE has achieved impressive developments in various social and economic sectors leading to high human development indicators at the national and international levels. Mohammed Shihab (2001, 258) notes that the

> successful implementation of human development policy in the UAE, hand in hand with industrialization, urbanization and modernization, is one of the rare examples of a country which has successfully used income from its huge natural resources for its long-term development over a very short period (from the early 1970s to late 1990s).

The UAE's population has increased drastically from 180,000 in 1968 to more than four million in 2005 with 670,000 nationals and a larger number of expatriates representing one of the richest social, ethnic, and religious societies in the world (Heard-Bey 2005). In general, the Emirati national population has a very young profile with relatively similar percentages of males and females (Morris 2005).

Female Status in the UAE

The position, status, and role of women in the UAE have traditionally been limited by religious, social, and cultural norms (Nelson 2005; Erogul and McCrohan 2008). At the present time, the previously accepted roles of wife and mother have started changing remarkably with women being encouraged to pursue higher education and secure professional careers.

At the governmental and policy level, major initiatives are aiming at supporting female advancement and empowerment. A very good example is the National Strategy for the Advancement of Women established in 2002 to facilitate women's active role in education, economy, information, social work, health, legislature, environment, and the political and executive fields (UAE Ministry of Information and Culture 2004). Emirati women are entering the labor force in increasing numbers. The reasons for the increase relate to higher educational achievements and changing attitudes toward working women in the UAE and the region as a whole (Nelson 2005).

Nevertheless, there are various issues that still limit women's educational and professional choices and limit their entry into various public and private sectors (Erogul and McCrohan 2008). Presently, Dubai and Abu Dhabi house the largest number and the most prestigious universities in the UAE. As such, a major constraint for many of the women residing in the different emirates is geographic mobility, which limits their access to education (Baud and Mahgoub 2001). Another limitation is enforced by cultural norms, whereby Emirati women tend to marry and have children at a relatively young age, increasing their social and family duties and responsibilities. Together, family commitments and geographical locations tend to be the most prominent challenges that an Emirati woman needs to overcome while embarking on a formal education journey.

Theoretical Framework

From a theoretical perspective, Michael Moore (1989) distinguished three important types of interaction that are important in distance or online education: *student-student, student-instructor, and student-content.* A more recent meta-analysis by the CSLP systematic reviews team investigated the relationship among the three types of interaction and students' achievement (Bernard et al. 2009). The meta-analysis synthesized effect sizes from 74 empirical studies with findings indicating that more interactive setups, whether *student-student, student-instructor,* or *student-content,* are more favorable for students' achievement in comparison with less interactive treatments.

Although previously DE was limited to mere correspondence education, technology's progression has changed the picture drastically, particularly with the advent and widespread use of the Internet. In earlier DE courses and programs, students received course content and submitted assignments by mail while having limited options for interaction with the instructor and mostly no interaction with other learners. Educational institutions are increasingly taking advantage of developments in computer and communication technologies to offer a variety of DE modes with increased power, flexibility, and ease of access, which support all three forms of interaction. One of the emerging delivery modes is blended learning that combines the advantages of technology-enhanced face-to-face instruction and electronic-supported learning.

Particularly with regard to female empowerment, many researchers advocate DE and online learning as successful delivery modes for enabling females in different cultures and contexts. Natasha Patterson (2009) stresses that DE has a lot to offer to feminist pedagogies. Based on her review, the author argues that conceptions about feminist pedagogies need to be recontextualized with the virtual classroom in mind, research needs to focus on strategies and frameworks to support the large percentage of females in DE programs and courses, and administrators need to acknowledge that the use of technology in the DE context should be informed by the end users, namely the women who are using the technology in their DE studies. Although research in this area is still not extensive, findings reveal that DE is playing an important role in gender equity and female empowerment around the world. For example, research conducted by Walter Sukati, Esampally Chandraiah, and Nokuthula Vilakati (2006) with the Institute of Distance Education at the University of Swaziland revealed that DE is offering females increased access to university education and allowing them to enroll in more diverse programs. Similarly, Suchita Gokool-Ramdoo (2005) reported that online delivery modes could help in the democratization of women's access to education in Mauritius and support professional development in situations where the power relationships are properly understood and negotiated in the community. D. Janaki (2006) stresses the importance of DE for females based on personal experience and research findings at Mother Teresa Women's university in India. Janaki's survey of 200 female participants found that DE offered various advantages including increased self-confidence, updated personal skills, improved career opportunities, enhanced decision-making capabilities, and higher social respect.

Hamdan Bin Mohammed e-University—A Profile

In line with the ongoing initiatives for the continuous development of the country, the UAE government has allocated huge resources to establish a strong ICT infrastructure. In 2009 the country was ranked first (out of 133 countries) in the *Global Competitiveness Index* in terms of mobile phone subscribers and second in terms of Internet users. Other high scores for the UAE include fourth rank for technology integration and use in corporate firms, sixth for foreign direct investment and technology transfer, and eighth for the availability of the latest technology (Senteni et al. 2011).

In addition to the focus on economic growth, the UAE government has taken various steps aimed at making the best of the e-learning modality. Within this context, HBMeU seeks to cross boundaries between several generations of the educational system. HBMeU originally started as the e-Total Quality Management College (eTQM) in 2002, and later evolved into a university in 2009 that was renamed in honor of the crown prince of Dubai.

HBMeU is a coeducational university that combines face-to-face, online, and self-paced learning as part of its delivery strategy (See Figure 10.1). It uses a Virtual Learning Environment (VLE) that is a combination of the Moodle Learning Management System (LMS) and Wimba virtual classroom.

The face-to-face mode includes in-class physical sessions where the learners meet with their professor and fellow students during scheduled instructional sessions. It enables the learners to meet their professors and to get to know each other allowing for more effective interaction during subsequent virtual sessions. The online component includes synchronous sessions in which learners log onto a virtual classroom for prescheduled meetings with a professor in a collaborative environment. The self-study component includes guided periods of personal study that are enhanced by asynchronous or synchronous communication as needed. Such an approach optimizes the strengths of the various delivery models to provide a learner-centered environment conducive to meaningful learning and compatible with recent research findings in e-learning.

In general the blended learning approach allows learners to pursue professional development within a lifelong learning framework thus enhancing their knowledge without having to place their professional careers on hold. One of the key advantages of blended learning is the flexibility it offers to learners. The HBMeU model of blended learning specifically addresses

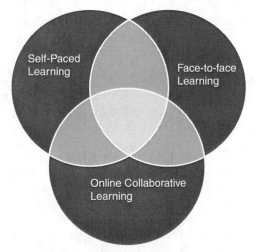

Figure 10.1   Hamdan Bin Mohammed e-University Blended Learning Approach.
Source: Created by the author.

twenty-first-century learners' need for flexibility while minimizing the feeling of isolation experienced by learners in 100 percent distance education models. A number of learners at HBMeU are professionals working in various fields. Moreover, many of them reside in different emirates and do not have the flexibility of attending regular classes in a traditional face-to-face university. In addition to catering for working professionals and geographically distant individuals, the university is providing formal education through an approach that is believed by many to allow for empowerment of minority groups and females in particular societies.

In the UAE, females marry and have their own families to take care of at a relatively younger age but are still highly motivated to complete their formal education, and their role in the UAE workforce is growing progressively. Considering the limitations enforced by the more conservative social and cultural setup of the UAE and the remoteness of some of the emirates, the utilization of technology for the delivery of formal programs while taking advantage of face-to-face sessions to enhance synchronous and asynchronous online communication seems to be particularly suited for women in the UAE.

The Moodle platform is the LMS used by the university.It provides a user-friendly and safe environment that enables learners to access and use the provided course material based on the syllabus, their own needs, and time availability. Through the different course portals on Moodle, learners can download course materials and documents, consult and download resources, participate in online discussions, hand in assignments, and communicate with the professors and other learners in an asynchronous fashion. Such a tool offers a particular level of interaction and flexibility that supports collaborative learning, which could not have been achieved through regular e-mailing tools.

In addition to Moodle, the university makes use of the Wimba virtual classroom for synchronous online delivery of courses. Faculty members can work with learners on a shared PowerPoint presentation, present information on the Electronic Whiteboard, send messages, browse the web, or chat with learners. In addition, learners can work on collaborative activities as designed and set by the instructors in breakout rooms that allow for student-student interactions.

Method

To allow for the collection of in-depth and substantive information, a combination of semi-structured focus groups and interviews were used to gather data for the purpose of this exploratory research. Requests for participation were presented during a number of individual classes while highlighting the focus and the objectives of the research. Seven women volunteered to participate.

Data collection was scheduled during the fall semester of the academic year 2010–2011 and included two focus groups and three individual interviews with the volunteers. Participants were prompted to answer as honestly and completely as possible. The focus groups and interviews began with some short demographic and general questions, and were audio taped after receiving the participants' informed consent. In case any participant did not provide the consent for audiotaping, the researcher took notes as the interview was conducted, with member checks being conducted afterward to ensure reliability of the data collection.

Participants

Participants included seven female graduate students enrolled in the different educational programs offered by the School of e-Education, with each reflecting a different academic and personal background. All participants were Emirati ladies, born and raised in different emirates. In addition, all were full-time professional workers in the academic field with varying numbers of years of experience. Further information about the participants' profiles will be provided in the findings section.

Focus Groups and Interviews

The focus group and the interview protocol started with general profile questions and then concentrated on issues related to the blended learning approach, its strong points, and added value to the participants. Following is a sample of the questions asked:

- Which program are you registered in, and why are you completing your studies?
- How did you know about the university, and what was your first impression about the blended learning mode?
- What were your other alternatives if this program was not offered in this format?
- Can you describe your overall experience with the blended learning approach (including how many courses); what are the strongest points; what are the weakest points?

- At a personal level, what is the most important added value for the program?
- Beyond the subject matter, what is the most important skill or competency that you believe you have gained through the program?
- What are the most helpful aspects of the program at both personal and professional levels?

Depending on the participants' responses, follow-up questions were presented to ensure capturing the essence of the participants' notions and ideas.

Analysis

The focus groups and the interviews were transcribed to help in the analysis process. Although an electronic tool for qualitative data analysis such as HyperRESEARCH could have been used, it was not deemed necessary due to the relatively small number of participants and due to the need to have a deep understanding of the data at hand. In light of these givens, manual analysis was conducted as suggested by John Creswell (2007). Data was coded using a content analysis approach (Patton 2002). The author and a research assistant reviewed the data independently to identify codes and meanings in addition to labelling the codes and organizing them. After the initial coding process, the researchers met to compare and discuss the codes leading to the emergence of a common classification. To identify the main themes, the two researchers analyzed the codes independently (Creswell 2007) and then met to discuss the themes and resolve any conflicting issues.

Findings and Discussion

All participants were full-time employees in the educational sector, with five being teachers at different grade levels, one administrator, and one instructional designer. The participants' ages ranged from 25 to 40 years, and their social profiles were varied with three being married, one divorced, and three being single. All except one of the participants resided in emirates other than Dubai where the university is located; one was from Abu Dhabi, two from Fujairah, two from Ras al-Khaimah, one from Ajman, and one from Dubai. A brief description of each participant's profile is presented below, followed by the findings of the interviews and focus group discussions. To maintain confidentiality, pseudonyms are used.

Shada is the most senior participant, both personally and professionally. She is a married, 40-year-old mother of four who resides in Dubai. Her children range in age from eight to seventeen, and she is currently a full-time administrator at a university. She has extensive teaching and administrative experience in different educational sectors in Dubai, including national and international schools. Shada stresses that she is a highly motivated individual who has always planned to continue her graduate studies. A few years prior to joining HBMeU, she attempted to join a graduate program in a traditional university in Dubai. Due to the rigid schedule and timetable that did not allow her to address family and professional commitments, Shada put the plan on hold. According to Shada, the blended learning approach has allowed her not to only pursue her graduate studies but to also start dreaming of the next step. Although working on her master's thesis, she is hoping that the university initiates a doctoral program so that she can fulfill her bigger dream.

Anoud is a single, 33-year-old mother of three children, aged eight to ten. She is an elementary English teacher with five years' experience. Anoud is a very shy individual by nature and resides in Fujairah with her parents. Like her colleagues, Anoud has always dreamed of pursuing her graduate studies but due to the unavailability of graduate programs in Ras al-Khaimah and various personal and family commitments that make it hard for her to commute to Dubai frequently, she had to put the plan on hold for some time. Not unlike Shada, Anoud is now dreaming of the next step beyond the graduate program.

Dallal is a 28-year-old mother of one boy. She is a primary school English teacher with five years of experience. Dallal lives in Fujairah and has been waiting for more than four years for the local university to open a graduate program in education. When told about the HBMeU programs, she was highly interested in joining, but her challenge was to convince her husband who was not convinced due to the coeducational nature of the programs. With further clarification regarding the blended learning approach and the limited physical attendance requirements, Dallal was able to gain her husband's support for embarking on her graduate studies. For her, the first few months were very challenging with regard to adapting to the new delivery approach, but she stresses that with her instructors' and friends' support she managed to adjust and get used to the new system. While Dallal is going to work and continuing her education, her mother takes care of her son along with his cousins whose mothers are also working full time.

Kholoud is a 25-year-old married lady who lives in Abu Dhabi and has no children yet. She is a secondary school math teacher with three years' experience. She is a highly motivated individual who completed the last two years of her undergraduate studies while being married and has been waiting for the chance to join a graduate program. Kholoud had previously thought about pursuing a master's degree at a traditional university how-ever, the time commitment with regard to the physical attendance resulted in putting the plan on hold. Her main reason for joining the program at HBMeU was the flexibility in the delivery and the attendance aspect, especially the ability to sit for classes from home.

Huda is a single, 25-year-old female who has a bachelor's degree in educational technology and resides in Ajman. She is currently a full-time instructional designer at the Sharjah branch of one of the bigger colleges in the UAE. Both her decision to pursue her graduate studies and the choice of the specific program were informed and influenced by her parents' and family members' input. Her personal first choice was the Interactive Technologies program but she opted for the Leadership and Management in Education program based on her family's advice that with such a pro-gram she will have more potential for advancement in her professional life as well as being able to serve the community better.

Maryam is a 32-year-old elementary school IT teacher with four years of experience. She holds a higher diploma in business information technology and a bachelor's degree in information administration. Maryam is the most religiously committed and conservative female among the participants, as reflected by her outfit and reference to religion in her discussions. Her desire to pursue graduate studies is fuelled by her commitment to lifelong learning and personal growth and is supported by her interest in proving to herself and others that her religious commitment is not hindering her personal growth and development.

Sara is a 28-year-old, single woman who resides in Ras al-Khaimah. She is an elementary school math and science teacher with seven years' experi-ence. During her undergraduate study years, Sara was looking forward to graduating and never imagined that she would pursue graduate stud-ies. She noted that she attended an orientation session that presented an overview of the university and the blended delivery approach at her school but was not convinced by it. Only after an in-depth discussion with her own colleagues was she willing to try the program out and embark on the graduate studies journey. At present, she is delighted about the fact that she is continuing her studies, and although it was hard in the beginning, she is feeling more confident about completing her course at HBMeU.

Drive for Joining Graduate Studies with Alternatives

Participants' responses with regard to the reasons behind their enrollment in the graduate programs reflected a high level of commitment and moti-vation. Although professional development and growth would have been the most expected response, the emerging theme was personal growth and achievement. The majority of the participants noted that it has been a long-standing objective and dream to go for graduate studies. Shada, Anoud, Dallal, and Kholoud noted that they had wanted to pursue their graduate studies since the time when they completed their undergraduate programs. Anoud particularly specified that to her learning and progressing in her studies is like a game as reflected in the following quote:

> Anoud: For me it is like a game, you finish one level and you have to go to the next level, next level, next level, so I am aiming to the next level ... and I like learning since I was in year two at college I wanted to do my master and now my aim is PhD ... that is the next level.

It is interesting to know that although Anoud is an English teacher, she is pursuing her graduate degree in interactive technologies for online learning because of her interest in the technological area, and hence her video and computer game language and analogy is not surprising.

Contrary to the majority of her colleagues, Maryam explicitly noted that whereas the degree is not what she is aiming for, she has always been focused on improving and advancing her own personal knowledge, and it is not all about the degree but rather the personal growth.

> Maryam: For me the degree was not the purpose for joining since I always wanted to keep learning. If I did not get this chance I would have done something purely related to IT. So it wasn't like I was hoping for master or PhD. Even if it meant me joining only courses I would have done that. Not even for certificate, even if it was like training courses only, just for the sake to be updated with whatever is happening.

The responses not only revealed the female learners' commitment but also reflected the high level of support and encouragement that they receive from their families. The feedback also gave clear and solid indications about the close family ties and social bonds in the UAE community. Huda explicitly indicated that her decision to pursue graduate studies and her selection of a graduate program was more of a family endeavor than an individual act on her side. When asked if she feels that such a family involvement may be intrusive or controlling, she genuinely dismissed the assumption noting that the whole process of family decision-making made her feel supported, cared for, and provided with well-informed guidance. Following are some excerpts of her responses:

> Huda: My family is very supportive, they are the reason for who I am and what I became ... they are not educated because they are from the older generation but they have always wanted us to learn more and achieve more ...

They are the ones who gave me the drive for learning and for continuously progressing and trying to reach the best in my life ... They are not giving me input with no alternative, they tell me what they believe is best for me with an argument. They encourage me and challenge me to bring out the best that I can and become better and advance more.

Similar indications of strong family connections and respect for elders were revealed by Maryam who noted that her greatest pride is knowing that her not highly educated father is supportive of her decision and is proud of her achievement. She explicitly noted that although she is single, young, and fully committed on the religious side, and although many individuals may consider it strange that she is pursuing her graduate studies, she takes pride in proving that she can be successful on the academic and professional levels.

Maryam: My strongest satisfaction is that my studies here at this university is appreciated by the person who I appreciate most, my father. He can read and write, but he is not highly educated. When I come all this way, he has fear for me, he is worried until I come home, still he never said you do not need to continue ... even though nothing will happen to my work, my position at work will still be the same but he was very supportive and motivating only because he sees the impact of my studies on me ... it is nice, it will not add that much value but it is important to be appreciated by the elders.

With reference to potential alternatives for their graduate studies, had the program not been offered through the blended learning approach, all the participants listed traditional university programs located in Dubai, since they offer graduate programs in education. One way or the other, they all stressed that although they seriously thought about those alternatives, they were not sure if they would have been able to make it work due to logistics and personal commitments. Dallal mentioned that another option was to wait for a geographically close university to start offering a graduate program in education. Anoud agreed with this but further highlighted that they have been waiting for that for the past five years to no avail.

Blended Learning Mode: Strengths and Weaknesses

The participants' responses to the question asking them about their overall perception about the blended learning approach were very positive. Some of the terms used were *new, exciting, attractive, incredible, and advanced.* Although participants mentioned that the technology used is an attractive feature in the blended approach, the flexibility provided was by far the

most positive aspect according to all of them. This is not striking, especially since the participants are mostly residing outside Dubai; however,
even Shada who is living in Dubai considered it to be the strongest asset,
since it allows her to manage her professional and personal life more easily
than a regular traditional university.

The mothers noted that it is much easier to deal with their children's
needs with the blended learning approach. Although the perception may
be that most of the families in the emirates leave their children to be cared
for by nannies and house maids who are employed by almost all Emirati
families, this is not true in most of the cases. Reflecting the strength of
family ties in the society, in most situations where the mother is absent, the
grandmother or an extended family member becomes the main support
for taking care of the children. This is especially true in the case of these
motivated women who are interested in their personal and professional
growth. In a regular traditional university, a female student with children
will have to take her children over to her parents' house before coming in
to attend classes. However, with the blended learning approach, the pressure is minimized, since the self-study and the synchronous sessions do not
raise the need to take the children out of their homes. Dallal sets a very
good example with the following excerpts:

> *Dallal:* When I go to work or come to university, my son stays with my
> mother and my mother has my sisters' children also, my nieces and
> nephews, and our house is like a kindergarten, full of children it is a big
> responsibility for my mother
> *Interviewer:* If I may ask, why is she willing to do this?
> *Dallal:* I do not know ... the mothers always do this in our society.
> My mother loves my son more than she loves me, because when I went
> back to work after two months of having my son, she has my baby, she
> takes care of him more than I do, really, because of my study and work.

In total, participants' responses reflected their beliefs that the blended
learning approach is catering for their needs and allowing them to overcome the two main obstacles, namely the logistic flexibility, and the need
to address social and family commitments without abandoning their personal dreams of continuing with their formal education.

In addition to the overall positive feelings and the importance of flexibility, Anoud considered that one of the strongest points of this approach
is that it is allowing her to provide a very strong and positive role model for
her children. She stressed that by seeing her commitment to her studies,
including the online sessions when she is at home, her children are having
the opportunity to appreciate the value of education more, and they are
even helping her in creating the positive and calm environment that she

needs. More importantly, she believes that the whole process is impacting her children's commitment to their school studies positively and is motivating them to achieve more.

In response to the question addressing the strongest points in the blended learning approach, as expected, flexibility came out as one of the most prominent. Shada considered things from the perspective of flexibility in studying and completing tasks and said: "I am a mother, working, demands, family, so I organize myself, I study the time that suits me, and no one is running after me. Now we want that assignment and now do that, you know the conventional way. It is very comfortable way of studying." Sara focused more on individual preferences and styles saying: "The flexibility, it is not just fit for one person or one class, you can use the time as you wish, someone will study at the morning, someone at night and it fits all persons who are working or not working, mother or single." Understandably, Anoud who has to worry about her children and commuting to Dubai focused on logistic flexibility saying:

> distance; it saved a lot, I am from east coast, it is very hard for me to come each week to the university, every Wednesday being in the university in face to face classroom so the blended learning made it easier to attend classes at home and I do not need to come to Dubai every week.

Another prominent theme reflected by many of the responses was independence and self-reliance, especially in the asynchronous self-study sessions. Most of the participants noted that they appreciate the fact that they have a stronger say in what they are learning, and how they are doing it. They stressed that they are able to prioritize and focus more on things they do not feel confident with as opposed to the need to follow the specific pace of all the other learners in class.

According to the respondents, the weakest point in the blended learning approach is related to the individual differences among faculty members' abilities to deliver and facilitate such forms of learning. The differences are many and include both technical and pedagogical aspects. It was noted by Anoud that although this is also the case in any other form of learning, the impact of such differences gets to be amplified in blended learning modes for various reasons especially the separation between the student and the professor. Following are some excerpts that reflect this notion:

> Shada: One weak point I find in the blended mode of learning is the instructor himself or herself. They need to be more aware that the blended learning model requires certain skills to deal with the learners. For example all instructors assume that during the asynchronous sessions we read which is not true.

> Kholoud: Some instructors are used to the virtual classroom and use it very properly. They know how to use most of the features in it. Other instructors are not at ease with it and waste a lot of time and spend a lot of time trying and discovering how to do things, and sometimes they have technical problems.

Another weak point that was raised refers to the amount and quality of interaction in the online sessions in the cases when students' numbers are low. Being in a graduate program almost always entails relatively small number of students per course. This is especially true in the case of elective courses where not all students are interested in a particular course, leading to very small enrolment numbers. Anoud noted that the problem tends to be augmented further in case of absence of some students on a given day. In her opinion, this could lead to a situation where the ability to maintain a high level of collaboration and communication among students tends to be harder.

Blended Learning Added Value and Personal Empowerment

With the blended learning approach, the participants felt that the learning process is focusing on them and their needs, rather than revolving around the instructor who, in their belief, is the center of the class in a traditional learning university. Anoud said that in a regular classroom "the teacher is the center of the lesson or the class ... the teacher is there and she is giving the information in one direction," but in the given delivery approach "you are the center of it all, you are experiencing it all and you are responsible for what you are learning" leading to more autonomy and responsibility at the same time.

Participants' responses regarding the added value of the program delivery mode focused mainly on its role in enabling them to develop a variety of skills and competencies. These included time management, decision-making skills, ability to take initiative, online communication and collaborative skills, sharing ideas, and self-confidence. More importantly participants noted that the process is allowing them to become better self-regulators and is enhancing their critical thinking skills. For example, Huda said that the approach is leading to "the growth in my critical thinking skills since the content is very challenging ... I have to search and find things and decide on what to do with it. I am becoming more critical with the content and with the feedback." In a country where the educational system is highly traditional and depends on the teacher-lead classroom, such skills and expertise tend to be of utmost importance, and may prove to be the most empowering at a personal level.

With aspects that are more related to the Emirati culture, the participants noted that the approach is helping some of them in breaking the boundaries and limits set by cultural norms and restrictions. Although many of the participants did not have major problems in joining the program from a cultural perspective, Dallal had to convince her husband who was not very supportive of her joining a coeducation university. She stressed that had it been in a traditional university her husband would not have allowed her to sign up for a graduate program where she might be studying and collaborating with male students on a regular basis. The only aspect that convinced him to support her in her endeavor was the fact that it is a blended learning mode where the physical attendance component was limited. Considering the experience from a totally different perspective, Huda noted that although in the Emirati university educational context she is used to communicating with expatriate male professors, she did not have previous experience with working and collaborating with male students. According to her, the blended learning experience at the university is allowing her to gain more confidence in her communication with male colleagues.

> The whole process made me improve my communication skills and improve my self-confidence. I am shy, but my self-confidence grew, especially with the notion regarding the presence of male nationals in the class with me and me talking in the class. I was used to being in a class where the professor is a male but not fellow colleagues and this experience is making me develop my communication skill and self-confidence. I never thought I will be able to but it is challenging and allowing me to move progressively in building my confidence.

Conclusion

This chapter has presented the HBMeU case study and the perceptions of female learners and how the blended learning approach adopted by the university is helping them reach their goals and empowering them in their personal and professional growth. Findings reveal that the Emirati female population is not lacking in motivation or commitment to complete higher educational levels, where most of the participants are pursuing graduate studies for personal fulfillment and growth. Findings indicate that the approach is helping female learners in overcoming geographical, social, and professional constraints with regard to the completion of their graduate studies. This may be mostly attributed to the self-paced and online-collaborative learning components of the blended learning approach. The findings are in line with researchers' calls advocating for distance education and blended learning for female empowerment (Janaki 2006) and previous findings indicating that DE is increasing women's access to higher education (Gokool-Ramdoo 2005; Sukati et al. 2006).

The participants indicated that the approach is enabling them to develop and enhance their organizational skills and self-regulation competencies while enabling them to build their self-confidence in different circumstances. The development of these abilities and skills are believed to be enabled by the different delivery modes utilized in the blended learning approach, and more importantly by the implementation of the student-centered course design. In addition, findings indicate that students are aware of and value the different forms of interaction advocated by Moore (1989) and supported by the 2009 meta-analysis of Robert Bernard, Philip C. Abrami, Eugene Borokhovski, Anne Wade, Rana M. Tamim, Michael Surkes, and Edward C. Bethel. This is evident in different responses including Huda's appreciation of the opportunity for student-student communication with male peers, and Shada's and Sara's comments regarding their ability to interact with the content at their own pace. Future studies need to focus on the specific advantages of each mode of delivery and the added value each one brings to the female learning experience. Findings from such research will be helpful in providing input with regard to the focus and the attention needed for each delivery mode. Furthermore, future research should move beyond the overall delivery mode and address specific pedagogical and course design issues that female learners believe are helpful to them and may be beneficial in enhancing their personal growth while enriching their learning experience.

REFERENCES

Baud, Isa and Hala Khalid Mahgoub. 2001. *Towards Increasing National Female Participation in the Labour Force Research Report 2*. Tanmia, Dubai: Centre for Labour Market Research and Information.

Bernard, Robert M., Philip C. Abrami, Yiping Lou, Eugene Borokhovski, Anne Wade, Lori Wozney, Peter Andrew Wallet, Manon Fiset, and Binru Huang. 2004. "How Does Distance Education Compare with Classroom Instruction? A Meta-Analysis of the Empirical Literature." *Review of Educational Research* 74 (3): 379–439.

Bernard, Robert M., Philip C. Abrami, Eugene Borokhovski, Anne Wade, Rana M. Tamim, Michael Surkes, and Edward C. Bethel. 2009. "A Meta-Analysis of Three Types of Interaction Treatments in Distance Education." *Review of Educational Research* 79 (3): 1243–1289.

Creswell, John W. 2007. *Educational Research: Planning, Conducting, and Evaluating Quantitative and Qualitative Research.* Upper Saddle River, NJ: Pearson Merrill Prentice Hall.

Erogul, Murat Sakir, and Declan McCrohan. 2008. "Preliminary Investigation of Emirati Woman Entrepreneurs in the UAE." *African Journal of Business Management* 2 (10): 177–185.

Gokool-Ramdoo, Suchita. 2005. "The Online Learning Environment: Creating a Space for Mauritian Women Learners" *The International Review of Research in Open and Distance Learning* 6 (3): 1–15.

Heard-Bey, Frauke. 2005. "The United Arab Emirates: Statehood and Nation Building in a Traditional Society." *Middle East Journal* 59 (3): 357–375.

Internet World Stats. 2011. *World Internet Users and Population Stats.* Bogota, Colombia: Miniwatts Marketing Group. Available online at: http://www.internetworldstats.com.

Janaki, D. 2006. "Empowering Women Through Distance Learning in India." Paper presented at The Fourth Pan-Commonwealth Forum on Open Learning, Ocho Rios, Jamaica, 1 November 2006.

Moore, Michael G. 1989. "Three Types of Interaction." *American Journal of Distance Education* 3 (2): 1–7.

Morris, Mervyn J. 2005. "Organisation, Social Change and the United Arab Emirates." Paper presented at the Social Change in the 21st Century Conference, Brisbane, Australia, 28 October 2005.

Nelson, Caren. 2005. *UAE National Women at Work in the Private Sector, Conditions and Constraints.* Abu Dhabi: UAE Ministry of Information and Culture.

Patterson, Natasha. 2009. "Distance Education: A Perspective from Women's Studies." *Thirdspace: A Journal of Feminist Theory and Culture* 9 (1).

Patton, Michael, Q. 2002. *Qualitative Research and Evaluation Methods.* Thousand Oaks, CA: Sage Publications.

Senteni, Alain, Rana M. Tamim, and Bryn Holmes. 2011. "A Smart Technology Enhanced Learning for the Post-Oil Arab Gulf." In *The New Post-Oil Arab Gulf: Managing People and Wealth,* eds. Nabil Sultan, David Weir and Zainab Karake-Shalhoub. London: Al-Saqi.

Schmid, Richard F., Robert M. Bernard, Eugene Borokhovski, Rana M. Tamim, Anne Wade, Michael Surkes, and Gretchen Lowerison. 2009. "Technology's Effect on Achievement in Higher Education: A Stage I Meta-Analysis of Classroom Applications." *Journal of Computing in Higher Education* 21: 95–109.

Shihab, Mohamed. 2001. "Economic Development in the UAE." Abu Dhabi: UAEInteract. Available online at http://www.uaeinteract.com.

Sukati, Walter, Esampally Chandraiah, Nokuthula Vilakati. 2006. "The Role of Distance Education in Gender Equality and in Empowering Women–A Case Study of the Institute of Distance Education." Paper presented at The Fourth Pan-Commonwealth Forum on Open Learning, Ocho Rios, Jamaica, 1 November 2006.

Tamim, Rana M., Robert M. Bernard, Eugene Borokhovski, Philip C. Abrami, and Richard F. Schmid. 2011. "What Forty Years of Research Says About the Impact of Technology on Learning: A Second-Order Meta-Analysis and Validation Study." *Review of Educational Research* 81 (3): 4–28.

UAE Ministry of Information and Culture. 2004. *United Arab Emirates Yearbook 2004*. Abu Dhabi: Trident Press.

Chapter 11

Educational Accessibility for African Refugees
Challenges and Opportunities

Safary Wa-Mbaleka

Millions of people live in either refugee or internally displaced people (IDP) camps across the globe due to wars, ethnic conflicts, and natural calamities. Although away from home and in critical living conditions, refugees and IDP are in need of, and have the right to, accessible education. To meet this need, educational researchers and practitioners developed a special interest in refugee education in the late 1980s and early 1990s (Penz 2004). However, little research has been reported on these settings, and it is important to take the particular circumstances of refugee and IDP camps into consideration given the number of people affected and the scope of the needs. The discussion in this chapter is geared toward refugee and IDP education in the central African context, a region where several wars keep millions of people either in refugee or IDP camps (Geisler and De Sousa 2001; Kaiser 2006; Salisbury 2006; Burton and John-Leader 2009). It discusses the challenges of implementing educational programming in refugee/IDP camps, based on a review of the literature. It also suggests ways in which information and communication technologies can provide important opportunities to address some educational challenges specific to refugee/IDP camps.

Background

Due to several civil wars that have plagued the central African region, millions of people live in refugee/IDP camps for an extended period of time (Bearak and Crossette 2001; Geisler and De Sousa 2001; Penz 2004). Table 11.1 synthesizes important statistics on refugees and IDP in central African countries as reported in January 2012 by the United Nations High Commissioner for the Refugees (2012), and demonstrates the vast number of refugees and IDP in the region.

Particularly, the Great Lakes region (Democratic Republic of the Congo, DRC; Rwanda; Burundi; and Uganda) seems to host the majority of refugees and IDP. These statistics reflect closely the result of civil wars and interethnic conflicts that have plagued the region since the mid-1990s. The inclusion of IDP in this analysis is important because in the DRC, hundreds of thousands of people have lived in IDP camps for several years. While IDP may not have access to as much assistance from the international community as refugees, who cross international borders, their life challenges are similar to those of the refugees.

Educational Expectations

Organizations and individuals involved in providing education to refugees and IDP face specific educational challenges that are particular to refugee/IDP camps. The leading question in facing these challenges is that of knowing how educators should effectively teach refugee/IDP learners

Table 11.1   Statistics on Refugees in Central Africa1

	Refugees	Internally Displaced People	Total Number
Burundi	29,365	157,167	186,532
Cameroon	104,275	0	104,275
Central African Republic	21,574	192,529	214,103
Democratic Republic of Congo	166,336	1,721,382	1,887,718
Equatorial Guinea	0	0	0
Gabon	9,015	0	9,015
Republic of Congo	133,112	0	133,112
Sao Tome & Principe	0	0	0
Rwanda	55,398	0	55,398
Tanzania1	109,286	0	109,286
Uganda1	135,801	125,598	261,399
TOTAL	764,162	2,196,676	2,960,838

Source: United Nations High Commissioner for the Refugees (2012).

(Waters and Leblanc 2005), using relevant information and communication technologies. Maybe one of the best answers to this question is the one provided by the United Nations High Commissioner for Refugees (United Nations Security Council 2000). This organization stated that education has the goal of helping rebuild the lives of refugee/IDP children. This goal is achieved through social interaction and the development of knowledge and skills needed for these children's future lives. According to Tony Waters and Kim Leblanc (2005), children and young people who are not involved in any activity are vulnerable to military recruitment and sometimes, criminal l activity involvement. So, education plays the role of healing the wounds of the past, providing means to deal with current challenges, and preparing children for their future.

People expect education to "heal psychosocial wounds of war, solve youth unemployment, deliver ... democracy, build peace and promote economic and social development" (Buckland 2006, 7). School is a place where students should receive counseling services, a place where young people should develop marketable, vocational skills, and learn how to resolve conflicts peacefully. Although education does not cause war, it is expected to help fix most of the ills that result from war (Kaiser 2006). Peter Buckland (2006) stated that good investment in children's education in refugee/IDP camps could be one of the most sustainable solutions to peacebecause education provides the means to prevent conflict while promoting peace, reconciliation, and reconstruction. Educators in charge of planning refugee/IDP education must keep in mind that education for refugees and IDP is more than just reading, writing, and arithmetic that have characterized the mainstream education. It is also a means by which to bring psychological and social healing, and prepare a brighter future for refugee/IDP learners.

Many of the refugees and IDP certainly need some type of education to meet their long-term education goals (formal education) and/or some skills-based education to address their basic needs, such as food, health, and safety (Strekalova and Hoot 2008; World Refugee Survey 2009). However, such education meets a number of constraints (Matthews 2008), including economic, social, political, psychological, and environmental issues that affect both the ability to offer programs and the outcomes.

Frequent mass movements of millions of refugees and IDP occur from seven countries of Africa that are torn by closely linked conflicts (Ogata 2000). These countries are Uganda, Sudan, Rwanda, the Republic of Congo, the DRC (formerly known as Zaire), Burundi, and Angola. The conflict in these countries is generally based on the control of minerals and other natural resources or ethnic cleansing, which is also linked to the control of power (Waters 1999; McBrien 2005; Newbury 2005; Waters and LeBlanc 2005; Tadesse 2007; Marwaha 2008; Lin et al. 2009).

Although government soldiers are involved in some cases, rebel groups seeking to gain power frequently create a situation that causes massive movements because people are afraid of systematic looting, rape, systematic killings, systematic ethnic cleansing (Global Witness 2009), and other similar atrocities that people in central Africa have experienced. Some of these atrocities include, but are not limited to, mutilations, massacre, human rights abuse, and gender-based violence (Ward and Vann 2002; Wakabi 2006). The latter also has other effects, including a large number of unwanted pregnancies and health issues for the victims. In addition, ethnic conflicts have been frequent since central Africa comprises thousands of ethnic groups. When they escalate to violent levels, people have no other choice but to flee for their lives. These seem to be the two major causes of massive movements of populations in central Africa that cause the need for the creation of refugee/IDP camps (United Nations High Commissioner for Human Rights 2010).

Obstacles Particular to Refugee/IDP Learners

Ekaterina Strekalova and James Hoot (2008) analyzed seven major obstacles that refugee/IDP children face, each of which make education in refugee/IDP camps difficult. These challenges include living with traumatic experiences, gender-based violence, language diversity, parental resistance to education, cultural identity issues, discrimination, and socioeconomic challenges, creating a complex environment for designing appropriate education programs for refugee/IDP learners. These obstacles often lead to behavioral problems in the classroom: explosive anger, problems with authority, inability to concentrate, rule testing, withdrawal, age-inappropriate behavior, and lower academic achievement.

Young learners who have witnessed horrible situations can easily get angry, even at the smallest provocations. They may become extremely sensitive because of issues that go on for weeks, months, or even years without proper diagnosis and proper remedial assistance. In addition, past experiences may convince IDP/refugees that those who claim to be in authority positions commit atrocities (Global Witness 2009). Additionally, even in refugee/IDP camps, some gender-based violence has been reported, especially for women. Such violence can either create new traumatic experiences or accentuate past ones.

Another challenge that refugee/IDP children face is language diversity (Strekalova and Hoot 2008). Because of the great linguistic diversity found in central Africa, it is easy for thousands of people to get to a new place where there is limited communication with local populations

(Ethnologue: Languages of the World 2009). This challenge can easily happen in Africa where a country may have up to four national languages (the DRC, for example) not to mention hundreds of other languages and dialects not considered as official languages. Educators must choose the language of instruction, and although French and English are the major mediums of instruction in central Africa, educational organizations struggle to decide whether refugee students should study in the language of their host country or the language of their country of origin (Ahlen 2006).

Although high schools throughout Africa generally use English or French as the language of instruction, in the case of elementary school education, most learners study in their local or national languages. IDP learners may be torn between studying in the language of the host community and the language of their place of origin. The language of the host community may be less known or not known to IDP learners, and if learners study in the host country's language, they may have difficulties surviving in their country of origin upon their return. However, if they study in the language of their country of origin, they may not be able to use their new knowledge and skills in their host country while they live in refugee camps.

Parental resistance is another challenge that refugee/IDP learners may face (Strekalova and Hoot 2008). Due to long periods of living in fear, parents may develop an unusual, if understandable, resistance to anyone who would like to take their children away from them (Szente et al. 2006). Parents may be overprotective of their children, a feeling that may extend to not allowing children to participate in educational programs.

Refugee/IDP children also struggle with identity issues. While living in a long-term refugee/IDP camp, young learners end up developing multiple identities (Bash 2005). While at home children may be told to be careful about "strangers" and to develop some self-defense mechanism based on past experience, they may be told at school to be nice to everyone and participate in collaborative activities, and at church to forgive and love their enemies. Additionally, when children are playing with others, who might have come from different cultural and linguistic backgrounds, they may internalize or develop new identities for the sake of their new friendship. These identities develop as a result of different expectations imposed on them from leaders of such different social groups. The effort to meet competing sets of expectations may lead refugee/IDP learners to develop different identities for different situations. Refugee/IDP learners may have the tendency to test the rules because they have lived in different settings with varied expectations and values. They may want to challenge rules that are in place in a classroom until they reach the point where the teacher can no longer tolerate it. In this case, they are not challenging the classroom rules simply because they are bad students; they are challenging rules to find out where their limits of freedom are set (Strekalova and Hoot 2008).

Refugees and IDP face a serious level of discrimination. Their needs are often considered less important than those of their host community or host country (Kaiser 2006; Westhoff et al. 2008). In fact, such discrimination against children can negatively affect them to the extent that they can develop low self-esteem, lose all types of motivation for learning, and thus develop inhibition against personal achievement (Strekalova and Hoot 2008). This discrimination is due to both linguistic diversity and cultural diversity (McBrien 2005). Effective education planning for refugees/IDP must incorporate sensitivity to cultural diversity (McLoughlin and Oliver 1999; Burton and John-Leader 2009). Additionally, it cannot be emphasized enough that most refugees and IDP usually face difficult socioeconomic challenges. Most of them are not involved in any socioeconomic, income-generating activity. Many refugees and IDP live on only one meal a day.

Designing educational programs for refugee/IDP learners will be different from designing them for regular classrooms found in villages, towns, and cities that are peaceful. Trying to provide education to refugee/IDP while ignoring their background experiences and their current socioeconomic, psychological, physiological, linguistic, and cultural needs may not yield expected results.

Structural Challenges in Providing Education in IDP/Refugee Camps

There are disparities in access to financial support needed to deliver effective and efficient education to refugee/IDP learners (Brown 2006). There is a clear distinction between the level of support given to IDP and refugees. Refugees are more likely to receive more financial assistance than IDP, especially in most central African countries, because they receive assistance from the international community while, by law, countries are required to provide for the needs of their own IDP.

In central Africa, several thousands of refugees and IDP pitch their makeshift huts in the thick of the jungles, where few people and organizations, if any, canever reach. Refugee/IDP camps that are more accessible are more likely to receive needed financial assistance than those that are much less accessible. The level of funding of refugee/IDP education determines the quality of education, the type of instructional materials, the level of teacher's qualification, and the level of comfort of the instructional setting. Many of those who have the chance to access some type of education do so literally under a tree.

In addition, large numbers of children and young people in IDP/refugee camps have not been exposed to the educational opportunities needed to be successful in life. Since wars go on for months and even years in different parts of central Africa, many people miss out on education. Either they never had any organized schooling program in their refugee/IDP camps or whatever education is provided there does not meet the level of standard education in the host country or the country of origin.

Another issue is that of limited educational facilities. Makeshift tents are often provided for refugees. In such tents, families live in the smallest space imaginable. In some cases, people make their own makeshift huts from tree branches that can hardly withstand the tropical rains of central Africa. Building a school in such settings is the last item on their to-do lists. Then, when war comes to an end and people return to their villages or towns of origin, rebels have already destroyed or burned everything to the ground. Large numbers of former refugees and IDP have nowhere to sleep, let alone a classroom in which to study.

One of the constraints frequently reported in the literature is the lack of formally trained teachers in refugee educational programs (Ahlen 2006). Because of the pressing educational needs, programs must oftentimes be put in place in a hurry (Drechsler et al. 2005). In many refugee/IDP camps, most teachers have received little or no teacher preparation training (Brown 2006). According to Buckland (2006), many teachers in refugee/IDP camps are under-qualified (those who received little teaching training) and others are simply unqualified (those who have never had any teacher training at all). People who plan educational programs should expect teachers who will use their programs to know exactly how to deliver the instruction. Most teachers need some type of professional training to either develop or improve their teaching skills (Burgoyne and Hull 2007) and to meet students' educational needs (Winthrop and Kirk 2004; Kirk and Cassity 2007; Kirk and Winthrop 2007). They also need to develop necessary skills to help in learners recover from their past experiences and prepare them for better learning experience and success in their future life.

Another educational challenge is the curriculum that needs to be adopted. From the perspective of IDP education, Martin Greeley and Pauline Rose (2006) suggested that educational administrations should create a specific curriculum that can be used for IDP learners. This uniformity of curriculum could help provide the same education to all IDP learners. From the refugee perspective, some educational experts have recommended that refugee students receive the curriculum of their country of origin (Kaiser 2006; Kirk and Winthrop 2007; Dumbrill 2009). The challenge with this recommendation is that some refugee learners may stay in host countries for several years until they reach a college-going age. In this case, their primary and secondary education may not necessarily be appropriate in preparing these learners for tertiary education in the host country. Greeley and Rose's (2006) suggestion seems appropriate for refugee learners: an international curriculum for refugees that are located in the same geographical area, for instance, central Africa. Although central Africa is a vast region that covers several countries, the curriculum provided to refugees in that region should be acceptable in educational systems in all central African countries. However, due to ethnic and linguistic diversity, such a curriculum would have to be translated to the major national languages of the central African region, especially at the primary education level. The curriculum for the high school level could simply be developed in English and French.

Yet another important educational challenge that is commonly experienced in refugee/IDP education is that of providing vocational training that promotes marketable skills needed to cope socioeconomically at the local level. Indeed, some refugee/IDP experts claim that in those settings, education does not develop practical and relevant skills needed to teach vocational skills or knowledge that can be marketable in the learners' communities (Brown 2006). Although formal education is important for younger learners, vocational training for the socioeconomic needs of refugees and IDP is equally important, especially for older learners. Buckland (2006) stated that such education helps decrease youth unemployment and reduces their chances of getting lured into joining rebel groups.

In African communities, some people hold negative attitudes toward women's education (Brown 2006). Failing to address gender discrimination in education may promote social inequalities that can generate other social ills that, in turn, need to be addressed. Educational policy makers should make education equally accessible to both male and female learners, even when information and communication technologies are used in instruction.

Using ICT to Address Educational Needs in Refugee/IDP Camps

Information and communications technologies are frequently cited in strategies to address unmet educational needs in this population. For example, the United Nations High Commissioner for Refugees' education strategy for 2010–2012 focuses primarily on three major goals: increasing access and enrollment of refugee learners, improving the quality of education, and enhancing the protection of all refugee learners (United Nations High Commissioner for Refugees 2009). The strategy notes the importance of integrating open and distance-learning programs; however, it does not indicate which specific programs will be implemented, what type of ICT-based solutions might be needed, or the technical infrastructure needed to deliver those open and distance-learning programs.

Challenges That Might Be Addressed through ICT

How can ICT address adult education issues and promote lifelong learning in refugee/IDP camps? A review of ICT programs that have been successful in providing educational services in Africa in recent years may be a good place to start when searching for applicable models.

In recent years, Kenya and Rwanda have both promoted technology literacy by using solar-powered mobile labs equipped with laptops. Funded by the World Bank, the ICT Bus Project in Rwanda, launched in 2009, is a US$200,000 lab that provides training for and access to Internet applications to rural areas of Rwanda. The initial project consisted of two buses equipped with Internet connection, 20 laptops, printers, scanner, and photocopiers. The buses are equipped with electric power generators, so they can also be used in remote areas without electricity. According to e-learning Africa, 1,500 people, including many small farmers, local entrepreneurs, police officers, students, and women traders have used their facilities (Kyama and Kabeera 2011).

Another program based on the same model is the solar-powered Mobile Computer Lab Project launched in Kenya in 2010, comprising mobile labs containing 22 computers each. Funded by Computer Aid International from the United Kingdom in collaboration with Computers for Schools Kenya, this program focuses on delivering Internet services and access to information technology training in the rural areas of Kenya. Because the target areas for these labs have no electricity, this project's reliance on solar energy is an excellent solution. The self-contained battery pack within the computers can run for seven days. The solar panels can recharge with one day of sunlight. Another similar solar-powered computer lab has been reported in Zambia (Balancing Act 2010).

A mobile lab of this kind could definitely benefit refugee/IDP learners. One of the challenges for educating refugees noted in this chapter is related to undereducated and unqualified teachers. With the use of solar-powered mobile labs, educators in refugee/IDP camps can have access to different types of instructional materials to train people in teaching skills-based and basic health courses, and workshops on how to deal with posttraumatic experiences and gender-based violence. Skills-based education would focus on marketable skills that can help refugees/IDP generate income, thus successfully addressing socioeconomic challenges. Such labs can also help teach reading, writing, and arithmetic to refugee/IDP learners. Additionally, mobile labs can decrease the cost of building large schools that may not be of much use after refugees or IDP return to their home country or home place.

In addition, for the refugee/IDP learners (adult or young), a mobile lab could deliver language-learning applications (such as Rosetta Stone), basic health training, conflict resolution, computer literacy, and other skills-based workshops. People could be trained in first-aid skills that are so needed in refugee/IDP camps based on dynamic multimedia presentations and technology-based, reusable learning objects. These courses and training materials could be developed in advance with different teams of experts. These mobile labs can be moved to different locations as the need arises and, if solar resources are utilized, they would not need to rely on electricity.

A second type of technology innovation that could be utilized in a refugee/IDP context would be the smart phone. The Dunia Moja (One-World) Project, initiated by Stanford University in California in recent years, is a successful model that can be replicated through the use of smartphones to deliver education to refugee/IDP learners (see their website at http://duniamoja.stanford.edu). In collaboration with Makerere University (Uganda), Mweka College of African Wildlife Management (Tanzania), and the University of Western Cape (South Africa), Stanford University developed and delivered audiovisual instructional lectures. In this project, learners could also submit assignments using smartphones. The project is funded by Stanford University, the Whitehead Foundation, and the Communication for All Program at Ericsson. The Dunia Moja Project's curriculum is specifically geared toward international environmental issues. The curriculum is the product of the collaborative effort of the faculty of the four institutions that are involved. Students from each of the three participating higher education institutions are the first beneficiaries of this project.

To use such ICT tools in refugee/IDP learning, a few smart phones could be offered to schools for instructional purposes. Such smart phones could even be used for teachers in training to access materials for their own learning purposes. Additionally, because most people have cell phones in refugee/IDP camps, some simple texts could be used to disseminate practical instructional information to teachers or even high school learners.

A similar example is Africa Aid, a US-based nonprofit organization with the mission to develop poverty-alleviation programs that focus on empowering Africans. Africa Aid has launched three major programs in the areas of healthcare, microfinance, and feeding (Africa Aid 2011). One of the three programs is especially ICT-based: the Mobile Doctors Network (MDNet). In this specific program, Africa Aid creates free mobile phone networks to connect physicians in different African countries. These networks are used for knowledge transfer and emergency response capabilities, thus improving healthcare and saving more lives than usual. MDNet Ghana, launched in January 2008, was the first countrywide mobile doctors' network in Ghana. Since its inception, more than 1,900 physicians in Ghana have registered for the MDNet program, logging more than a million calls and creating a total of 2,266 hours of medical discussion within Ghana in one month (Africa Aid 2011). In Liberia, the MDNet launched in August 2008 is reported to have already connected all physicians.

Smartphones could be similarly used in refugee/IDP camps to deliver less complex training, tips, and techniques for skills-based workshops in the areas of agriculture, safety, basic literacy and arithmetic, and basic health. Teams of education experts could develop some curricula written in short texts, short audio and video clips, and educational applications to be delivered on smart phones. Just like the case of the Dunia Moja Project, educational leaders could partner with national mobile telephone companies in the delivery of ICT-based instructional materials. In the case of the MDNet project where physicians are connected through a free network in Liberia and Ghana, this ICT-based approach should be funded and expanded in refugee camps to deliver relevant healthcare in a timely manner. With MDNet-like programs in refugee camps, physicians and other health experts around the world can deliver high-quality healthcare and health education without having to physically go to the refugee camps. This system could also function as a basic warning or security system for this vulnerable population.

The fact that many refugee/IDP already own personal mobile phones makes this technology an extremely viable solution for education and to disseminate information to refugees/IDP.

For the challenges of gender-based violence and the challenges related to traumatic experiences, ICT tools can be developed to help learners alert the relevant services when someone is going through posttraumatic stress or gender-based violence. It could be as simple as pressing a button to alert counseling services (for posttraumatic experiences) or the refugee/IDP camp security services (for gender-based violence). Some coordination is needed to choose a specific structure to follow for both the training and the delivery of such services.

For language diversity, ICT can help deliver interactive English and French language-learning activities to students. In fact, programs such as Rosetta Stone, if available in a (mobile) computer center, could increase refugee/IDP learners' motivation. For parental resistance to education, ICT can still be used, although it would require much planning and coordination. A teleconference where parents and their children watch an interview with a person (who could even be in another country) who became successful because of education could be held from time to time. Because resistance to education is claimed to be more with female learners, more interviews would be needed with successful women to encourage girls and their parents to embrace education. This approach could even help decrease gender-based discrimination that is commonly reported in refugee/IDP schools.

Last, cultural identity issues may not be directly solved by ICT. However, ICT can be used to raise cultural diversity, and thus help learners to be more tolerant and more accepting of other cultures. Videos from National Geographic about the cultures of the world could be saved on refugee/IDP school computers as instructional materials. As refugee/IDP learners, sometimes with local learners, learn about other cultures, they can begin to appreciate their own cultures and develop a cultural identity based on universal cultural values such as courtesy, care, love, respect, freedom, and the promotion of greater good for all.

Meeting Teacher and Counselor Training Needs

Information and communication technologies could also help address the problem of teacher training by providing reusable teacher training. With a solar-powered mobile lab that has 20–50 computers connected to the Internet, training can be offered for teachers and counselors. Teachers can complete intensive training that is prepared in advance and saved on the lab network in the areas of teaching theories and methods, classroom management, content matter, and the whole curriculum that is adopted in any defined region. Because refugee/IDP learners have major psychological problems that need appropriate interventions, the mobile lab could help deliver materials that are needed for the counseling services in diagnosing and addressing behavior problems, multiple identities problems, and posttraumatic stress. Additionally, because some refugees and IDP may be owners of cell phones, some applications could be developed to deliver some simple teaching techniques on the refugee/IDP teachers' cell phones to complement the programs offered by the mobile lab. In fact, they could use such applications to submit a request or question related to some specific teaching approach.

While ICT cannot solve the knotty problems of what curriculum—that of the host country or the country of origin—or what language the curriculum should be offered in, it can provide the tools to make proposed solutions more viable. For example, if the United Nations High Commissioner for Refugees were to develop regional curricula accepted in all the countries of that region, the lab could be used to provide easy accessibility to the curriculum. In addition, language-learning tools could be provided to help both teachers and students access resources to alleviate the issue of language diversity.

The mobile lab could provide facilities and content to expand the availability in training in marketable skills as well as basic health and welfare issues. Although it may be almost impossible to give computer access to all refugee/IDP learners, it is definitely feasible to use the limited information and communication technologies found in a mobile lab to train the teachers in the marketable skills that they would teach to refugee/IDP learners. The lab could also be used to provide easy accessibility to the curriculum.

It is obvious that technology integration in the classroom is still a major educational challenge whether it is in or outside the refugee/IDP camp, especially in central Africa. However, mobile labs could provide an opportunity for refugee/IDP students to access knowledge that would have otherwise been difficult, if not impossible, to access. In this case, not all courses need to be offered using the mobile lab. However, offering some specialized courses using information and communication technology can significantly enhance meaningful learning for refugee/IDP students and direct self-paced instruction for refugee/IDP learners.

Conclusion

Millions of people live in refugee/IDP camps in the central African region, with potentially hundreds of thousands of learners. Accessibility to any type of education is still a serious challenge in those contexts. Information and communication technology has the potential and opportunity to play an important role in significantly increasing that accessibility. Using ICT may be more effective and efficient than trying to financially support large numbers of experts to travel internationally to assist refugee/IDP learners in central Africa. Rather than simply providing a quick-fix approach to the educational needs of refugee/IDP learners, such an ICT approach should focus on empowering learners by empowering teachers and by striving to make education accessible to as many of the learning constituencies (K-12, vocational, family and health education, etc.) within the refugee/IDP population as possible. Furthermore, utilizing technology that has already been adopted and is widely used by refugees/IDP learners, such as mobile phones, provides an opportunity for implementation that could not be addressed with other technology tools.

Although ICT solutions such as mobile phones or computer labs do provide numerous possibilities for improving the accessibility for teachers and students in refugee/IDP camps, they will not solve all problems. Questions of appropriate curriculum for diverse learners or appropriate language of instruction, for example, require more attention at the policy level. More research is thus still needed to develop best practices for employing ICT solutions on the ground in refugee/IDP camps.

Note

1. Although not part of central Africa, Uganda and Tanzania have been added to this table because they host large numbers of refugees from central African nations. They are, therefore, directly affected with the issue under discussion.

References

Africa Aid. 2011. *Programs*. San Francisco: Africa Aid. Available online at: http://www.africaaid.org.

Ahlen, Eva. 2006. "UNHCR's Education Challenges." *Forced Migration Review* (Supplement): 10–11. Available online at: www.fmreview.org.

Balancing Act. 2010. *Solar-powered computer brings internet to North of Kenya*. Available online at: http://www.balancingact-africa.com/news/en/issue-no-529/computing/solar-powered-comput/en

Bash, Leslie. 2005. "Identity, Boundary and Schooling: Perspectives on the Experiences and Perceptions of Refugee Children." *Intercultural Education* 16 (4): 351–366.

Bearak, Barry, and Barbara Crossette. 2001. "The New Refugees: For Millions of Refugees Around the World, Home is a Ragged Tent and Hunger is the Norm. Does Anyone Care?" *New York Times Upfront*, September 3.

Brown, Tim. 2006. "South Sudan Education Emergency." *Forced Migration Review* (Supplement): 20–21. Available online at: http://www.fmreview.org.

Buckland, Peter. 2006. "Post-Conflict Education: Time for a Reality Check?" *Forced Migration Review* (Supplement): 7–8. Available online at: http://www.fmreview.org.

Burgoyne, Ursula, and Oksana Hull. 2007. *Classroom Management Strategies to Address the Needs of Sudanese Refugee Learners*. Adelaide, Australia: National Centre for Vocational Education Research.

Burton, Ann, and Franklin John-Leader. 2009. "Are We Reaching Refugees and Internally Displaced Persons?" *Bulletin of the World health Organization* 87 (8): 637–638.

Drechsler, Helmut, Holger Munsch, and Jurgen Wintermeier. 2005. *Basic Education for Refugees and Displaced Populations*. Bonn, Germany: German Technical Cooperation. Available online at http://www.gtz.de.

Dumbrill, Gary C. 2009. "Your Policies, Our Children: Messages from Refugee Parents to Child Welfare Workers and Policymakers." *Child Welfare* 88 (3): 145–168.

Ethnologue Languages of the World. 2009. *Languages of the Democratic Republic of Congo.* Dallas, TX: Ethnologue Languages of the World. Available online at: http://www.ethnologue.com.

Geisler, Charles, and Ragendra De Sousa. 2001. "From Refuge to Refugee: The African Case." *Public Administration and Development* 21: 159–170.

Global Witness. 2009. *Natural Resource Exploitation and Human Rights in the Democratic Republic of Congo 1993 to 2003: A Global Witness Briefing Paper.* London: Global Witness Ltd. Available online at: http://www.global-witness.org.

Greeley, Martin, and Pauline Rose. 2006. "Learning to Deliver Education in Fragile States." *Forced Migration Review* (Supplement): 14–15.

Kaiser, Tania. 2006. "Between a Camp and a Hard Place: Rights, Livelihood and Experiences of the Local Settlement System for Long-Term Refugees in Uganda." *Journal of Modern African Studies* 44 (4): 597–621.

Kirk, Jackie, and Elizabeth Cassity. 2007. "Minimum Standards for Quality Education for Refugee Youth." *Youth Studies in Australia* 26 (1): 50–56.

Kirk, Jackie, and Rebecca Winthrop. 2007. "Promoting Quality Education in Refugee Contexts: Supporting Teacher Development in Northern Ethiopia." *International Review of Education* 53 (5–6): 715–723.

Kyama, Reuben, and Eric Kabeera. 2011. "ICT Buses Delivering the Internet to Rural Rwanda." *Elearning Africa News Portal*, June 8. Available online at: http://www.elearning-africa.com.

Lin, Nancy J., Karen L. Suyemoto, and Peter Nien-Chu Kiang. 2009. "Education as Catalyst for Intergenerational Refugee Family Communication About War and Trauma." *Communication Disorders Quarterly* 30 (4): 195–207.

Marwaha, Alka. 2008. "Battle for Congo's Mineral Assets." *BBC News*, November 25. Available online at: http://news.bbc.co.uk.

Matthews, Julie. 2008. "Schooling and Settlement: Refugee Education in Australia." *International Studies in Sociology of Education* 18 (1): 31–45.

McBrien, J. Lynn. 2005. "Educational Needs and Barriers for Refugee Students in the United States: A Review of the Literature." *Review of Educational Research* 75 (3): 329–364.

McLoughlin, Catherine, and R. Oliver. 1999. "Instructional Design for Cultural Difference: A Case Study of the Indigenous Online Learning." Paper presented at the Annual Conference of the Australasian Society for Computers in Learning in Tertiary Education, Brisbane, Australia, 5–8 December 1999. Available online at: http://www.ascilite.org.au.

Newbury, David. 2005. "Returning Refugees: Four Historical Patterns of "Coming Home" to Rwanda." *Comparative Studies in Society and History* 47 (2): 252–285.

Ogata, Sadako. 2000. "The Situation of Refugees in Africa." *Migration World Magazine* 28 (1–2): 23–27.

Penz, Peter. 2004. "Dams, Guns and Refugees." *Alternatives Journal* 30 (4): 8–12.

Salisbury, Mary. 2006. "Internally Displaced People and Refugees." *Social Studies Review* 46 (1): 56–60.

Strekalova, Ekaterina, and James L. Hoot. 2008. "What is Special About Special Needs of Refugee Children? Guidelines for Teachers." *Multicultural Education* 16 (21): 21–24.

Szente, Judit, James L. Hoot, and Dorothy Taylor. 2006. "Responding to the Special Needs of Refugee Children: Practical Ideas for Teachers." *Early Childhood Education Journal* 34 (1): 15–20.

Tadesse, Selamawit. 2007. *The Education of African Refugee Preschoolers: Views of Parents Toward Appropriate Practices, Experiences of Parents/Teachers and Encouragement/Barriers to Greater Parent Involvement.* PhD diss., Department of Learning and Instruction, University of New York at Buffalo, Buffalo, NY, USA.

United Nations High Commissioner for Human Rights. 2010. *Democratic Republic of the Congo, 1993–2003: Report of the Mapping Exercise Documenting the Most Serious Violations of Human Rights and International Humanitarian Law Committed Within the Territory of the Democratic Republic of the Congo between March 1993 and June 2003.* New York: United Nations.

United Nations Security Council. 2000. *Resolution 1325.* New York: United Nations. Available online at: http://www.un.org

UNHCR (United Nations High Commissioner for the Refugees). 2000. *UNHCR Website.* Geneva, Switzerland: UNHCR. Available online at: http://www.unhcr.org.

UNHCR. 2009. *UNHCR Education Strategy 2010–2012: "Education for All Persons of Concern to UNHCR."* Geneva, Switzerland: UNHCR. Available online at: http://www.unhcr.org.

Wakabi, Wairagala. 2006. "Landmines Pose Further Danger to Uganda's War Refugees." *The Lancet* 368: 1637–1638.

Ward, Jeanne, and Beth Vann. 2002. "Gender-Based Violence in Refugee Settings." *The Lancet* 360: S13-S14.

Waters, Tony. 1999. "Assessing the Impact of the Rwandan Refugee Crisis on Development Planning in Rural Tanzania, 1994–1996." *Human Organization* 58 (2): 142–152.

Waters, Tony, and Kim Leblanc. 2005. "Refugees and Education: Mass Public Schooling without a Nation-State." *Comparative Education Review* 49 (2): 129–147.

Westhoff, Wayne W., Guillermo E. Lopez, Lauren B. Zapata, Jamie A. Wilke Corvin, Peter Allen, and Robert J. McDermott. 2008. "Reproductive Health Education and Services Needs of Internally Displaced Persons and Refugees Following Disaster." *American Journal of Health Education* 39 (2): 95–103.

Winthrop, Rebecca, and Jackie Kirk. 2004. "Teacher Development and Student Well-Being." *Forced Migration Review* 22: 18–22.

World Refugee Survey. 2009. *Report Card: Congo-Kinshasa.* Washington, DC: US Committee for Refugees and Immigrants. Available online at: http://www.refugees.org.

Contributors

Trish Andrews is a senior lecturer in Higher Education (e-learning) in the academic unit in the Teaching and Educational Development Institute (TEDI) at the University of Queensland in Australia. She has a particular focus on integrating technologies into higher education programs and has been extensively involved in the design and support of innovative learning spaces at the University of Queensland. Trish has been presented with two UQ awards for programs that enhance learning (2009 and 2010), and she has also received Australian Learning and Teaching Council (ALTC) awards for programs that enhance learning in 2010 and 2011. Trish has had several educational development and research grants including two recent successfully completed ALTC grants and is currently working on a new ALTC grant that is exploring online learners' use of technology and space.

Stacy Austin-Li is an analyst and consultant with Boston based conferencing and collaboration market intelligence firm, Wainhouse Research. She specializes in market research and consulting related to Asia and China in particular. Fluent in Chinese, Ms. Austin-Li lived for more than ten years in China accumulating expertise in localization of sales & marketing strategies, cross-cultural communication, and training. Ms. Austin-Li co-organized online symposia regarding technology in education with Rebecca Clothey in 2008 and 2010. She has also conducted studies to benchmark the effective use of conferencing technologies in higher education in China. Ms. Austin-Li holds an M.A. in International Relations from the University of Hawaii, where she was an Asia Pacific Scholar.

Jason Bordujenko is the videoconferencing manager for the Australian Academic Research Network (AARNet), which provides the backbone Internet connectivity to all Australian higher education institutions. He provides extensive technical knowledge, practical experience, and access to professional videoconferencing networks, which supported the investigation of the Leading Rich Media Technologies Collaboratively project described in this volume and on which Bordujenko served as a project coleader.

Richard Caladine is an associate professor and the manager of Learning Facilities and Technologies at the University of Wollongong in Australia. He is responsible for the operation of University of Wollongong's audio-visual and rich media educational systems. As well, he is responsible for podcasting, webcasting, and streaming services. He is actively involved with the training of staff in the pedagogically appropriate use of these systems and other educational technologies. Since 1994 he has researched the use of rich media in higher education and has published a number of papers, book chapters, and a book all on the appropriate pedagogical use of educational technologies. He is the author of the book "Enhancing E-Learning with Media-Rich Content and Interactions," published in 2008. Richard is currently on the reference group for a Carrick funded project titled "The Impact of Web-Based Lecture Technologies on Current and Future Practice in Learning and Teaching." The lead institution for this project is Macquarie University and the partners are University of Newcastle, Murdoch University, and Flinders University.

Ellen Clay is an assistant professor of Mathematics Education and a mathematician in residence at the Math Forum at Drexel University in the United States. She has over 20 years of experience in the field of mathematics and mathematics education. She holds a PhD in Mathematics from the University of Louisiana, has taught middle school, and works extensively with mathematics teachers in the School District of Philadelphia. Her research interests focus on the learning and teaching of mathematics, especially in teachers' learning of mathematics. She uses the affordances of online learning to provide mathematical access to a diverse group of teachers who share their local knowledge with each other while she shares her mathematical expertise and then takes advantage of the permanent records of the online learning environment to further study the acquisition of mathematics knowledge.

Rebecca Clothey is an assistant professor of higher education at Drexel University's School of Education with a research interest in equity issues in higher education, particularly in China. She developed an interest in the potential to provide educational access to underserved populations through various uses of technology while serving as the program director of distance learning programs at Drexel University, first in higher education (2007–2010) and then in global and international education (2009–2012). Dr. Clothey lived in China for five years working and researching in various higher education institutions throughout the country. She speaks Mandarin Chinese and has a working knowledge of Uyghur, a Turkic language spoken in China's northwest region of Xinjiang. Dr. Clothey presents internationally on the topics of higher education policy, Chinese education, and equity and access in higher education and is the author of numerous journal articles and book chapters on these topics. She has been awarded two Fulbright Fellowships for her research, one to China and one to Uzbekistan. She has a PhD in Administrative and Policy Studies from the University of Pittsburgh School of Education.

Tricia Coverdale-Jones is a principal lecturer in the School of Languages and Area Studies, University of Portsmouth, UK. She teaches Intercultural Communication and International Business Communication; formerly she also taught German language and culture, and Linguistics. Coverdale-Jones has also had roles as faculty e-learning coordinator, and faculty Learning and Teaching coordinator. She has presented papers at many conferences and published papers on e-learning, CALL, and CMC, and has an interest in cross-cultural issues in online contexts. She has also done work in raising the profile of international students' needs and in the dissemination of good practice to colleagues. Her publications include a special issue of *Language, Culture and Curriculum* on the Chinese learner (2006) with Paul Rastall and a coedited book *Internationalising the University: the Chinese Context*. From October 2011 to February 2012 she was visiting professor at Nagoya University, Centre for Studies in Higher Education.

Mercedes del Rosario has an EdD in International Education Development with a concentration on International Education Policy and an EdM in International Education Development with concentration on Language, Literacy and Technology from Teachers College, Columbia University. She also has an MA in Instructional Technology from San Francisco State University and a BS in Development Communication (major in Journalism) from the University of the Philippines. She is currently director, ePortfolio Initiative–City University of New York, LaGuardia Community College. Dr. del Rosario has many years of professional experience in instructional design and technology training for teachers, both local and international. Her scholarly interests and educational research experience focuses on the use of ICT in national development and educational reform through innovation. She has also conducted international research on dropout issues in postsocialist countries.

Dorothy Ettling, a professor in the doctoral program in the Dreeben School of Education at the University of the Incarnate Word, San Antonio, TX,

USA, holds an MSW and an MA and PhD in Transpersonal Psychology from the Institute of Transpersonal Psychology in Palo Alto, CA. She has worked extensively in personal and organizational development and change and assumed leadership roles in local, national, and international organizations. She has received academic and civic awards and was chosen a piper professor in the State of Texas in 2009. Her research interests focus on change processes, women's empowerment, transformative learning, and cross cultural, participatory research. Professor Ettling is a member of the Sisters of Charity of the Incarnate Word, a Catholic religious community of women. She is also the cofounder of Women's Global Connection (WGC), a virtual gathering place for women across the globe. On the ground and online at www.womensglobalconnection.org, WGC develops capacity building programs in collaboration with women in Tanzania, Zambia, Peru, Mexico, and the United States.

Kalpana Kannan is a project manager in the Department of Computer Science and Engineering, at the Indian Institute of Technology Bombay, Mumbai, India. She is also pursuing her doctorate in the Department of Humanities and Social Sciences at the same institute. She is pursuing her research in the area of ICT enabled education, professional development of teachers, and evaluation. She has over 12 years of experience at the managerial and administrative levels. She holds a master's degree in management from Bombay University and an undergraduate degree in physics from Delhi University.

Joyce P. Kaufman is a professor of Political Science and the director of the Center for Engagement with Communities at Whittier College in the United States. She is the author of a number of books and articles that address various aspects of national and international security, foreign policy, and teaching and pedagogy. She is the creator of the International Negotiation Project for high schools and the International Negotiation Modules Project for community colleges, both of which use simulation to internationalize the curriculum and to teach students about current international issues. As both are technology based, they are also important tools to integrate technology across the curriculum in a meaningful way. She received her BA and MA from New York University and her PhD from the University of Maryland. Prior to joining the faculty of Whittier College in 1985, she served in Washington, DC as a foreign affairs specialist in the office of the assistant secretary of defense, and worked with a number of defense contractors.

Minghua Li is a professor at the School of Public Administration, East China Normal University. He earned both his master's degree in economics and a PhD in Economics of Education from Stanford. He has taught courses in economics, economics of education, higher education reforms, the emerging educational markets, comparative education, and social science foundations of education policies and leadership. Besides Chinese students, he also has master's students from Africa and many other developing countries. His research interest is in community college models, migrant worker education, education markets, for-profit education, and education reforms. He was the principal investigator of the Ford Foundation sponsored action research project 2005–2008 to address migrant workers' continuing education problems, an internationally cooperative project participated in by teams from East China Normal University, Peking University, and Columbia University. Currently he is the principal investigator in a project titled "Social Choices and Their Efficiencies of Higher Education Accreditation Institutions Among Nations," sponsored by China's National Natural Science Foundation. In 2011 he published a book in Chinese titled "Demand and Supply of Higher Education for the Migrant Workers and Its Accreditation Systems."

Maria Eliza Marquise is a doctoral student pursuing a degree in Higher Education at the University of the Incarnate Word in San Antonio, Texas. She received her MA in Adult Education in 2010 from the same university. She is currently employed as a graduate medical education coordinator in the CHRISTUS Health System. Her current research interests lie in the fields of women's empowerment from a technological standpoint, the learning styles of students based on culture, and a group project involving electronic portfolios for graduate students.

Elsa Mentz is a professor in Computer Science Education and project leader of self-directed learning research group in the Faculty of Education Sciences at North-West University in South Africa. She studied at the University of Pretoria, University of South Africa, and the Potchefstroom University for CHE (Christian Higher Education). Her doctorate was awarded in Computer Science Education (CSE). Her research focuses on cooperative learning in CSE as well as on the fostering of Self Directed Learning (SDL) skills in the Computer Science classroom. She has received national and international funding for her research projects on cooperative learning as well as on the empowerment of information technology (IT) teachers especially in rural areas and has been actively involved in the training of IT teachers for the past 12 years.

Michel L. Miller is an assistant professor in Drexel University's School of Education in the United States, and the director of Drexel's Special

Education Programs. She has over 20 years of experience in the field of special education. She holds a PhD in Special Education from the University of Miami and has completed extensive course work in educational administration at Widener University and Temple University. She holds certifications in early childhood, elementary education, special education, and supervision of special education. Her research interests focus on autism, special education leadership, accessibility of online learning, and program evaluations. Dr. Miller created Drexel's special education teaching and special education leadership programs, which are offered online and on campus. She cochairs the online accessibility subcommittee of the Online Learning Council at Drexel and presents on the topic of accessibility. Dr. Miller is an active member of the Council of Exceptional Children (CEC) and Council of Administrators of Special Education (CASE) subdivision and serves nationally on CASE's research committee. Dr. Miller was a supervisor of pupil services in East Pennsboro Area School District with direct supervisory responsibilities over all of the district's special education programs, which included programs for students with autism. She also has teaching experience in life skill and inclusive settings.

Krishnan Narayanan obtained his PhD in Economics from the Delhi School of Economics, Delhi, India, and carried out postdoctoral research at the Institute of Advanced Studies United Nations University, Tokyo, Japan during 2000–2001. His research interests span the areas of industrial economics, international business, socioeconomic empowerment through ICT, environmental economics, economic impacts of climate change, and development economics. He has a number of publications in the field of industrial competitiveness, technology transfer, ICT, trade, and vulnerabilities due to climate change. He has published in multiple international journals and most recently published an edited book called *Indian and Chinese Enterprises: Global Trade, Technology, and Investment Regimes* (jointly with N. S. Siddharthan). He is actively engaged in a web-based research group, Forum for Global Knowledge Sharing, which interfaces scientists, technologists, and economists. Narayanan is currently professor and head, Department of Humanities and Social Sciences, Indian Institute of Technology Bombay and president, Academy of International Business India Chapter.

Ferdinand Potgieter studied at the University of Pretoria and University of South Africa. His doctorate was awarded in History of Education at the University of South Africa. He is currently an associate professor in Philosophy of Education and Education Theory at North-West University,

Potchefstroom Campus, South Africa and was previously a senior lecturer in Education Management, Law and Policy Studies at the University of Pretoria. He has published widely in the field of spirituality and education, morality and education, sources of inspiration for student teachers, as well as in Philosophy of Education.

Gregory P. Rabb is an associate professor of Political Science and coordinator of global education at Jamestown Community College in the United States–the first community college in the State University of New York (SUNY) system. He also serves as president of the Jamestown City Council. Greg holds a juris doctor degree from SUNY, Buffalo. In May 2011 he was awarded the SUNY Chancellor's Award for Excellence in teaching. Greg has been the past recipient of a Fulbright Fellowship to study the Netherlands, a Holocaust Education Foundation Fellowship through Northwestern University to study the Holocaust, and a Freeman Foundation Fellowship to study East Asia at Columbia University. Greg is a revision author for an introductory textbook in American Government and Politics. He is also a consultant to the college board conducting workshops for middle and secondary school teachers throughout the United States in pre-Advanced Placement (AP) skills as well as Advanced Placement courses in US Government and Politics and Comparative Government and Politics.

Rosalind Latiner Raby is a senior lecturer at California State University, Northridge, California, in the Educational Leadership and Policy Studies Department of the College of Education. She also serves as the director of California Colleges for International Education, a consortium whose membership includes 86 California community colleges. Raby is also the Education Abroad Knowledge Community chair for community college education abroad programs and the Region XII Community College chair for NAFSA. Raby received her PhD in the field of Comparative and International Education from UCLA. Since 1984, Raby has worked with community college and secondary school faculty and administrators to help them internationalize and multiculturalize their curriculum, their college programs, and their college mission statements. Among her many publications on the topic of international education and community colleges are: *Financing Community Colleges* (2011); *Community College Models: Globalization and Higher Education Reform* (2009); *International Reform Efforts and Challenges in Community Colleges NDCC Series* (2007); "Community Colleges and Study Abroad" in *NAFSA's Guide to Education Abroad for Advisers and Administrators*: 3rd Edition

(2005); *Internationalizing the Community College Curriculum: Theoretical and Pragmatic Discourses*, NAFSA Monograph (2000); and *Looking to the Future: Report on International and Global Education in California Community Colleges* (1999).

Robyn Smyth is a senior lecturer and academic developer for the Joint Medical Program working from the University of New England, Armidale, NSW, Australia. She has been using and researching synchronous communications technologies for more than a decade, with particular interest in the educational uses of personal and room-based videoconferencing systems and pedagogical innovation in higher education. Her doctoral work concerning large-scale curriculum change underpins her work, providing theoretical frameworks from which to understand implementation of technology and its implications for curriculum design. She served as the project leader for the Rich Media Technology project described in this volume.

Hennie Steyn was appointed in 1976 as a lecturer at the Potchefstroom University in South Africa after serving three years as Teacher, and has served, since 1997, as a professor in Comparative Education. Since the beginning of 1999 he was appointed as a rector of the Potchefstroom College of Education. Because of the incorporation of the college into the Potchefstroom University, he was appointed as the dean of the Faculty of Education Sciences. After the conclusion of his contract as dean, he resumed in 2006 the position of professor in Comparative Education at the North-West University (Potchefstroom Campus). His expertise is primarily in Comparative Education. He has taught Comparative Education at the under- and postgraduate level. Twenty-six MEd and nine PhD students have completed their studies under his leadership, and he acted as author and coauthor of sixteen subject-related books. He has published 35 articles in peer-reviewed scientific journals and 15 articles in nonpeer reviewed scientific journals. His research specialization is the structure and functioning of the education system with a recent focus on planning of the education system, education provision to minorities, and productivity in the education system.

Rana Tamim is an assistant professor at the College of Education at Zayed University, in the United Arab Emirates. She has a PhD in Educational Technology from Concordia University with extensive teaching experience in Canada, Lebanon, Saudi Arabia, and the United Arab Emirates. Tamim is a collaborator with the *Centre for the Study of Learning and Performance* in Montreal, Canada and is an active participant in national and international meetings with an established publication record.

Her research interests include: (a) learners' empowerment through the use of educational technology and instructional design, (b) the impact and role played by computer technology in facilitating learning in general and in science education in particular, (c) appropriate pedagogical approaches to the integration of technology in the design of learning environments based on student-centered principles, and (d) knowledge synthesis through systematic reviews particularly meta-analyses, in addition to knowledge dissemination and mobilization for the purpose of improving practice in educational contexts.

Safary Wa-Mbaleka is an associate faculty at the University of Phoenix Online, in the curriculum and instruction doctoral program, where he has been teaching for the past three years. He studied in three different countries and has worked in Africa, Asia, the United States, and the Caribbean in the fields of education, online instruction, educational technology, and applied linguistics. Originally from the Democratic Republic of the Congo, in central Africa, Wa-Mbaleka saw firsthand the challenges of internally displaced people and refugees. Because of the strong impression this experience has made, he began to focus his research on refugee education, in addition to his usual focus on applied linguistics and online instruction.

John C. Weidman is Professor of Higher, Comparative and International Development Education, University of Pittsburgh, USA, where he teaches courses on education policy, planning, capacity building, and sector analysis. He was Chair, Department of Administrative and Policy Studies, 1986–93 and 2007–10; and Director, Institute for International Studies in Education (IISE), 2004–07. He has also been Visiting Research Fellow, Graduate School of International Development, Nagoya University in Japan (2011); Guest Professor at Beijing Normal University in China (2007–12); UNESCO Chair of Higher Education Research at Maseno University in Kenya (1993); and Fulbright Professor of the Sociology of Education at Augsburg University in Germany (1986–87). He has consulted on education development projects funded by USAID in Egypt, Indonesia, Kenya, and South Africa; and by the Asian Development Bank (ADB) in Indonesia, Kyrgyzstan, Laos, Mongolia, Vietnam, and Uzbekistan. Many of the results from this work have been published in refereed journals, edited books, and research monographs. His books are *Beyond the Comparative: Advancing Theory and its Application to Practice* (Ed. with W. James Jacob, Sense, 2011); *Socialization of Graduate and Professional Students in Higher Education: A Perilous Passage?* (with Darla J. Twale & Elizabeth L. Stein, Wiley, 2001); *ASHE Reader on Finance in*

Higher Education, 2nd Ed. (Co-ed. with John L. Yeager, et al., Pearson, 2001); and *Higher Education in Korea: Tradition and Adaptation* (Ed. with Namgi Park, Falmer, 2000). He is co-editor of the Pittsburgh Series in Comparative and International Education (PSCIE) from Sense Publishers (https://www.sensepublishers.com) and the electronic journal, *Excellence in Higher Education* (http://ehe.pitt.edu), launched in 2010 in cooperation with the Consortium of Indonesian Universities-Pittsburgh (KPTIP) (http://kptip.uns.ac.id). Dr. Weidman holds degrees from Princeton University (BA, sociology, *cum laude*), and the University of Chicago (MA, social science; PhD, sociology of education).

Charl C. Wolhuter studied at the University of Johannesburg, University of Pretoria, University of South Africa, and University of Stellenbosch. His doctorate was awarded in Comparative Education at the University of Stellenbosch. He is currently Comparative Education professor at North-West University, Potchefstroom Campus, South Africa and was previously junior lecturer in History of Education and Comparative Education at the University of Pretoria and senior lecturer in History of Education and Comparative Education at the University of Zululand, South Africa. In the winter semester of 2012 he was a visiting professor of Comparative and International Education at Brock University, Ontario, Canada. He has published widely in History of Education and Comparative Education and is the current president of SACHES (Southern African Comparative and History of Education Society) and editor of the electronic journal *SA-eDUC*. He is coeditor of the book *Comparative Education at Universities Worldwide* published by the World Council of Comparative Education Societies in 2008 and coeditor of the *International Handbook on Teacher Education Worldwide* published in 2010 and republished in 2012.

Index

Printed in the United States of America